THE

REFRAMING

OF

REALISM

D1249638

THE

REFRAMING

OF

REALISM

Galdós and

the Discourses

of the

Nineteenth-Century

Spanish Novel

Hazel Gold

DUKE UNIVERSITY PRESS *Durham and London 1993*

© 1993 Duke University Press
All rights reserved
Printed in the United States of America on acid-free paper ∞
Typeset in Bodoni Book by Tseng Information Systems.
Library of Congress Cataloging-in-Publication Data appear
on the last printed page of this book.

For my parents

Contents

Acknowledgments

This project represents a number of years of work on an author who, in the time it took me to complete this one study, would undoubtedly have been able to write several novels. This verbal facility, coupled with an astonishing command of social history and narrative technique, is what initially drew me to Galdós's work. The subsequent evolution of my ideas on the nineteenth-century novel owes a great deal to my conversations with other Galdós scholars, whose critical input and encouragement have left an indelible mark on this book.

Some of the research for this project was conducted with the aid of a summer travel grant from Northwestern University, whose support is much appreciated. I would also like to express my gratitude to the American Council of Learned Societies. The fellowship that the Council awarded me in 1988 enabled me to write several sections of this volume. The services of the interlibrary loan offices of Northwestern and of Emory University also proved invaluable, particularly when time was short and the material I had requested seemed impossible to locate. The unflagging support and good cheer of my family provided a reassuring sense of continuity as I tackled the various stages of this project.

The material in some of the chapters of this book, now considerably revised and expanded, was first published in the following articles: "Francisco's Folly: Picturing Reality in Galdós' *La de Bringas*," *Hispanic Review* 54 (1986): 47–66; "Problems of Closure in *Fortunata y Jacinta*: Of Narrators, Readers, and Their Just Deserts/Desserts," *Neophilologus* 70 (1986): 228–38; "Galdós and Lamennais: *Torquemada en la hoguera*, or the Prophet Deposed," *Revista Canadiense de Estudios Hispánicos* 13.1 (1988): 29–48; "A Tomb with a View: The Museum in Galdós' *Novelas contemporáneas*," *MLN* 103 (1988): 312–34; "Looking for the Doctor in the House: Critical Expectations and Novelistic Structure in Galdós' *El doctor Centeno*," *Philological Quarterly* 68 (1989): 219–40; and "Back to the Future: Criticism, the Canon, and the Nineteenth-Century Spanish Novel," *Hispanic Review* 58 (1990): 179–204. The chapter on *Tormento* appears here for the first time; however, some of the ideas I develop in it were first set forth in "*Tormento*: vivir un dramón, dramatizar una novela," *Anales Galdosianos* 20.1 (1985): 35–46. I would like to express my thanks to the publishers for their permission to use this material.

Introduction

The frame is no longer the wall, a merely func-
tional part of my surroundings; but it is not yet the
enchanted surface of the painting. A frontier be-
tween both regions, it serves to neutralize a brief
strip of the wall and acts as a trampoline that
launches our attention toward the legendary dimension of the aesthetic isle.
—José Ortega y Gasset, "Meditación del marco"

In the course of a brief meditation on the picture frame Ortega y Gasset compares the painting to an island, an unreal territory adrift in the ocean of its "vital surroundings." The frame is the isolating barrier ("aislador," derived from "isla") that permits viewers of the painting to recognize that they have completed the transit through the turbulent waters of circumstances and have disembarked on the banks of art's "imaginary precinct," the source of aesthetic pleasure.

In his recourse to the metaphor of the island, further reinforced by a footnote on the Latin origins of the Spanish *isla* and its more erudite form *ínsula*, Ortega inevitably stirs up associations with that other seeker of islands of unreality, Sancho Panza. Cervantes's novel is, among other things, an object lesson in the grief that comes to characters who dwell overly long in the archipelago of ideality because they are unable to perceive frames and interpret them correctly: the covers of books of chivalric romances, the curtains drawn across Maese Pedro's puppet stage, the costumes donned by the Duke and Duchess, the formulaic remarks that conclude the intercalated tales and return the listeners to their lived present. Readers, too, are implicated in the game along with don Quijote. Presented with Cide Hamete Benengeli's manuscript, its anonymous translation, and subsequent publication by yet a third party, they must try to navigate their way through this play of narrative frames enclosing the story of two characters who, in a mirror of their own experience as readers, stumble between the spheres of the imaginary and the real, miscalculating or on occasion willfully mistaking where their shared perimeters lie.

It is only fitting, therefore, that the Cervantine legacy should be especially pronounced in the works of the prolific Spanish author Benito Pérez Galdós (1843–1920). For Galdós, as the most innovative and insightful of Spain's nineteenth-century novelists, similarly displays an acute understanding of the ways in which both historical and literary experience are structured and evaluated, not least of all in the acts of composing and reading fiction, according to a variety of narrative, social, and epistemological frameworks that directly influence human behavior and judgments. Galdós's frame-building skills are evident in his reliance upon narrative pictorialism, his deft use of scenes set within summaries, and his increasingly sophisticated and ironic handling of novelistic overtures, endings, intertexts, and embedded narratives. Moreover, critics have universally acknowledged that the treatment of the principal issues that sustain his fiction—the changing constitution of contemporary society, the dynamics of the historical process, the aesthetic, ludic, and ethical functions of literature—reveals him to be an artful framer of experience in his own right as well as a trained observer, by turns tolerant or deprecating, of how his fellow Spaniards framed it.

Hence the principal thread guiding my examination of what distinguishes Galdós's singular novelistic voice from the chorus of European realists is the multifaceted concept of the frame as perceptual mechanism, narrative artifice, and institutional construct. This concern with frame strategies extends in two directions. On the one hand, it is a question of seeing how Galdós manipulated a literary apparatus that would allow him to delimit and then interpret what he perceived to be the distinctive and frequently disheartening historical experience of bourgeois liberalism in nineteenth-century Spain. On the other, it is a matter of seeing how readers and critics in turn have framed Galdós's novels in accord with changing literary fashions and theoretical models, ideological alliances, and even national prejudices.

Concretely, this book will first explore how Galdós created narratives that in their paradoxical and sometimes transgressive uses of framing either undermine or flatly negate many of the restrictive conventions of so-called high or orthodox realism, thus contributing to the expansion and revision of the larger generic frame we call the novel (chapters 1–3). Narrative frames are in principle symmetrical, thus providing readers with a comforting regularity of pattern; they normalize their content "by attributing to it an origin and a context."[1] On the contrary, Galdós repeatedly constructs narrative frames that resist formal closure, duplicate themselves in abyssal structures, or perversely circumscribe an empty field, thereby admonishing readers they must look elsewhere for a repository of stable meaning. At the same time, the normally elastic boundaries of the novelistic genre are further stretched to encompass variants that seemingly cannot be so easily accommodated to the standard realist roster.[2] In these first chapters, close readings of the texts are performed with the aid of studies of the role of the frame in cognitive activity and its application to the artistic text during the successive processes of composition and reading.

Simultaneously, by shifting focus alternately from the contours of this narrative envelope or container to what is contained within it, it becomes possible to identify specific frames of knowledge—ways of organizing and purposively manipulating the data of reality—that seen through Galdós's works define nineteenth-century society and its discursive practices (chapters 4–5). Particularly, the museum and the theater occupy Galdós's attention as models of representation, at once visual and epistemological in nature, that inform Spanish Restoration society's politics and culture. Literally, they are frames: the museum as a defined space for works of art that have themselves been framed for exhibition, the theater for the play being acted in front of the proscenium and the curtains. Figuratively, they propose a means of delimiting and hierarchizing knowledge of society and the material world based on the oppositions of artistic sublimity to prosaism, illusion to reality, imitation or performance to authenticity. The worth of these institutions is incessantly interrogated in Galdós's fictions and the effectivity of their framing capacities found wanting. Since, however, his *Novelas contemporáneas* repeatedly borrow elements of dramatic form and mimic the museological enterprise by virtue of their compendious presentation of "cuadros sociales" 'social pictures,' the challenging of the legitimacy of these two vehicles responsible for the dissemination of culture necessarily entails a similar challenge to the realist fictions that are their homologues.

For this second line of inquiry into the notion of framing the purely cognitive model is not wholly adequate. Because such a model tends to confine the critic to a highly formalist, immanent reading of texts, it must be complemented by a broader inquiry that begins to take into account the complexities of exchanges between culture and power, one that is attentive to details of historical record and the cultural matrix that informs it. The methods of classifying information, the metaphors that allude to this classificatory activity, even what counts as knowledge in the first place: these kinds of frames are not simply perceptual phenomena but above all social constructs designed to validate a given society's self-image, to authorize and perpetuate its value systems through policies that are institutionally driven and implemented. Cognitive psychology proves by and large to be an insufficient tool to analyze this; it is "curiously insensitive to the fact that what in a given domain counts as knowledge is always institutionally determined."[3] One might add that this is also true of the knowledge readers use and acquire in processing texts, which is similarly shaded by its institutional character. Critics especially are aware that when they engage in the sense-making operations that subsequently inform their talk about Galdós's narratives, they do so not solely on the basis of the codes and conventions that circulate within the economy of realist writing, nor their familiarity with the historical and cultural landscape of nineteenth-century Spain. The readings they produce may also be colored by the knowledge that at any given moment some modes of reading are likely to be more readily endorsed than others, especially by the official agencies that sponsor such activity.

Finally, moving in ever-widening circles from text to (meta)context, the readings that comprise this volume also seek to prize apart frames that for too long have boxed Galdós within a confining critical discourse, one that rather disingenuously fails to take note of the author's strategies for bypassing or imploding the inherent contradictions and limitations of the realist aesthetic (chapters 6–7). In one particularly tenacious strand of Hispanic criticism, Galdós's works have been and continue to be categorized as either archetypical specimens of narrative of a very traditional order, strictly obedient to the static conventions and codes of nineteenth-century realism, or, equally conservatively, as social documents whose principal values are qualified as archaeological rather than literary.[4] Counter to this fossilization of an immense body of work with respect to both its form and its expressive function, the successive chapters of *The Reframing of Realism* examine those facets of Galdós's fiction that gesture toward breaches in the continuity of the frame, either of the novel or of the belief systems that ground it. Such gaps are symptomatic of the problematic nature of language and representation with which, however, the writer is unable to dispense altogether. This is a point which has been forcefully argued in recent critical studies by John Kronik, Germán Gullón, Diane Urey, and Akiko Tsuchiya, among others.[5]

In moving from the structure of individual nineteenth-century texts to the structuring of discourses of knowledge and culture in which these texts participate, and from there in turn to the various critical theories that circumscribe both these aspects, I have not attempted a comprehensive typology of the repertoire of framing strategies that can be found in Galdós's fiction. The difficulties inherent in presenting an exhaustive analysis of the incidences of framing in the novels of an author as prolific as Galdós present an immediate deterrent to such an approach. Moreover, such features of a text as its internal and external frame boundaries can assume different meanings depending upon the manner of their juxtaposition against the whole. "The catalogue approach to a text is always ineffectual," Jurij Lotman writes, "since an artistic device is not a material element, but a *relation*."[6] Rather, the readings offered here represent selected and often interlocking examples of framing within and around salient texts of Spanish realism, and are themselves organized as a nesting series of frames within frames. Lest readers conclude that these demarcations will be too rigidly enforced, I hasten to point out that all three of my focuses— narrative, social, and critical—share overlapping boundaries. Such intersections are seemingly inevitable, for margins and borderlines have always posed an irresistible challenge to be violated.

It is clear that frames are everywhere present in human life and art as a means of organizing perception. Constructed out of mental data, their function is to allow individuals to comprehend various aspects of the reality through which they move. In its current elaboration, frame theory annexes a wide range of concepts drawn from Gestalt perception psychology, phenomenology, and mathematical set theory, and has applications to research in fields as diverse as education, narratology, cognitive linguistics (especially frame semantics), and artificial intelligence. In the basic terms outlined by Marvin Minsky, a frame is a data-structure, stored in the memory and activated by each successive perceptual experience, used to represent a stereotyped situation.[7] Thus the frame simultaneously is a representation of knowledge, a method of recognition and reasoning, and a tool for processing information. On the basis of further refinements of Minsky's model, theorists have concluded that frames are akin to definitions, in that they describe classes of properties associated with certain objects and events. The knowledge embraced by the frame (Kuipers's "domain of expertise") functions both normatively and predictively. It tells the viewer or user what to anticipate in future encounters with the situation or object under scrutiny. Conjointly, when there occurs a mismatch between predicted values and those actually observed on any single occasion, the frame can be used to process a corrective account. As helpful as frames are in approaching the study of natural language, works of visual art, and social behavior, it is easy to see that they are equally as instrumental in understanding texts. Writers use frames to assemble series of narrative predicates into organized configurations that encode meaning. Readers rely upon these same frames or schemata to activate the signifying process. Since they come to the text equipped with foreknowledge derived from their previous experience of literary codes and conventions, their encounters with the text amount to a "continual interplay between modified expectations and transformed memories."[8] Because it is performed through preexisting frames that are revised where necessary, reading can in fact be viewed as a productive response and the text as an event rather than a stationary artifact.

In his in-depth study of frame analysis, Erving Goffman points out that frameworks are both situational and relativistic. Although governed by rules of organization mutually agreed upon (consciously or unconsciously) by users, they represent not a fixed reality but rather a perspective on, or interpretation of, events.[9] Yet, although framing may be a relative concept, its relevance to cognitive activity is absolute. Notwithstanding their artificially constituted nature, frames are an indispensable tool necessary for the management of both physical environments and social structures, the flow of events and signs.

At their most basic level, frames combat anarchy. In the face of reality's overwhelming multiplicity and simultaneity, the manufacture of frames permits the perceiving subject to demarcate and manipulate with autonomy a specific segment of experience with the expectation of gaining ascendancy over it. The frame attributes a specific, univocal focus to the episode, activity, or object that has been singled out as having primary importance, and concomitantly provides mechanisms to screen out and suppress distracting and/or subordinate events—"disattention," in Goffman's terminology (*Frame Analysis* 210)—that might confuse or dilute that focus. What the frame leaves out, resultingly, is of no less significance than what it includes. The restrictive or exclusive quality of framing is a requisite of its function to impart instructions for ordering and expressing experiences, both past and future. Individuals can more easily master a given situation or assess more completely the data concerning an object by narrowing their purview to a limited domain and following the directions for its interpretation that the frame affords. For this reason, Gregory Bateson speaks of the framing process as metacommunicative: the message *of* the frame is to interpret the message(s) contained *within* the frame.[10]

Of course frames cannot always be relied upon as a foolproof means of contending with experience and ensuring the continuing intelligibility of the external world. When the frame is either deliberately or accidentally broken, when it proves invalid or inadequate to the situation it has been used to define, users experience a change in the degree of their engrossment in the frame and a weakening of their belief in its future applicability (*Frame Analysis* 378). If all participants do not share the same reading of the framework, or if in their involvement with framing conventions they are subjected to purposeful deception or involuntarily fall prey to illusion, or again, if their competence in dealing with rules of framing is underdeveloped, the resulting ambiguities and contradictions of interpretation will frequently conclude in an epistemological impasse. An individual who previously presumed to command certain and positive knowledge of the real may discover that "in fact what is happening is plainly a joke, or a dream, or an accident, or a mistake, or a misunderstanding, or a deception, or a theatrical performance, and so forth" (*Frame Analysis* 10). Such errors and miscues may lead to the revision or even the removal of the particular frame whose credibility is suspect, but not the abolition of frames generally. It is only through the activity of framing that given behaviors, events, relationships, and experiences become meaningful.

So basic is the concept of framing that it can be seen as informing all speculation on the nature of art and its relation to reality. Frameless activity, "the convention of the conventionless—speaking from the heart, from nature, from a privileged place of signification," can be shown, as in Susan Stewart's analysis of folkloric and literary materials, to be frankly a myth. There are only two categorizations of experience possible: social gestures and activity, including the extreme example of nonsense, which are all inevitably subjected to framing; and purely natural ones, which stand, alienated, outside the realm of the frame altogether.[11] Consequently, given their ubiquitousness in social life, it is not sufficient simply to point out the existence of frames. It is also necessary to explore what exactly constitutes them, how they function, and what sorts of transformations they effect on the relationship between that which is framed—this might be a painting, photograph, scene observed through a doorway or window, stage play, textual fragment, game, ritual or other organized social activity—and whatever lies beyond the frame's borders.

Whether they occur spontaneously in nature (for example, the outline of a yard made by a stand of trees) or are man-made (the pedestal interposed between a sculpture and the floor or tabletop it rests upon), frames are by definition a device that in some way isolates an activity or object from the field surrounding it. Most frequently, the segregation realized by the frame is temporal or spatial. In a literary text, the framing of a particular passage or scene may rely on visual, verbal, conceptual, or even gestural techniques.[12] In all cases, this detachment or decoupage is accomplished by means of a set of boundary markers, an armature of enclosure. Frame analysts are in agreement that such markers are for the most part highly conventionalized. To cite only one obvious example, that a rectangular sheet of paper is today unreflexively accepted as the customary surface for writing and drawing is evidence of the extent to which the boundaries of fields can become naturalized and recognition of them become a learned response. As Meyer Schapiro's study attests, no such prepared and regularly bounded field existed for prehistoric cave painters or the earliest wielders of the writing stylus. Until such an organized space of representation had evolved, the practice of framing visual art was unknown. As both artifact and idea, then, the frame has a lengthy history as an emergent perceptual and cultural convention.[13]

Setting a frame into place establishes a series of important distinctions analogous to the figure/ground opposition that governs Gestalt psychology of perception or the redundancy/innovation binarism that operates in information theory. First, the presence of a frame implies the demarcation of an inside from an outside and thereby makes it possible for the framed object to possess a structure and a content. Second, framing may be considered a form of representation, ultimately invested with symbolic meaning. Thus Boris Uspensky states that "in order to perceive the world of the work of art as a sign system, it is necessary (although not always sufficient) to designate its borders; it is precisely these borders which create representation."[14] The viewer (or reader) is encouraged to draw comparisons between the framed object, regarded as a kind of copy or imitation, and the actual elements in ordinary life it is modeled upon. Framing in this sense supplies a process "for articulating texts from contexts and for arranging texts and contexts in a hierarchical relationship throughout social life"; as Stewart illustrates, it allows for the marking off of " 'the real' from the nearly real, the nearly nearly real, and so on." [15] The spectator relies upon the hierarchical nature of framing procedures in order to make sense of something always *in relation to* something else.

Finally, the existence and superimposition of frames is what makes possible any and all discourse on aesthetics. It is not only that without the signals that frames provide we would be incapable of recognizing the sublime, the beautiful, or the aesthetically noteworthy—in a word, art. Rather, as Jonathan Culler indicates, the entire critical enterprise is enabled by the assumption that there exists a distinctive boundary between criticism and literature, the former constituting a commentary or framing discourse bracketing the latter. [16] So deep is the psychological (not to mention ideological) demand for framing to provide clear and uninterrupted lines of demarcation that when previously established borders are moved or dismantled outright, as, for example, deconstruction has managed to do in its refusal of text/*hors-texte* boundaries, the result has been a marked unease felt by some critics, among them traditional historicists, philological and textual positivists, and formalists descended from New Criticism, who find themselves in disagreement with the increasingly aggressive role assumed by theory in recent decades. The suggestion that critical discourse is a field coextensive with literary discourse, its equal rather than its descriptive and supporting framework, has proven to be a disquieting notion to those who see the map of exegetic practices being redrawn along unfamiliar lines, or erased entirely. Poststructuralism defines an indivisible, unbounded web within which all writing is imbricated, a field which, given its infinitely dilatory nature, referring from signifier to signifier and permanently deferring arrival at the site of the signified, can never achieve closure. Such a notion of text and textuality in many ways makes obsolete the traditional critical frame that encapsulates the poem or narrative sequence as a discrete entity. The erosion of rigidly established borders between high and popular culture, the reformulation of literary canons, and the blurring of genre distinctions are likewise elements of a contemporary critical practice that has destabilized previously accepted applications of framing to literary texts. [17]

The activity of framing, so obviously central to a general theory of aesthetics, is equally important to the compositional practices that ground the art of the novel. Novelistic beginnings and endings, frequently characterized by their formulaism, are intended to serve as frontiers separating the fictional from the factual, literature from life, although metafictional texts including Galdós's own "La novela en el tranvía," *El amigo Manso*, and

Misericordia demonstrate how easily such fictive fences may be undermined or simply circumvented.[18] Nor does the ever-contingent framing process cease with the initial delineation and subsequent closure of a fictional world in contradistinction to a real one. Within the novel itself there occurs a continual shifting and reframing of its contents, effectively dividing the macrotext into numerous minimal sequences or microtexts. Such reframing can be accomplished by a variety of formal techniques: syntactic and structural divisions of the text into sentences, paragraphs, chapters, and parts; shifts in focalization, whereby the events of the novel are presented from the perspective of first one and then another character (or, in the case of omniscience, from no consistently localizable angle of vision); alternation between external observation of the type that dwells upon the physical environment and outward appearances and internal observation that locates the narrative instance within the characters' minds; juxtaposition of contrasting spatial and temporal sequences; constant switching among the polyvalent registers of discourse (direct, indirect, free indirect, and recounted speech); embedding of one story directly within another, creating a metadiegetic narrative (the so-called frame tale) that depends for its effects upon the interaction of multiple planes of narration arranged in infinite regress; inclusion within the text of overt narratorial commentary, either in the form of interpretation, judgment, or generalization, upon the story or its discourse.[19] Many other examples could surely be added to this list. To define all the occasions and strategies of framing that may occur over the length of a novel is an exceedingly complex charge, part of the task that in fact has long occupied narratologists and semioticians in their study of the surface features and deep structures of both verbal and nonverbal representations.

As important as framing is to all novels, its status relevant to the forms and objectives of the nineteenth-century novel is paramount. The exponential proliferation of information over the course of the last three centuries, metaphorized in the figure of the encyclopedia, provoked changes in the manner in which the corpus of all available scientific and historic knowledge was codified. Such changes account in part for the genesis and structures of the realist novel which, in attempting a similar codification, comes to depend specifically upon the aesthetic principle of framing.

In his archaeology of knowledge, excavated from the recorded transformations that overtake such disparate epistemological fields as biology, economics, and philology, Foucault maintains that the rupture between the classical and modern periods occurring at the end of the eighteenth and the beginning of the nineteenth century is signaled by a significant shift in the organization of human knowledge: from horizontal to vertical, from relations of identity and difference to relations of analogy, from the unity of tabular representation to the discontinuity of temporal succession. In Foucault's description of the evolving western *episteme*, the nineteenth century represents the crowning stage of an era during which the loosely seriatim accumulation of data is challenged and ultimately supplanted by their rigorously temporal (in other words, historicized) arrangement: "Thus, European culture is inventing for itself a depth in which what matters is no longer identities, distinctive characters, permanent tables with all their possible paths and routes, but great hidden forces developed on the basis of their primitive and inaccessible nucleus, origin, causality, and history."[20] Although he does not do so, Foucault might well have included in his remarks on the emblems and fields of inquiry pertinent to nineteenth-century thought a discussion of the realist novel, for it, too, symbolizes a focal point in the struggle between an earlier theory of representation ("the sovereignty of the Like") and a theory of signification that will eventually come to replace it (*Order* 43).

Fiction written under the aegis of realism confronts a daunting and ultimately self-defeating task. It is charged with constructing a description, distinguished by its precision and thoroughness, of the hidden inner mechanisms that animate and explain those movements of the social community as a whole and of its individual members that are accessible to superficial observation. The emphasis on the anthological completeness of social portraiture (Foucault's horizontality of the visible) is thus immediately accompanied by an exploratory expedition into underlying motivation and causality (Foucault's invisibility of the vertical). Using a vocabulary laced with adjectives that imply considerable drudgery, critics have long pointed out how realism undertook in herculean and frequently distended fashion the labor of classification of individuals—by sex, class, trade, physical attributes, psychological temperament, national or regional provenance, and so on—and of the nature and varieties of their interactions.[21] Propped up by a veneration of the document and a cult of the detail, realism drew upon several basic assumptions: the consequentiality of even the smallest particles, the most modest attributes and inconspicuous circumstances of the *hic et nunc*, and, concurrently, the imperative agency awarded mimesis, the aesthetic formula considered most capable of translating the multiplicity of the real into a work of words.

The reasons for this insistence (a neurotic drive, some would maintain) upon the novel of totality are not hard to discern. Bourgeois society, the wellspring of the realist impulse in fiction, was uniquely structured as a culture of institutional and also private spaces. In this culture, individuals were as likely to be submerged in the minutiae of the quotidian as they were to experience events on a grand scale, in all their vast historical sweep. Seized with the narcissistic desire to contemplate its own image in a fictional mirror, even at the risk of discovering that the reflection might be unflattering in the extreme, the middle class demanded that the novel reproduce both these domains, the public and the intimate, in all their infinitesimal particulars, conferring upon them a newly dignified significance. Singling out individuals of non-aristocratic ancestry and occupations and ennobling them by the very act of representation was a way of validating the bourgeoisie's status, of lessening its anxieties of origins. Accordingly, the realist novel normally passes over the sensational *faits divers* of the great men in favor of the now-decorous trivialities of middle-class existence.

The impetus for the creation and cultivation of a totalizing novel can also be traced to the fact that the nineteenth century is in large measure characterized by its submission to a pressing epistemological mandate, what Ortega labeled an "explicative furor." [22] Under the influence of such burgeoning disciplines as evolutionary biology and the experimental sciences, historiography, and philosophical positivism, all of them predicated upon a firm faith in the capacity of empirical reason to arrive at a definitive explanation of the real, the novel of Spain and Europe, as much as any sociological treatise or historical chronicle, also sought to "ballast its giddy imagination with the weight of truth, and submit its forms, conventions, and consecrated attitudes to the purifying ravishment of fact." [23]

In what would prove to be the first of many ironies governing the realist project, however, authors found themselves obliged to accept from the outset that in comparison to the variegated universe of physical, psychological, and social particulars that served as their inspiration and prototype, their novels could offer only an approximation of life's infinitude. Noting that the nineteenth-century novel exults in its "impenitent intercourse with the outer world," Harry Levin comments that realism "has the pluralistic advantage of recognizing that there are more things in heaven and earth than any one system can comprehend." [24] Nonetheless, as regards questions of formal execution, this unencompassable pluralism worked to the novel's disadvantage. Achieving realism's ends as a totalizing structure meant, paradoxically, engaging in a process of selection and reduction, since representation is inevitably and intrinsically synecdochic. In D. A. Williams's words: "Knowing the dream of total absorption of the real to be impossible, the Realist resigns himself to working with a scaled-down model of reality."[25]

This scaled-down model—what Williams alternately tags "discriminated occasions" (265) and other critics have identified with the terms *paradigm, pattern,* or *slice of life*—is, of course, nothing other than a segment of the continuum of the observed real along with the frame that distinguishes it. In fact, the quarantined field of activity that is the subject of the realist novel corresponds precisely to what Goffman in his examination of framing dynamics has labeled a strip: "an arbitrary slice or cut from the stream of ongoing activity, including here sequences of happenings, real or fictive, as seen from the perspective of those subjectively involved in sustaining an interest in them" (*Frame Analysis* 10). Commentators on the novel in Spain, including José María de Pereda, Leopoldo Alas, Emilia Pardo Bazán, and Galdós himself, spoke repeatedly of the composition of realist fiction in terms of a chained succession of scenes ("cuadros") or snapshots ("instantáneas") that freeze and outline moments whose typicality is guaranteed by the supposed randomness of their selection.[26]

The metonymic character of representation that is a feature of all realist writing is magnified in importance in Galdós's case by several factors peculiar to nineteenth-century Spain and the author's own artistic penchants. Stephen Gilman notes that in creating miniatures of society in which fictional biography allegorizes national life, Galdós employs "representational techniques derived not only from political cartoons but also from the basic tenets of 'krausista' social theory."[27] The satirical cartoon, appearing in newspapers, broadsides, and humorous reviews such as *Madrid Cómico*, was an expressive vehicle well known to Galdós, who drew pictures of individuals, places, and events in freestanding sketches and also in the margins of his manuscripts. The cartoonist has but a single panel to communicate a premise or hammer home a criticism; hence the inseparability of the production of the cartoon from the activity of framing and the strong visual and structural impact which this undoubtedly exercised on Galdós's works.[28] Krausism, as the most influential current in later nineteenth-century Spanish thought and a frequent intellectual backdrop for Galdós's writing, similarly favors a metonymic approach to representation, since it posited that microcosm and macrocosm would ideally be united in a harmonic rationalism and that the ills of the whole could be diagnosed and cured piecemeal by restoring health to its various parts.

Clearly, then, in its general conception or its specific embodiment in Galdós, conventional narrative realism is inevitably linked to the contrast of framed segment and open field. As Fredric Jameson intimates, realism portrays events as taking place "within the infinite space of sheer Cartesian extension, of the quantification of the market system: a space which like that of film extends indefinitely beyond any particular momentary 'still' or setting or larger vista or panorama, and is incapable of symbolic unification." [29]

The insurmountable paradox of the realist enterprise, nonetheless, cannot remain unacknowledged for long, for what at first appears to be realism's primary framing activity in fact is revealed to be a case of framing in the second degree. Addressing the issue of the preeminence of the pictorial code in literary mimesis, Barthes describes realist authors as transporting always with them an empty frame, more important even than their easels, which they must then fill: "the writer, through this initial rite, first transforms the 'real' into a depicted (framed) object; having done this, he can take down this object, *remove* it from his picture: in short, de-depict it (to depict is to unroll the carpet of codes, to refer not from a language to a referent but from one code to another. . .)." [30] By preceding the act of writing with this prior act of symbolic or imaginative framing, the novelist ends up copying a copy, while reality in its pure and unmediated state is displaced to a realm where it must forever remain inaccessible.

In his analysis not of literary operations but of social behavior, Goffman arrives at a remarkably similar conclusion. This, despite the fact that his approach and objectives are altogether different from Barthes's: where the latter rehearses a demythification of realism's ideological presuppositions, the former advances a phenomenological inquiry into the nature of perception. Goffman notes that it is normally assumed that "everyday activity provides an original against which copies of various kinds can be struck." Yet a closer inspection reveals that an individual's daily behavior does not necessarily reproduce an actual real-life model but may instead adhere to a series of predetermined cultural standards and social roles that offer an idealized, fabricated representation of conduct suitable for members of a particular society. "So, everyday life, real enough in itself, often seems to be a laminated adumbration of a pattern or model that is itself a typification of quite uncertain realm status," Goffman writes. And he concludes: "Life may not be an imitation of art, but ordinary conduct, in a sense, is an imitation of the proprieties, a gesture at the exemplary forms, and the primal realization of these ideals belongs more to make-believe than to reality" (*Frame Analysis* 562).

These strongly parallel observations on the nature of framing as mimesis of the second order strike at the heart of the correspondence theory that underpins the realist enterprise. The stability of literary realism as an aesthetic system derived from the conviction that there exists an untroubled similitude between the world as depicted and the world as lived, an isomorphic relationship between the sign and the object, language and truth. The stability of realism as an ideological construct was comparably predicated upon this same hypothesis. So long as the discourse of realism was deemed perfectly natural, there was little likelihood of a formal contestation of the bourgeois values that it depicted as universal and yet were contingent upon the organization of social power relations at a certain historical moment. Qualifying mimesis as a multi-tiered process of mediation belies the disinterestedness of realism's claims and conclusions regarding the ordering of the social world. At the same time, establishing the doubly imitative nature of mimetic representation effectively banished the referent from view and consigned the novel to a ghostly display of shadows in the cave.

Nineteenth-century authors were consequently faced with the choice of crying over lost signifieds or accepting the novel for what it truly was: a frame which, like all frames, extends not just passive support but also active definition. Proponents of naïve realism liked to claim that it was a transparent medium, a window on the world. Yet one could just as surely argue that in actuality "the window makes the scene" (*S/Z* 55). The language and the selective framing characteristic of realism do more than simply transcribe or ornament reality; they creatively configure it. The frames with which the nineteenth-century writer surrounds narrative are themselves a fabrication, no less so than the core texts they bound. The act of framing, thus fictionalized and incorporated into the novel, is engulfed by the very fictional content it was meant to frame. Outside becomes inside, referentiality becomes self-referential, the frame dissolves into the ambiguity of its own liminal position.

The more reflective (better still, the more reflexive) among the century's readers and writers, Galdós foremost among them in Spain, came to discern these essential paradoxes and aporias of the realist program. Description and enumeration, they intuited, can never be exhaustive. Neither can they lay claim to full presence, if they are based on prior models. The transcription of reality in a novel is reduced to a semiotic convention, an imaginary verbal construct that can never be truly objective or unmediated. Once authors sensed that an aesthetic project grounded in totalization and reproductive fidelity to the referent was in fact hopelessly utopic, literature saw the breakup of realism during the final decades of the 1800s. Henceforth, material reality would be elided as writers instead began to restrict themselves to conveying only that which could be known with certainty: the perceiving consciousness of the individual. As the novel looked beneath, or beyond, what Levin terms the "habitual surfaces of realism" (*Gates of Horn* 460), its center of gravity—its frame—shifted to the mind of the novelist. To borrow Germán Gullón's visual analogy, if the space of representation of the realist and the naturalist novels of Pereda or Pardo Bazán is a "frame charged with signs," a stage setting defined by the obtrusive curtains that hang on either side, then the modern novel exemplified by Unamuno has been stripped down to a "pure scaffolding, the space of a maquette," that for lack of a mimetic context must erect "its own frame of references."[31]

Galdós is perhaps the most prominent example of a Spanish writer situated on the cusp between the novel of realism and that of modernity. Readers of his texts can find numerous instances that seem to indicate that he has abandoned the hope of ever truly touching bottom in his dive into what constitutes the truth of the world around him. Such is the conclusion to be drawn from his ironically titled pair of novels, *La incógnita* and *Realidad*, in which the characters are haunted by a series of enigmas whose ostensible explanation only creates further ambiguities. Still, his works never totally relinquish a basic reliance upon the capacity of language to be meaningful and of art to record and censure egregious social imbalances and historical blunders in the hopes of redressing them. Resultingly, what is most notable is the unsteady status of the frame in Galdós's narratives. In a study of reading frames from Jane Austen to Henry James and Virginia Woolf, Mary Ann Caws observes a shift in the novel's emphasis from reading what is framed to reading the frames themselves, a shift which she accounts for by asserting that literary modernism is characterized by the impulse to "set aside aesthetic beauty."[32] One might object that if what characterizes modernity and its cultural manifestations is in fact not the adulatory setting apart of beauty but rather the destruction of logic and linearity, causality, and transcendentalism, then the modern novel is engaged more than anything in the destruction of the frame. Even Thomas Pavel, who in the face of the conventionalist-structuralist rejection of referentiality remains an eloquent defender of the philosophical legitimacy of the links between the universes of fiction and referential discourse, is inclined to agree: "Critics of contemporary culture have not failed to notice the trend toward a drastic reduction of fictional distance that brings fictional worlds as close as possible to the beholder. Frames and conventional borders seem to vanish, and the purpose becomes achievement of immediacy." [33]

Between these two extremes of fictional discourse, the one adamantinely framed and the other unbounded and indeterminate, Galdós's texts remain suspended in an almost preternatural equipoise. As the fictional plane more and more intrudes upon the verisimilar, as novelistic form is increasingly infiltrated by dramatic structures, as narrative self-consciousness and traditional omniscience collide and collude, the narrative frame moves in and out of focus. Meaning is held in abeyance, the better to see the process of its construction, but then is restored from its temporary exile. Evolving technically throughout the decades of the 1880s and 1890s, the *Novelas contemporáneas* continually oscillate between the word as representation and the word as a sign of its own nature and making. The depth that Galdós achieves in his work is in large part owing to the fact that readers are not asked to choose one pole over the other. They are instead expected to shuttle between the two realms indefinitely, becoming more deeply aware of each alternative, each ambiguity, a reading strategy that finds its equivalent in those visual paradoxes that involve what E. H. Gombrich labels "switching." In such well-known examples as Rubin's vase (the outlines of a vase reverse to form the profiles of two heads turned to face each other), the Winson figure (which may be read visually as an Indian or an Eskimo), or the rabbit-duck sketch, the location of the subjective contour oscillates and the viewer's attention is captured, first by one figure, then the other, always on an alternate basis. Eventually, the viewer remembers one reading when executing the other, but cannot hold both interpretations at once since they are mutually contradictory. [34] Many of Galdós's most challenging texts behave in comparable fashion, sending readers from story to discourse, referent to fictive universe, and back again. In the process, both sets of readings are problematized, and enriched.

Before concluding any discussion of frames and framing activity, it seems only fitting to address a few final remarks to the problem of margins. Even though certain historical periods have been characterized by their delight in large, heavily carved frames that surround pictorial fields with their obtrusive material reality, perhaps the better to guarantee the value of what they encompass, frames are by definition the designators of edges and borderlines, which do not partake of such corporeality. Derrida writes, echoing Ortega, that "the frame is in no case a background in the way that the milieu or the work can be, but neither is its thickness as margin a figure. Or at least it is a figure which comes away of its own accord."[35] The brackets that segment and segregate a field—a social event, a text, a piece of art—enjoy an odd status that is at once internal and external to the field; the site of their inscription is apparently undecidable. As Goffman insists, "these markers, like the wooden frame of a picture, are presumably neither part of the content of activity proper nor part of the world outside the activity but rather both inside and outside, a paradoxical condition . . . not to be avoided just because it cannot easily be thought about clearly" (*Frame Analysis* 252). Quite evidently, what transpires at the margins of any perceptual or conceptual framework cannot simply be pushed aside as unworthy of attention. Elements of a literary text, or of a reading of a text, are often relegated to the periphery because they do not fit well-established and accepted frameworks, suggesting vulnerabilities in the frame's adequacy and authoritativeness that demand reexamination. Often it is the case that previous interpretations of the text, by partitioning it into a meaningful center and an insignificant outer rim, establish an identity for it that the text's own borderline components, its semantic and structural leftovers, work to contradict.

One of the strategies at work in *The Reframing of Realism* is, therefore, that of reading and writing at the margins of Galdós's fiction. This logic of the residual has led to an examination of actual textual margins (opening and closing chapters and the framing tropes they employ), of minor or popular art forms that are interwoven into the fabric of mainstream nineteenth-century Spanish realism (kitsch, melodrama, serial novels), of varieties of discourse or genres marginalized by classical rhetoric (ekphrasis and novelistic description) or by the stylistic protocols and ideological postulates of late nineteenth-century realism (most forms of romantic expression, including utopian socialist political treatises), of ignored textual motifs and novels and novelists outlawed wholesale from the canon. By challenging traditional notions of what is considered relevant to a text or group of texts—notions which often act unwarrantedly to immunize readers against the idiosyncratic—I have attempted to present in my readings a fuller understanding of the competing aesthetic and ideological discourses that erode realism's monolithic vision and foreshadow its eventual (self-)immolation. Surely it has become increasingly necessary to pursue these successes and failures, these laws and loopholes of the theory of representation that undergirds realism and referentiality, given the fact that narrative paradigms are themselves increasingly being applied in the interpretation of such diverse fields as history, anthropology, psychology,

philosophy, and science. In Wallace Martin's words: "Mimesis and narration have returned from their marginal status as aspects of 'fiction' to
inhabit the very center of other disciplines as modes of explanation necessary for an understanding of life." [36]

Finally, while it never ceases to amaze scholars who have found in Galdós's enormous novelistic production a seemingly inexhaustible lode to be
mined, the fact is that his work still remains largely unexcavated by those
otherwise conversant in the fortunes and foibles of nineteenth-century
European fiction. In that sense, reading Galdós continues to be, regret-
tably, an exercise in reading at and against the margins of the contemporary
discourse on realism. This is a forceful reminder that in many ways critical
readings of realistic fictions are, like realism itself, consensual patterns,
too often sclerosed by inattention and convention, but always potentially
susceptible to reassessment and reframing. Whether my own book succeeds in establishing a dialogue with scholars and dedicated readers of the
nineteenth-century novel will eventually be judged by the ways in which
it, too, is framed anew in subsequent discussions of the embarrassment of
riches to be found in Galdós's fiction.

ONE

Narrative

Frames

1

Narrative

Beginnings

in

La de

Bringas

He who has no feeling for art lacks the disposition for collecting, activity, the spirit of observation, and the tenacity needed to study the genre he chooses (it is impossible to undertake them all); he loses time and money and risks being carried off to a lunatic asylum. What nature doesn't give . . . . —Romualdo Nogués y Milagro, Ropavejeros, anticuarios y coleccionistas

La de Bringas, Galdós's justly famous novel of domestic and political revolutions, opens with a gesture toward revolution in narrative as well. Experienced readers of Galdós were a faithful lot, buying up his *Novelas contemporáneas* and especially his *Episodios Nacionales* with a regularity as rhythmic as that with which their author produced them. Yet their prior encounters with Galdós's texts scarcely prepared them for chapter 1 of *La de Bringas*, where they discovered neither a cast of characters, nor a budding intrigue, nor the customary introduction of a concrete social milieu. Looking for the standard interpretive clues they had come to rely upon, what they found was a densely packed description of something (exactly what they would not know until the chapter's final sentence) divorced from any relevant explanatory context. Instead of the expected signals that might fix their position relative to the narrative universe, once inside the novel's inaugural frame they discovered yet another framed entity to contend with, in the form of a lengthy ekphrastic set-piece. And within the borders of this verbal presentation of a picture, still another box, in the form of a mausoleum. The nesting boxes of the first chapter so interiorize the space of representation that readers are immediately situated *in medias res*, literally in the middle of the thing, whatever that thing might be.

The suspension and deferral of meaning that occurs as readers pass from one frame to the next, either withholding or revising judgment on what they perceive, appears to contradict the logic of the function of the beginning in narrative, which Lotman specifies as nothing less than the provision of a comprehensive cultural model: "It [the beginning] is not only evidence of existence, but also a substitute for causality, a category of later origin."[1] Addressing a series of general remarks to the problem of framing, Uspensky similarly notes that "the concepts of the 'beginning' and the 'ending' have a particular significance. Their importance becomes manifest in the formulation of systems of culture which we understand to be systems of the semiotic representation of the world view (or more precisely, systems relating social and personal experience)."[2] And speaking of the role of beginnings in novelistic, historical, philosophical, and critical discourses, Edward Said notes that "beginning is not only a kind of action; it is also a frame of mind, a kind of work, an attitude, a consciousness. It is pragmatic—as when we read a difficult text and wonder where to begin in order to understand it, or where the author began the work and why. And it is theoretic—as when we ask whether there is any peculiar epistemological trait or performance unique to beginnings in general."[3] Said affirms that a beginning establishes a time, place, object, principle or deed; some beginnings introduce several of these cues at once (*Beginnings* 41). The initial descriptive chapter of *La de Bringas* does in fact intimate a historical past: "Era" 'It was' is the novel's first word. However, the necessary clarifications regarding the other elements Said mentions are not introduced until very belatedly in the chapter.

Readers do eventually learn that the first chapter of *La de Bringas* is a representation of a funeral tableau fashioned out of hair clippings, but this knowledge does little to reconcile for them the contradictory maneuvers of the text. No matter how gilded or ornate it may be, it is not the frame that should occupy the viewer's attention but rather the picture. This particular picture, however, is worthless. Truly *de trop*; although the bathetic scene mounted under glass is freighted with detail, there is nothing in the image worth lingering over. Figuratively speaking, the frame demarcates an empty field. Literally, the image is a depiction of a cenotaph, a funeral monument that is purely symbolic, for although it mimics in form a sepulchre it contains no mortal remains of the deceased honoree. Once again, the reader, conditioned to anticipate the plenitude of information and significance that realism promises, reaches the center and finds nothing there. Clearly, the cenotaph, as an inaugural frame within a frame, is a key to understanding Galdós's devastating critique of representation and the society that so firmly trusts in it.

In *Galdós, novelista moderno*, Ricardo Gullón points out the empire occupied in Galdós's novels by objects of everyday life submitted to the ruthless scrutiny of their chronicler.[4] Indeed, the contemporary reader, at a considerable remove from the world so surveyed, is struck by the diversity of artifacts Galdós singles out. Clearly, his purposes are twofold: to transcribe mimetically the particulars of nineteenth-century Spanish social reality and embody symbolically certain truths in the psychological makeup of his characters. In Galdós's fictional universe, the old *topos* of the similitude that exists between an individual's physiognomy and his inner moral being, the former functioning as a visible mark or sign of the latter, is also amplified to include all manner of inhabited human space and the personal possessions which fill it. Furthermore, such extended metaphorical appendages to a character's physical person no longer serve the sole function of moral definition. In light of the realist novel's impulse toward documentation and naturalism's emphasis on the power the environment wields in channeling the course of individual development, seemingly trivial details of decor and decoration become part of both the cultural and hermeneutic codes of the novel. In a quite graphic sense, these details allow the reader to locate a given character upon a complex grid of factors: religious convictions, political affiliations, economic standing, educational background, and so forth. They come to constitute, as the author explains in *Tristana*, "the expressive language of things" (5: 1545), a language whose signs bristle with the idiosyncratic detail of the *realia* they represent.

Galdós's use of settings and domiciliary objects are crucial elements in the narrative economy of his works, as William Risley has shown to be the case in the first six *Novelas contemporáneas*.[5] Among them, Risley finds the dramatization of mood, the expression of personality or will, the creation of a verisimilitudinous illusion of a "real" world within the novel corresponding to the extratextual world, geographical emplacement, and the revelation of subjective authorial evaluation of characters. Almost as varied are the formal techniques used in the presentation of these settings and objects: expository description offered by an omniscient narrator, dramatization filtered through the perceiving consciousness of the characters themselves, monologic interludes, or indirect free discourse. Not surprisingly, the rhetorical tone employed by the narrator in these segments is equally kaleidoscopic. It traverses the gamut from the broadly satirical (the doll-like image of the infant Jesus dressed in underclothes by Rosario in *Doña Perfecta*), to the endearingly foolish (Frasquito Ponte's toilet in *Misericordia*), to the clinically sober or downright ominous (the dissected cat in *El doctor Centeno*).

The lingering gaze of the character and the narrator wrenches the object from its typifying context and inflates it to extraordinary proportions, even while acknowledging its conventional denotative signification. Correspondingly, the relationship linking the fictional characters with their assorted accoutrements is immediately invested with psychic significance and energies. Not content merely to represent a neutral or zero-degree narration of the simple ratio "owner:possession," Galdós situates objects in terms of the relationship of miser to treasure, curator to rarity, addict to narcotic. Maxi Rubín's piggy bank, Rosalía Bringas's cape, and the manuscripts of José Ido's serial novels transcend their own referential function. They are by turns obsession, crutch, hallucinogen, or fetish.

Of all the items spilling from the cornucopia of descriptive delights with which Galdós has stocked his novels, perhaps none is quite so minutely dissected nor so bizarrely exalted in its inconsequentiality as the cenotaph, laboriously emerging under the tireless hands of Francisco Bringas before the uncomprehending eyes of the reader. What is one to make of this most peculiar object whose description comprises the entire opening chapter of *La de Bringas* and which occupies its maker until blindness overtakes him in chapter 20? Beyond the triteness of the image (a mourning tableau composed of symbols taken from romanticism's iconography of death) and the disconcerting nature of the material in which it is worked (human hair of various members of the Pez family), there is the fact that Galdós places precisely this ludicrous emblem in novel-initial position.

Compared to other texts that begin with an exchange of letters (*La familia de León Roch*), an exchange of dialogue (*Tormento*), or a lengthy relation of the personal history and genealogical antecedents of a character (*Lo prohibido, Fortunata y Jacinta, Torquemada en la hoguera*), *La de Bringas* stands apart as a novel whose narrative movement is inaugurated by a frame that encapsulates the prolix description of a thing. The thing, moreover, happens to be worthless, its sole distinction seeming to derive from its rather dubious artistic value. It meets "only the most relaxed aesthetic standards," as Michael Nimetz dryly comments.[6] Also puzzling is our observation that, verbosity notwithstanding, the actual description conceals almost as much information as it reveals. The identity of the object's creator is withheld from the reader until the final sentence. The disclosure that it is Francisco Bringas only succeeds in raising further inquiries, none of which is addressed within the confines of the first chapter. What is the object's intended function? Who is to be its recipient? What is its connection with other characters in the novel, or even with Bringas himself, who appears so indefatigably dedicated to this piece of sentimental junk? Indeed, if the novel's title promises that center-stage will be occupied by Rosalía, what sort of compositional logic dictates her absence from any active speaking role until chapter 10 and, instead, invokes as the novel's point of departure the profoundly unprofound labors of her husband? The questions where?, when?, who?, why?, questions of place, time, subject, and subjectivity which arise, Victor Brombert suggests, whenever a reader crosses the threshold of the opening lines of a text, are insinuated but then subsequently sidestepped by Galdós's narrator.[7]

Since the description of the hair work unfolds spatially rather than temporally and because it seemingly has no story to tell, *La de Bringas* paradoxically begins with a pause, even though no action or plotting has preceded that pause. Galdós's ingenious opening gambit, that is, arresting the narrative movement before it has even had a chance to get under way, apparently justified the worst fears of many critics of the novel regarding the role of description in general as ornamental and immobilizing, tending to disperse meaning among its particulars. Clarín is not unique in counseling that authors beware of crossing the line between realism, an art that subordinates the observation of accidental and petty details to an underlying knowledge of essences, and copying, a mechanical skill devoid of inspiration. He carefully explains and qualifies his praise of writers such as Ortega Munilla who, according to less forgiving critics, "paint for painting's sake and concede too much importance to the most insignificant objects, to trifles worthy only of being passed over in silence."[8] Even his great admiration for the artistic achievements of Galdós's *Novelas españolas contemporáneas* does not blind him to the fact that in novels such as *Miau* and *Fortunata y Jacinta* "the author pauses to describe and narrate certain objects and events that hardly matter and add no element of beauty nor even of curiosity to the work of art." Such passages are qualified as "digressions and details that tire certain readers and which, while they may not be superfluous, should not, however, be abused."[9] In his review of *La de Bringas*, the critic Orlando put the charges rather more bluntly: "Some [readers] have been unable to exit the labyrinth that Pérez and his companion enter in search of don Francisco Bringas; others have choked on the hair picture the latter is making . . . many individuals of both sexes have found themselves practically smothered amid so many ribbons, bows, and dresses."[10] Given the margination of the genre of ekphrasis in classical treatises of rhetoric and the frequent censure of nineteenth-century descriptive practices by professional critics and the lay public alike, Galdós's act of beginning his novel with the meticulous verbal portrait of the cenotaph, at once repulsive yet comical, represents a challenge to preexisting canons of novelistic composition and framing, a "hairy" endeavor in and of itself.

Generally, chapter 1 of *La de Bringas* has been analyzed for the manner in which it initiates certain major themes of the novel. Often the cenotaph has been considered as yet one more extravagant piece of kitsch in a novel literally strewn with the dissociated shards of bourgeois life. V. S. Pritchett, for example, sought to ground the use of the work's opening image in nineteenth-century romanticism's cult of death and its veneration of ceremonial funeral objects.[11] Here such morbid fascination is lampooned in the description of a piece of mourning jewelry, as exaggerated as it is representative of a fad that held Spain and much of Europe in thrall. Of course trinkets and costume jewelry commemorating the death of a loved one date back much further than the usage recorded by Galdós. The seventeenth century favored bejewelled skulls and enameled skeletons under glass, while the eighteenth century was fond of neoclassical designs taken from late Georgian memorial sculpture: broken columns and statuary, weeping willows, tearful madonnas, images which later made their way into Romantic symbology and eventually into Bringas's picture. Though already known in France during the Empire and Regency periods, mourning jewelry worked not in precious stones but rather in intrinsically cheap materials—seed pearls, ivory, black enamel, jet, and especially hair—enjoyed enormous popularity during the Victorian era.[12]

However, despite the patience and manual dexterity of amateurs and professionals, recruited in the manufacture of whole hair landscapes adorning large pendants and brooches framed in gold, the characteristic features of mortuary jewelry were its overt sentimentality and its cheapness. Always it was relegated to the status of minor art. All in all, an excellent opportunity for the narrator, apparently well acquainted with Iberian specimens of this form of ornamentation, to satirize a particularly ineffectual way of rendering homage to the dead. Francisco Bringas, in his slightly anachronistic enthusiasm for the cenotaph, becomes one more example of middle-class intranscendence in matters of both death and art.[13]

A second line of approach, also thematic in nature, treats the cenotaph as a metaphor for the anemic character of the Isabeline monarchy, thus linking two levels in the novel which, although separately delineated by the narrator, are nonetheless the warp and woof threads of the proverbial social fabric: the private circumstances of the individual and the broader scheme of historical events in the public domain. The most obvious are the formal coincidences and similarities establishing the links between biography and history. As Gullón so rightly notes, the description of the cenotaph emphasizes above all its chaotic, labyrinthine qualities.[14] When, in chapter 4, both the narrator and don Manuel Pez become hopelessly lost in the maze of apartments where Bringas lives, directly above the royal family's own quarters in the palace, an explicit parallel is drawn between the two spheres. Confronted by spiral stairways that lead nowhere, doors that do not open, winding passageways, and dead ends, the narrator comments that "we didn't recognize any part of that labyrinthine city," which appears to him "a capricious architecture and a mockery of symmetry" (4: 1592). Galdós's recounting of Rosalía's and Francisco's petty and insubstantial lifestyle as exemplified by the cenotaph reproduces on microcosmic scale the narrow circle of bureaucratic inaction, ceremonial pomp, and convoluted rhetoric within which the already doomed queen and her consort Francisco de Asís had been moving. By the same token, Bringas's sudden loss of his sight, the result of so much close work on his picture, allows him to fall back on a moral blindness to his wife's economic trespasses and sexual infidelities, much the same way in which the ruling forces of prerevolutionary Spain had lost sight of their responsibilities to the nation, even as Isabel II reportedly dallied in her boudoir with men other than her husband.

The analogy between the cenotaph and the monarchy has also been drawn from a Bachelardian perspective that emphasizes the symbolism of enclosed spaces in a world of bourgeois values. For Chad Wright, Bringas's withdrawal to one corner of the Gasparini salon to work on the tableau represents a voluntary exile to a "secret space" far removed from "the reality which exists outside in troubled Madrid" or, for that matter, in his own home, in the Camón.[15] One can easily adduce a parallel retreat from the most pressing economic and political issues on the part of Isabel II's government during the decade immediately preceding *la Gloriosa*, the "glorious" Revolution of 1868. So, as Nicholas Round succinctly concludes, not just Rosalía's world (the hyperactive life of the court) but also Francisco's (the sluggish civil-service bureaucracy) is "insulated against the demands of external reality": "Unrealism is the unifying theme of the book."[16] From the inventory of objects belonging to this one married couple, and from the cenotaph in particular, *La de Bringas* deftly extrapolates the moral and political tenor of an entire nation.

So much exploration of the thematic implications of the hair picture has tended to slight the role played by the cenotaph in the structuring of the novel and the destabilizing of its narrative voice.[17] To appraise this role more fully, readers must focus their attention once again on the lengthy excursus of chapter 1, reexamining the linguistic as well as the visual structures of the text, the better to trace the echoes that reverberate through subsequent chapters. The problem of Bringas's self-proclaimed masterpiece demands consideration from a dual perspective that evaluates the cenotaph as both content and as activity, that is, as object and as method. What becomes clear is that in his choice of incipit for *La de Bringas*, that is, the mock-epic presentation of Francisco's "handsome sepulchral design," Galdós lays as the foundation for his novel a triad of closely related concepts: the miser's compulsion to hoard capital, the artist-collector's impulse to assemble museums for private enjoyment, and the fetishist's drive to eroticize a fragmented and highly personalized object. In each instance, there occurs a deracination of an object from its quotidian context. Money is removed from circulation; the art work is divested of any and all utilitarian functions and is instead enshrined in the gallery; the whole person as erotic stimulus is discounted in favor of the isolated part. In each case, too, an air of covertness or the clandestine accompanies the activities of seeing and possessing. The miser's furtive hiding and counting of his or her treasure is comparable to the private viewing of art in a personal collection or the shameful and secretive contemplation of the fetish. Naturally enough, when the object is removed from its natural environment and its prestige disproportionately exaggerated in relation to its raw worth, the result is an actual or figurative distortion of the fields of perception and representation. Examples of such distortion in *La de Bringas* include the disruptive effects of radical myopia (microscopic effect), extreme tunnel vision (telescopic effect), and a generalized breakdown of optic structures that takes place as highlights and relief outlines are submerged and disappear into a sea of minutiae (a sort of reverse pointillism).[18]

In this way, *La de Bringas* sets up a system of interlocking activities— seeing, possessing, displaying—engaged in by the protagonists and others in their circle. *La de Bringas* is in the final analysis a novel about perception and acquisition, voyeurism and exhibitionism. That these complementary activities are shown to be self-defeating stands as one of Galdós's more scathing indictments of the Spanish middle class, poised for a revolution which would effect no real and lasting transformation of society, a revolution that was itself all show or empty display. The interlaced impulses of the miser, the collector, and the fetishist governing the fabrication of the cenotaph as a consequential object in the initial chapters introduce numerous elements of plot and characterization that will be expanded upon in later portions of the novel. Viewed in this context, the description of the hair landscape is no mere descriptive digression or vestige of *costumbrismo* but rather a principal device in the signifying systems of the work: "Very frequently, especially when the search for a beginning is pursued within a moral and imaginative framework, the beginning implies the end—or, rather, implicates it."[19]

No less importantly, the techniques Bringas uses in making his hair picture—the cenotaph viewed as method rather than product—provide the reader with an indicator of Galdós's concept of what should be the true function of art and artistic creation, to what extent realism can help achieve these aesthetic goals, and how an artist's mistaken interpretation of realism can prevent him or her from ever successfully entering art's domain. The discrepancy between Francisco's positive opinion of his own creation and the contradictory judgment evinced by the narrator, already transparent in the inaugural chapter and hence vital to the undermining of Francisco's authority and objectivity, is truly vast. However, the disparity between Bringas's theory of art and that of Galdós as evidenced by his novelistic practice is greater still.

Just what sort of object does Galdós offer on the first pages of his novel? The little image that Bringas mounts under glass is an oppressively over-ornamented mausoleum. An angel in near-supine position is draped over the tomb. Flowers and willows surround it; an inscription punctuates it; and behind it can be discerned a landscape of trees, a distant city, mountains, and bodies of water, all receding toward the horizon. If the pictorial composition is hackneyed, then the art form itself is obsolete. This fact is acknowledged by the narrator, who explains how in 1868, in response to Carolina Pez's desire to pay tribute to her late daughter Juanita, and Francisco's own wish to repay (but only at nominal cost) Manuel Pez's help in securing young Paquito Bringas a government post, Francisco begins work on "an ornamental, commemorative work of the kind that now are only found, faded and dirty, in the shop windows of old-fashioned hairdressers or the burial niches of some cemeteries" (4: 1588). First introduced in the text's opening margins, the hair work is by all accounts marginal: in its standing relative to the arts and even to other crafts, in its preterition by current standards of taste, even in its use of the pilar medium, for hair is a nonliving excrescence that grows at the margins of the human body.

Bringas's picture reminds readers of the old adage about not seeing the forest for the trees, since by its very nature it is a chaotic jumble of undifferentiated components. The description of the cenotaph contained in the novel's introductory chapter proceeds by enumeration and accumulation of its many parts, and the resulting image's most striking quality is its ineradicable heterogeneity. The mausoleum is a disordered mix of architectural styles (classical, Gothic, Plateresque, late Renaissance, and Tyrolean), borrowing details from sources that include the monuments of Egypt ("pyramidal staircase"), the temples of classical antiquity ("Graeco-Roman socles"), and the buttresses, ogival arches, and gargoyles of the great cathedrals of the Middle Ages.[20] The sepulcher's surfaces are covered with virtually every icon of death known to Romantic painting and sculpture, including torches, urns, amphorae, owls, bats, winged water-clocks, scythes, palm fronds, coiled serpents, and floral crowns of everlastings. The angel in center foreground position groans under a cumbersome apparatus of flowers, wings, feathers, beribboned garlands, even an hourglass; its footgear is part boot, part sandal, part cothurnus. The ground itself is carpeted by an assortment of daisies, pansies, sunflowers, lilies, and tulips. The overall arrangement of the tableau suggests a juxtaposition of wildly disparate motifs appropriated from many sources, as is later confirmed in chapter 3:

> The willow came from *The Tomb of Napoleon at St. Helena*; the weeping angel had come from the catafalque placed in the Escorial for the funeral of one of the wives of Fernando VII, and the background was taken from a little engraving in I don't know what Lamartinesque volume that was syrupy sweet. Finally, Bringas picked the flowers from the garden of an illustrated book on the *Language of Flowers* in Doña Cándida's library. (4: 1590)

Compounding the confusion, the cenotaph in its execution is simultaneously reminiscent of every major form of printmaking, including etching, engraving, woodcut, pen and India ink drawing, and pencil sketch. Even the medium used to construct the picture claims provenance from several different sources; hair samples covering the full tonal spectrum from grey to blonde to brown to black are taken from at least five members of the Pez family.

As is readily apparent, *La de Bringas* deals with the social climbing of an acquisitive bourgeoisie which measures its status against the variety of luxury goods found in the home. But the Bringas household is not nearly as wealthy as Rosalía or Francisco might wish, and the funeral picture, although bound for the Pez family's drawing room, is no elegant bibelot. On the contrary, don Francisco is faced with the oxymoronic task of gifting Pez with "something original, admirable, and valuable which wouldn't cost the blessed señor any money" (5: 128). If, indeed, it is when people are poor(er) that they indulge in the "multiplying absurdities of displacement of materials and decorations and functions,"[21] then not just Rosalía's remodeled gowns but also her husband's pseudoartistic endeavors are an illustration of this pointless merging of items and materials. The purchasing power Rosalía wields at the Sobrino Hermanos emporium is indiscriminate; so, too, Francisco's middle-class standing is most clearly defined by his nonselectivity. The blur of indifferentiation which clouds his existence is nowhere more evident than in the cenotaph, that monument to miscellanea and superfluity where he has unsuccessfully combined visual images, architectural styles, and artistic media with no attempt to order these elements in any sort of hierarchy. As the narrator's critique affirms, the end result is an "aggregate of details," never a "whole." This is only fitting, as Galdós views the contemporary society out of which the Bringas household emerges as itself a kind of alphabet soup in which a still-amorphous bourgeoisie drifts amid the flotsam of older social structures now in decomposition.[22]

The verbal and visual processes used in the presentation of the cenotaph follow very closely the narrative operation that the Russian Formalists described by the term *defamiliarization*.[23] By beginning at the heart of the image and working out piecemeal toward the borders of pictorial space, by refusing to identify the tableau or what it is made of until the closing sentence of the chapter, the description of the object under examination is subject to an estrangement from normal perception. This contributes to the bizarre impression that the reader forms of the cenotaph, and of course heightens the irony surrounding its conception and execution. The first two paragraphs, overflowing with their catalog of details, deliberately create the sense that narrator and reader alike are confronting some vast sculptural unit. What is the reader's surprise, then, when two-thirds of the way into the description it is revealed that the entire tableau "was enclosed in an oval that might have measured *media vara* at its greatest diameter," about sixteen inches by modern standards?

This sly undercutting of previously established impressions, which sets up reader expectations only to give the lie to them, crops up whenever the cenotaph is being discussed. It is an integral part of Galdós's demythification of materialism as a governing principle of the Spanish middle class: so much effort and pride of ownership lavished on a truly inconsequential object. It is, further, a symptom of the clash of scale between the miniature and the colossal, the bounded and the boundless, that troubles Francisco Bringas. Unable to cope with the ever-widening implications of the course of his nation's politics, he withdraws from the sprawling palace, itself set within the even larger public space of the modern city that is Madrid, and instead turns inward to the safety of a tiny, private world that is kept framed under glass and so under control. It is also, however, no less a warning to the reader as regards the untrustworthiness of the narrator who in chapter 6 pretends to remove "el estorbo de mi personalidad" 'the impediment of my personality' in favor of a neutral and omniscient point of view, but whose subjective presence will reemerge at certain key moments of the narrative.

The defamiliarization of the cenotaph is due at least in part to the extreme angle from which it is contemplated. The narrator's lens zooms in for a strabismic close-up, and only reluctantly backs up to allow for a panoramic view of the work as a whole. The similarity between the narrative approach in Galdós's novel and the visual techniques deployed by Bringas in his picture—a confluence of the textual and the textural, it is tempting to say—is unmistakable.[24] Compared to an actual scene in nature, the image Bringas creates has also undergone an estrangement of perspective. A quick look at two of the most influential systems of European painting that flourished during the decade when Galdós wrote *La de Bringas* will confirm this.

As impressionism and pointillism attempted to demonstrate, all images are composed of inherently infinite divisions and subdivisions of hue and mass occurring under the effects of light. The images, although transferred to canvas in the divided state, can once again be fused into a coherent whole on the retina of the eye of the viewer, provided he or she stands at a proper distance. Pressing one's nose up against a painting by Monet or Signac reveals seemingly random groupings of hazily delineated splotches in the former example, a series of primary-colored dots in the latter. Yet by stepping back, the viewer discovers an organically harmonious composition that suddenly sharpens into focus. The impressionist sought to convey a subjective truth about the world's appearance, the pointillist a more purely objective one, but although their philosophical and expressive approach varies, the mechanics of perception remain unchanged. By contrast, Francisco's picture follows the laws of a reverse pointillism in which the nearsighted perspective is never abandoned and no formal coherence ever emerges. Bringas carefully tries to re-create the illusion of depth, but the end result is still, hopelessly, a picture of indifferentiation. All the component parts are treated with equal importance; there is no visual subordination of minor elements to major ones. All fight to capture the attention of the spectator: "These objects climbed all over each other as though disputing, inch by inch, the space they were to occupy" (4: 1587). In subsequent chapters Bringas will be shown to be oblivious to the changing course of national politics and his own marital situation, but this myopia is really first introduced as a novelistic motif in the initial chapter, by way of the actual visual deformation that characterizes the cenotaph in all its "tangled prolixity," its *mare magnum* of detail.[25]

Yet another outstanding feature of the emblematic mourning tableau is the narrative tension between monumentality and trivialization which animates the language of its description. Although the passage describing the cenotaph corresponds grammatically to the voice of the first person narrator-witness, two distinct types of expression emerge. The more obviously pejorative language which damns the object for its vulgarity is easily identified with the narrator's own. Other circumlocutions which seem to praise the design of the object and the ingenuity of its manufacture belong to Francisco, Carolina Pez, and all those who dutifully admire the hair picture. However, since they issue verbally and syntactically from the lips of the narrator, they deliver an incongruous and highly ironic message to the reader. In adopting the mode of expression of these characters claiming only doubtful artistic credentials, the narrator subverts the literal meaning of their words. Thus references to the picture as a "handsome sepulchral design," a "very daring architecture," or a "difficult piece of work" are repetitions in a parodic mode of the comments of artistic innocents like the little friends of Isabelita Bringas, who crowd into the salon and exclaim: "How preeetty, how preeecious . . . ! Praaaised be God . . . , what angel's fingers!" (4: 1598). On the other hand, the greater part of the description closely follows the narrator's own more skeptical evaluation of the picture, and so emphasizes a large repertoire of reductive verbal techniques: for example, the numerous uses of the diminutive ("arbolito" 'little tree,' "caballerito" 'little gentleman'), the ironic superlative ("atrevidísima" 'very daring,' "pequeñísima" 'extremely small'), and the unflattering augmentative ("lagrimones" 'big tears,' "angelote" 'ungainly angel').

The angel in the hair picture, it should be noted, is demoted to the level of ordinary human being. Endowed with "ample flesh," the seraph suffers from a notable androgyny. It has women's feet yet is shown to be male because its weeping is accompanied by acute embarrassment: "covering its eyes with its hand as though ashamed to cry." Not just the epicene angel but also the willows and the letters forming the inscriptions on the tomb cry in the snivelly manner common to children. So the process of miniaturization begins with the microscopic physical scale of the cenotaph and then continues as an analogous reduction is carried out on all other levels: linguistically, by the peppering of the text with diminutives; sentimentally, by the predominance of a plangent sensibility that manifests itself in "moco y baba," the 'snot and drool' of the mewling toddler; and transcendentally, by the negation of the majestic gravity of the angel, the latter accomplished by diluting its gender distinction and endowing it with an anthropomorphized concern for human fashions, sentiments, and gestures. Conversely, while man and the divinity are belittled, inanimate objects are exalted, even burlesquely personified. The sculptural embellishments on the sepulcher fight each other for breathing room. The "melancholy letters" are disconsolate; the willow sheds leaves described as "fainting" and "suffering."

The tension between monumentality and trivialization has been observed by critics elsewhere in *La de Bringas*. Its particular significance in chapter 1 is nonetheless unique, because this tension is no less intimately connected with the narrator and his discourse than with the object being described. That is, by referring to the cenotaph as a "beautiful work" while tacitly implying its garishness, Galdós's narrator is established from the outset as a duplicitous character. He is, in fact, a kindred spirit to his friend Manuel Pez, who tells Bringas to his face that his picture "is a marvel" while thinking to himself that it is a piece of junk that only Bringas could dream up and that, fittingly, only his wife Carolina could appreciate: "What a ridiculous object . . . It's as though it materialized out of that thick skull of yours. Only you, you big fool, make such preposterous things, and only my wife likes them . . . You're made for each other" (4: 1615).

This early parallel between Pez and the narrator is crucial. It will be revived in the last chapter, where the basis for comparison turns from their shared aesthetic preferences to their sexual and political opportunism. Like Pez, who is able to ingratiate himself with whichever faction is in power, the narrator is not only not dispossessed by the revolution, but becomes the functionary presiding over the fate of those who are: "My luck, or my misfortune, determined that I was the person designated by the Junta to be the custodian of the Colossus and the administrator of everything that had belonged to the Crown" (4: 1682). And like his slippery friend Manuel, the narrator confesses to an involvement with Rosalía which appears to have ended when the price tag accompanying her favors grew too high. The novel concludes with the following lines: "We were then at the height of the revolutionary period. She [Rosalía] tried to repeat the proofs of her ruinously costly friendship, but I hastened to put an end to that. For if it seemed natural for her to be the support of her unemployed family, I didn't see myself in that role, in violation of all the laws of morality and domestic economy" (4: 1683).

One particular framing strategy found in certain folk tales and literary narratives is the sudden and unprecedented appearance of a first-person narrator at the end of the text, or conversely, the disappearance of such a narrator after the text's beginning pages, in each instance signaling the imposition of a point of view external to the story.[26] The blatant interruption of the narrator's voice in the final chapter can finally be seen as it links up with similar, more subtle intrusions in the initial chapter, at last making the novelistic frame clearly perceptible. The reader is now forced to reevaluate the message of the story of the Bringas family in light of this new evidence of the storyteller's own moral laxity and his final, self-righteous reform solely for reasons of economic expediency.

Once more the cenotaph can be seen as an integral part of the novel's structure. What might have been considered a trick ending—the narrator's confession of a potential liaison with Rosalía—turns out to have been carefully plotted.[27] Pez despises the hair tableau; so does the narrator. When Pez goes to visit Bringas at home, the narrator accompanies him. As his name indicates, Pez swims with ease through the turbulent waters of national politics; in this respect the narrator is also a survivor. And finally, Pez has his amorous tryst, although the adulterous encounter between him and *la de Bringas* is shortlived, their relationship unstable. And the narrator? Most likely he, too, is an unreliable paramour, as his snubbing of Rosalía in the final chapter makes clear. Yet the note of deception is sounded as early as the first chapter in the slippery, double-edged description of the cenotaph. In fact, the character whose voice speaks to the reader from the novel's incipit betrays with his words as well as with his actions; he is an inconstant lover and an inconsistent narrator.

By now it must be apparent that despite its subject matter, the hair picture has very little to do with the commemoration of death in general or Juanita Pez's death in particular. From heartfelt funeral tribute it has degenerated into a purely decorative object. "Era aquello . . . , ¿cómo lo diré yo? . . . , un gallardo artificio sepulchral" 'It was . . . how shall I describe it? . . . a handsome sepulchral design': so muses the narrator in the inaugural phrase of Galdós's text. The free-standing clause, "how shall I describe it?", may simply be one more indication of the control exercised by the narrator over the story and here metanarratively reflected upon in his discourse. The question asked is not "How was it?" (what was the cenotaph like?) but rather "How shall *I say* it was?" After such an introduction, it is certain that there is manipulation to follow—both of the text and the characters within that text. At the same time that Bringas is observed creating the hair landscape, the narrator is engaged in his own special brand of creation: the imposition of meaning upon the text, following his own partisan interpretation of the events he recounts. "How shall I describe it?" points to narrative caprice as regards the reproduction of reality. It is a red alert signaling to the reader that the feigned objectivity of the narrator's discourse is a sham.

But the narrator's self-directed question may also point to underlying expressive difficulties of a more serious nature. The narrator is in effect searching for linguistic signs which will convey to the reader the essential significance of the hair work. But the cenotaph means virtually nothing; it is a monstrous, depersonalized cliché. Clichés, overused and overly generalized, cease to signify precisely because they deal with the typical rather than with the individual or the distinguishable. As an object of indifferentiation, the cenotaph would thus seem to escape language, which is characterized by a most obvious process of differentiation on all levels, from the phonological to the syntactic and the semantic. Pictorially overcrowded and sentimentally demonstrative, the tableau is nonetheless empty of meaning, as befits its etymology (*cenotafio*, from *kenotaphion*, Gr. *kenos* + *taphos* "empty tomb," "a monument erected in honor of a dead person whose remains lie elsewhere"). The narrator's momentary hesitation of speech indicates by its tiny silence the colossal void of meaning and artistic value that is the hair picture's outstanding trait.

Steven Kellman has written that "the first words in a work of literature bear a uniquely demanding responsibility both to the corporation they represent and to the magistrate they petition."[28] The court of the reader is indeed a demanding one, and the pivotal opening sentences of the nineteenth-century novel were expected to provide information and orientation, to index and frame the real, to hasten the crossing of a verbal threshold that was symbolic of an ontological border. The function of the novel's overture was to effect somehow the transition of the readers' consciousness into the fictional universe which, not coincidentally, offered a simulacrum of the real world they had just left behind. In this regard, the question "how shall I describe it?" breaks up more than just the hypotactic syntax of the novel's initial line. It ruptures the continuous perception of lifelike surfaces; at the very least it clouds the mirror that would project the illusion of an unmediated representation of reality. In attempting to answer his own query, the narrator, relying on an empirical, encyclopedic description, seemingly holds out the promise of knowledge of the real. Yet by merely raising the question in the first place, he interposes language, thereby denying the possibility of ever fulfilling that promise. The chapter devoted to the presentation of the hair picture exemplifies the notion that every description is "a sort of internal metalinguistic apparatus inevitably led to speak about words instead of things."[29] And once the narrator begins speaking about words rather than things, the discussion of the cenotaph threatens to proliferate unendingly. After all, what is there to stop him? What law exists to force him to conclude his description and return to the business of narrating the story of Rosalía and Francisco? Regardless of what the chapter does or does not say about Bringas's tableau, it tells us a great deal about the narrator, especially about his exercise of an unlimited textual authority which long precedes (in the reader's experience, at least) the actual political authority that will be granted him in the hectic days following the September Revolution.

The first chapter of *La de Bringas*, it will be remembered, is marked by a halting and only partial revelation of the information necessary to make the wealth of detail expended on the cenotaph intelligible and meaningful to the reader. A few hints are thrown out along the way (one thinks, for instance, of the statement that the colors of the cenotaph are "brown, black, and blonde"), but these are the exception rather than the rule. Instead, it is only after the reader has formed a judgment of the unknown object as a life-sized mausoleum that the narrator reveals its true dimensions; only after we have been led to admire "the minuteness, the scrupulousness, and the steadiness of such a difficult piece of work" that the narrator announces the triviality of such labors; only after we are led to believe that Bringas is an artist that the narrator exposes his friend as a devotee of kitsch, the sort of man who would make a rosary out of grains of sand or reproduce the cathedral of Toledo inside a nutshell (4: 1590). Thus is delivered the coup de grâce that will hereafter cripple the reader's ability to take seriously don Francisco's opinions on such topics as art and the human imagination, his wife's faithfulness, or the unwavering allegiance of the Spanish navy to the Bourbon monarchy.

Philippe Hamon, himself an indefatigable classifier of the rhetorical operations governing the descriptive mode, observes that in many instances the incrustation in a text of a description (an announcement of the theme followed by its predicative expansion) is remarkably similar to the structure of a dictionary entry (presentation of the word followed by its definition). When, however, the identifying nomenclature (proper name, thematic term or lexia) is contradicted, temporarily elided or omitted altogether, the readability of the description becomes questionable: "But the term may be . . . rejected, even omitted, *at the end* of the description, which proliferates without the reader knowing *what* is being spoken about, and even gives rise to a narrative, a *quest* for knowledge, a *quest* for naming."[30] And not just a search for denomination, but for domination as well. The narrator finds himself in the position of being able to tell something because he is the one, etymologically speaking, who knows (Lat. *narrāre*, from *gnārus*, "knowing"). By controlling the amount of knowledge he chooses to dispense or conceal, he touches off a struggle with the reader who will attempt to wrest this knowledge from him.

In *La de Bringas*'s final paragraphs, the narrator divulges conclusive evidence of his duplicitous behavior with Rosalía. In surrendering this information from which he derives his power, he effectively surrenders a goodly portion of his narrative authority over the text and its readers. By way of compensation for this loss, he can console himself with the exercise of other forms of authority, both political (who may remain and who will be evicted from the residential quarters of the palace) and sexual (whose favors he will condescend to accept in exchange for his guarantee of preferential treatment under the new revolutionary government). And even from his position of diminished narrative authority he continues to flex his muscles, explaining that Rosalía claims that it will now be up to her to support and defend her family, but coyly refusing to say how: "How she managed things to this end is something that does not fall within the scope of this story. The new schemes of this señora have yet to be written" (4: 1683). In the absence of a sequel that would relate the subsequent history of this character, the reader remains indebted to the superior—because undisclosed—knowledge of the narrator.[31]

As the cenotaph moves further and further away from the representation of the realm of death, it draws ever closer to other categories of perception and experience far more germane to Bringas's existence, notably the financial, the aesthetic, and the sexual. In *La de Bringas* Galdós establishes Francisco in his triple characterization as miser, self-proclaimed artist, and fetishist, and, through a carefully controlled process of convergence, the cenotaph is transformed into the object of his affections on all three accounts. In *El amigo Manso*, Galdós had already offered in doña Cándida's friend Ponce an embryonic version of this character, blessed with an extraordinary manual dexterity yet incapable of seeing that his useless creations only bore people. "This man used to spend all the blessed day at my neighbor Cándida's house," the narrator criticizes, "either working on a cardboard palace to be raffled off, or else building a cage so big and complicated that he would never finish it. It was a *copy* of the Escorial made of wire. He knew how to make repairs and had a jigsaw with which he put together countless trinkets of wood, veneer, and ivory, all of them convoluted and in bad taste, fragile, useless, and never completed" (4: 1193). But whereas Ponce is dealt with in a few isolated paragraphs, it is with Francisco Bringas that the collector-fetishist-miser becomes the subject of the novel itself.

Bringas's inflated opinion of the value of the hair picture is something he intuits from the astonished reactions of those who visit the Gasparini salon to view the partially completed tableau: "All those who saw this marvel were enraptured by its originality and beauty and ranked don Francisco among the most famous artists" (4: 1590). This judgment is seemingly confirmed when Pez announces: "This work ought to go to a museum" (4: 1615). Undoubtedly don Francisco takes his friend's words at face value, thereby introducing the novelistic motif of the collector and broadening the use of the cenotaph as a point of reference associated not only with Bringas's stinginess but with his artistic preferences as well.

The history of the emergence in the nineteenth century of museums and private galleries implies the existence of several concomitant phenomena at work. On the one hand, the modern museum picks up where Kantian aesthetics leave off. The principle of disinterestedness, the self-sufficiency granted the category of forms of the beautiful in the *Critique of Judgment*, is recapitulated by the museum in its insistence upon isolating the items belonging to its collections for the sole purpose of scrutinizing them as art.[32] Even those objects that may have once responded to an extra-artistic, utilitarian function (say, church art or the artifacts of primitive civilizations) are removed from their surrounding cultural environment. A different and totally arbitrary relationship springs up between the museum and the newly uprooted art work, which is effectively transformed from functional object into pure sign as a result of the museum's framing action. On the other hand, by choosing to spotlight only certain works while rejecting still others, the museum is responsible for creating a dramatic rise in the intrinsic monetary worth of the favored pieces. And, finally, the museum can assure its continued existence only by holding on to its collection; its business, after all, is acquisition.

All these factors enter into play in Bringas's treatment of the hair picture, since the text highlights the apparent exclusivity and nonutilitarianism of this object which, left unfinished, never leaves his household. The display of the cenotaph to his neighbors as if it were a miniature masterpiece and his chimeric inflation of its value are not surprising activities coming from the miserly Francisco. As Maurice Rheims has pointed out, the miser resembles "the very type of person in whom one can recognize, as in the collector, 'the same need to possess, the same tendency to obtain quality.' These primordial traits are, in effect, common to misers and certain collectors."[33] In fact, the museological impulse, the compulsion to collect and view for one's private enjoyment, is burlesqued everywhere in *La de Bringas*, not just in the cenotaph. It is incarnated in Torquemada's house, described as a "museum of impossible luxury, of waste" (4: 1666), as well as in El Camón, the salon to which Milagros de Tellería and Rosalía withdraw to indulge their passion for the dressmaker's art. This same proclivity is associated with the cape purchased by Rosalía in chapter 10, which sets her on the road to economic perdition and is explicitly characterized by Galdós as "the passion of the collector in the presence of a rare specimen" (4: 1603). It is even identified with the boxes of bric-a-brac, the "treasure trove of knicknacks," which Isabelita and her father play with in the intimacy of Gasparini, his office and work area. Isabelita is plagued by poor digestion, nightmares, and epileptic convulsions, but not the least of her ills is the fact that "she suffered from the collector's mania" (4: 1663). These diverse examples of the collector's instinct run amok share the cenotaph's disequilibrium of scale. The amount of time and energy that the members of the Bringas family invest in the acquisition and contemplation of objects is out of all proportion to the collectibles' objective worth, a reminder of the same counterpoint between pseudoepic monumentality and trivialization which formed the cornerstone of the narrative treatment of the hair picture. The characters who indulge themselves in the pastime of collecting with no archaeological or aesthetic criteria to guide them simply repeat the initial error of non-selectivity in art exhibited by Bringas in chapter 1.[34]

Why should Galdós choose to focus in *La de Bringas* upon characters who collect things? Certainly it is not for the historical insights that collections may in potential provide their owners. While it is true that normally such activity carries with it the burden of cultural baggage, the cenotaph is essentially devoid of historical or folkloric connotations for don Francisco. In fact, Bringas's obsession with the hair picture is based precisely on its offering him an artificial refuge from the "revolutionary virus" (4: 1669) which threatens the fall of the monarchy and the loss of his own government position, events which when they finally come to pass he describes hyperbolically as "the end of the world" (4: 1680). The cenotaph he makes is a miniature, a narrative of nostalgia that stands outside the perimeters of temporality and causality: "The miniature does not attach itself to historical time."[35] Indeed, everything about the cenotaph bespeaks a flight from the historical present: Francisco's dedication to a meticulous labor involving eye and hand, suggestive of a rejection of the techniques of industrial production in favor of a return to an earlier age of artisanal craftsmanship; his recourse to pictorial elements which all derive from a specific iconographic vocabulary of the 1830s and 1840s but which, given their random juxtaposition, create no historical narrative; his portrayal of a moonlit landscape that pretends to exalt an idealized nature over culture; his creation of a tableau that eternalizes a moment in time and space that paradoxically reflects no lived human reality. As for Rosalía, her constant reshuffling of sleeves and bodices, fabrics and trimmings represents the pure present tense of fashion, a system whose pursuit of novelty erases all historical memory.

What distinguishes Rosalía, Francisco, and their children as true collectors is not so much the type of objects they hoard as the single-mindedness with which they pursue these pastimes, losing in the process all sense of time and creating a climate of secrecy and deceit surrounding the viewing of their treasures. Bringas is rapt with enthusiasm for his project and spends the first twenty chapters of the novel "submerged in the microcosm of the hair work" (4: 1601). His wife is no less intoxicated by the purchase of new clothes and the continual alteration of old ones. Resultingly, neither spouse pays any attention to time, or to each other. So absorbed is don Francisco in his creation that he spends all the leisure his job permits him working on the hair landscape. A similar temporal abstraction afflicts Rosalía. During her shopping trips with her friend Milagros, "time went by without their noticing it" (4: 1603).

With so many examples of aberrant behavior in *La de Bringas*, it must be obvious to the reader that both spouses have come to rely upon fragmentary material possessions as a source of much of their daily satisfaction. Dresses and hair landscapes have become transformed into fetish objects, and the act of collecting, viewing, and exhibiting them becomes an affective substitute in the absence of conjugal relations in the life of this mismatched literary couple. Rosalía's disparaging recollections of her first months with Bringas after their honeymoon are a clue to the sentimental void that now only a wardrobe crowded with dresses can fill. Right from the start she finds married life with her husband regimented and oppressive, a "domestic comedy": "Under the rule of such an ordinary man, she had learned her tepid role and played it mechanically, without realizing what she was doing. That insipid fellow had made her the mother of four children" (4: 1640).

Francisco seems no less indifferent to the Punch and Judy quality which marks their sexual encounters; by the period in which the novel's action unfolds (1867–1868), it appears that conjugal relations have been suspended altogether. With customary tact, Galdós alludes to the state of affairs in the bedchamber to which husband and wife retire separately and depicts Bringas as oblivious to Rosalía's chatter or, indeed, to her physical presence in the bedroom. Neither her conversation nor her disrobing have any impact on him, for his energies have already been spent: "When Rosalía returned home, don Francisco, his eyes and head fatigued after working on the cenotaph, would already be in bed and dozing." While removing her dress, petticoats, and corset, Rosalía dithers on about the gossip she has heard at Milagros's house, but she may as well be addressing a blank wall: "Don Francisco, now deeply asleep, was as far from all those miseries his wife was recounting as Heaven is from Earth" (4: 1609, 1611). The issue of Bringas's unresponsiveness to his wife is hammered home time and time again: "Don Francisco would fall asleep before her" (4: 1611). In the absence of matrimonial accord and intercourse, the compensatory value of the cenotaph to Francisco, as of dresses and accessories to Rosalía, is greatly increased. That Bringas uses human hair, mostly of female origin—one of the most common triggers of sexual fixation, as Freud saw—simply reinforces the fetishistic overtones of the cenotaph and Francisco's devotion to his craft.[36] The audacity of confronting the reader with an erotic fetish in the novel's very first chapter is surely unequaled in the always sexually circumspect nineteenth-century Spanish novel.

The hair picture turns out to be not just a thematic motif in *La de Bringas* but also a structural device, a means by which the field of vision and the textual field are made to coincide. It clarifies the ironically distanced stance of the narrator and establishes the counterpoint of voyeurism and exhibitionism—seeing and being seen, as applied to the perception of inanimate objects and to the psychology of sentient beings—as the compositional armature of the novel. At the same time, an examination of the role played by the cenotaph in *La de Bringas* must also include the manner of its conception and manufacture, which reveal Bringas's inadequacy as an artist in either the romantic or the realist mode.

The backward-looking don Francisco returns to the iconography of romanticism as the inspiration for his picture, although the sources he draws upon are at best second-rate. The description of the creative process he experiences, exaggeratedly recapitulated by the narrator, is similarly rooted in the romantic mythology of the work of art as a living organism born of a feverish explosion of uncontained expression: "He [Bringas] suffered from the epileptic malady of artistic gestation. The work of art, newly incarnated in his mind, was already announcing with internal tumult that it was a living being, and was developing extremely powerfully, pressing against the walls of his brain and exciting his nerve cells" (4: 1589). Nonetheless, the work he produces is stillborn, a true *naturaleza muerta*. Lacking the visionary quality intrinsic to romantic painting, it is simply "a frame within which all is glazed into sympathy and picturesque harmlessness," an airless tableau in which all sense of mystery has been neutralized.[37]

Of course Bringas's fortunes as a creative genius fare no better when considered in the context of the realist approach to art. In satirizing Francisco's particularly extravagant endeavors, Galdós demonstrates the pitfalls confronting the artist who mixes his stylistic sources indiscriminately or comes to rely upon slavishly imitative techniques in the execution of his or her work. In his address to the Real Academia in 1897 Galdós remarked that "the novel is an image of life." By contrast, the funeral memento that Francisco constructs is an image of other images, a simple line-for-line and strand-for-strand pastiche of fanciful Romantic engravings, statues, and paintings. Bringas does not duplicate nature in the cenotaph. Instead, observation of the real has given way to repetition of a previous artistic tradition which has itself rejected the *vraisemblable* in favor of the mythical. The mimetic activity thus engaged in by Bringas, twice removed from nature's domain, emphasizes fragmentation and the pure play of surfaces rather than the relationship of depth to surface ("souls" and "physiognomies") and the interaction of documentation and fictive creation ("exactitude" and "beauty") which are the objectives of Galdós's program of realism as outlined in his speech to the Academia. The weeping angel, the botanical specimens, the architectural fragments, and the moonlit landscape are all allegorical elements, signs of other signs, which demand a secondary decoding of their meaning. Allegory reinforces the semiotic status of a verbal or pictorial representation in inverse proportion to mimesis; the greater the degree of semiotic conventionality, the lesser the degree of realism.

In an effort to reproduce in his picture each and every detail of field, flower, and sky, Bringas outdoes nature itself, going so far as to include details which, according to the laws of optics and distance, should be blurred or obscured altogether to the naked eye: "ignorantly copying Nature to obtain the foliage, he had the saintly patience to put all the little leaves in one after the other. Some were so tiny they could only be seen with a microscope" (4: 1588). The effect achieved is less one of admiration before the trompe l'oeil illusionism of the picture than of an asphyxiating sensation produced by so much clutter. This obvious *horror vacui* appears to be characteristic of much of late nineteenth-century art. By way of compensation for such dreaded emptiness, Victorian painters such as William Holman Hunt filled their canvases far beyond the limits of spatial capacity. Their triumph, like Francisco's, is quantitative rather than qualitative. It represents the success not of the artist but of the technically skilled workman who has reduced the complex question of creativity to the dexterous execution of a piece of tracery or passementerie.[38] And indeed, this was one of the complaints lodged by critics such as Clarín against novelists in whom "the sometimes disproportionate grandeurs of inspiration have been replaced by the fine details of craft." Studying the French literary scene of the 1870s, Clarín rued the fact that "today what is preferred is a narrow and modest circle, an extremely limited horizon in order to make consummate filigrees, irreproachable miniatures."[39] So if in his choice of subject matter for his picture Bringas has strayed too far from the sphere of the real, in his style he clings too closely to it. He has turned into one of those middle-class aestheticians guided solely by what Jerome Buckley, writing on Victorian culture and art, has termed the "lamp of literalism," a position light years away from the revolution in twentieth-century art brought about by the realization that, in art, "exactitude is not truth."[40]

Galdós's conclusion is all too clear. No amount of secondary attention to detail in a picture, no number of particulars supporting the Barthesian "reality effect" in a text can rightfully lay claim to the descriptive label of realism if the work in question is not directly rooted in the world of contemporary human society and values.[41] Basing one's art, much less one's life, on some a priori notion of beauty or drawing one's inspiration solely from models of bad art or literature, as characters so often do in Galdós's fiction, cannot have a felicitous outcome: Isidora Rufete, Tristana de Reluz, José Ido del Sagrario, Alejandro Miquis, and Francisco Bringas all bear witness to this lesson. Peter Earle makes a most pertinent point when he states that the obsessive monotony and exaggerated laboriousness of don Francisco's work are symptomatic of "the desire to achieve an absolute and absurd realism in the impossibly crowded hair landscape."[42] That Bringas never achieves this absolute realism is not unexpected. Unable to perceive where reality lies in his own life, his attempts to picture reality in the cenotaph can never transcend the mechanics of technique. In perhaps no other Galdós novel does the reader find such a mordant critique of a certain brand of realism that paradoxically bears no allegiance to the real. Artists who dedicate themselves to such an undertaking, Galdós laments, produce images without coherence, form without substance; in brief, an empty tomb. Confronting the neatly framed tableau of the opening chapter-frame of *La de Bringas*, readers peer unexpectedly, vertiginously, into what, for all its minute detail, is the void to be found at the heart of what so often passes for the plenitude of realistic representation.

The "ending" of a novel is, for many persons, like
that of a good dinner, a course of dessert and ices,
and the artist in fiction is regarded as a sort of
meddlesome doctor who forbids agreeable after-
tastes.—Henry James, "The Art of Fiction"

Superimposed upon a spatial grid corresponding to the streets of Madrid, Galdós's *Fortunata y Jacinta* sketches out a map of the convoluted and convergent life histories of two wives and their families, set against the backdrop of the new economic, political, and social realities forged by the Revolution of 1868. It is generally acclaimed as the author's greatest achievement in fiction, a masterpiece of social observation and moral sensibility. Nonetheless, the manner in which the novel ends, including the disposition of the fates of the principal characters and the positioning and repositioning of narrative perspective, has not infrequently emerged as a matter of critical contention.

Much as a frame demarcates the shape and field of a painting, closure must inevitably play a large role in the determination of overall novelistic design. Lotman rightly notes that "the properties of structure and demarcation are interrelated," and Barbara Herrnstein Smith, in her examination of poetic closure, similarly agrees that the conclusion, however it is accomplished technically, always implies a principle of organization.[1] *Fortunata y Jacinta* offers a telling example of this organizational rule. When Jacinta and Guillermina Pacheco visit José Ido's flat in the tenement on Mira el Río, they find his wife Nicanora painting black borders on a stack of white pages which she will then sell as mourning paper for a nominal sum per ream, an instance of how the application of a frame imposes new meaning and function. At the same time, this novelistic vignette emphasizes that the

creation and subsequent interpretation of frames may in fact entail deception or ambivalence. José Ido assists Nicanora by lining up the sheets of
paper in graduated fashion so that each one exposes the edge to be inked,
a process referred to in the text by the verb "desmentir" 'to dissemble, to
contradict' (5: 1/IX, ii, 104).[2]

The notion of concealment or ambiguity is particularly apropos in considering the problem of closure in fiction, for repeated readings of *Fortunata y Jacinta*'s final chapters have not produced an easily identifiable
consensus regarding the novel's ultimate plan. In the same ending that for
Anthony Zahareas constitutes a tragedy Michael Nimetz finds the expression of an unbounded optimism and Geoffrey Ribbans a more modest tendency toward renewal and reconciliation within the bounds of the socially
possible.[3] While almost unanimously labeled a unified work, *Fortunata y
Jacinta*'s structure has been variously described as being patterned after
a circle, a succession of constantly shifting triangles, or a series of parallel lines that later change course, finally converging and intertwining in
labyrinthine tracery. The coexistence of so many competing explications
is sufficient temptation to take up the question of the ending once again.

Closure, obviously, is a fundamental aspect in the study of all narratives. Beliefs regarding history, eschatology, and social ordering undoubtedly invest the endings of realist novels with additional nuances of meaning unique to nineteenth-century culture. Yet to speak of closure without
also broaching the topic of the frame, as readers of *Fortunata y Jacinta*
have sometimes done, is somewhat deceptive, for the two concepts are
intimately related. Of those who have analyzed either frame or ending in
Galdós's novel, the majority have concentrated on such elements as the manipulation of narrative time and space, the rearrangement of relationships
among characters, and the treatment of ethical values. Another profitable
mode of inquiry, albeit one that is infrequently pursued, is to focus upon
distinctive uses of the element of language.[4] In fact, one possible frame
linking the novel's opening and closing sequences can be constructed from
a cluster of rhetorical figures that develop an analogy between the representation of certain foods and bodily functions and the process of fabulation. The theorizing about fiction that takes place in the novel's outer
frame is best understood in conjunction with the actual fiction-making that
goes on in the text's many embedded narratives. The presence of these
subordinate narrations signals the text's fractioning into countless inlaid
sequences, each in turn framed by shifts in narrative voice, register, and
focalization. It is in the context of this interplay between inner and outer

frames in *Fortunata y Jacinta* that the closure effected in the final chapter can best be understood, and from which emerges a poetics of fiction that alternately buttresses and erodes the structure of realist representation.

That closure could pose a daunting problem of form and intent was surely not lost on Galdós. The confirmed existence of two distinct endings for *La Fontana de Oro* (1870) and another two, possibly three variants, for the final pages of *Doña Perfecta* (1876) demonstrates that in the author's revisions of his works at various stages of the composition process from original manuscript to proofs to *princeps* and subsequent editions, the matter of the ending was occasionally resolved not without a fair amount of effort and only after earlier false starts had proved they were not artistically viable.[5] Similarly, the conspicuously marked final chapter titles that punctuate so many of his novels—"Conclusion" (*La Fontana de Oro*), "It was all over" (*Gloria*), "Farewell!" (*Marianela*), "Moral" (*La desheredada*), "Beginning of the End," "End," and "End of the End" (the last three chapters of *El doctor Centeno*), and *Fortunata y Jacinta*'s own "Finale"—strongly suggest an author conscious of end-designs and the possibilities for rehearsing or parodying traditional conventions of closure and completion.

It is easy to imagine that as a moment of narrative risktaking, the question of closure must have seemed an especially thorny one to the author of *Fortunata y Jacinta*. After having guided the reader through the four lengthy volumes of his novel, after having demonstrated the impossibility of ever appropriating (much less mastering) the inexhaustible totality of social and psychological portraiture that all skilled nineteenth-century realist writers are claimed to have pursued, Galdós was then faced with the equally onerous task of sealing off between title page and endplate the fictional world of his invention. Beset on the one hand by the demands and expectations of the readers of his novels, many of them schooled only in the stereotypes and formulas of the serial novel, and on the other by the difficulty of disengaging himself from the utterly convincing illusion of the autonomy of his paper entities—"Such incited lives want above all to go on creating themselves," Gilman notes[6]—Galdós ideally needed to construct an ending that would be artistically, ideologically, and psychologically congruent with all that had come before in the novel. Otherwise, the coherence of his work might be jeopardized: "The length of the nineteenth-century novel, elaborated as it is in subplots and digressions, runs the risk of detotalizing the form at the level of writing as well as at the level of reading."[7]

Galdós's own concerns are at once abstracted and intensified in the work of contemporary literary critics, who have investigated from a variety of perspectives both the structural and ideological ramifications attendant upon narrative closure. They are in general agreement that the conclusion is necessarily a major building block in any literary edifice. It is the textual sequence that realizes the modulation from language to silence and as such represents a site of convergence where passage is facilitated from the fictive universe to the extratextual world of the historical referent and the reader. Narrative endings, as Frank Kermode has argued, seem to dramatize conceptual patterns inherent in human thought. They mimic our perception of the tangentiality and arbitrariness of life while at the same time imposing order and system, thus expressing the "tension or dissonance between paradigmatic form and contingent reality."[8] They reveal the process by means of which the narratable elements of a novel ("instances of disequilibrium, suspense and general insufficiency from which a given narrative appears to rise") are neutralized by or transformed into the nonnarratable (elements which "complete a specified narrative lack" or resolve narrative enigmas and so produce a state of "quiescence" incapable of generating any further story).[9] Closure in a novel determines the outcome of the plot, thus gesturing toward thematic signification. It also fixes the structural relationship among the component parts as viewed from the perspective of the completed whole, exposing the compositional logic of the work. A novel, a poem, a conversation, a play are viewed as closed when the necessary protocols and terminating formulas have been observed, when further action or change is precluded, and the readers' or participants' experience of their structural dynamics is that of a single integrated, stable unit.[10]

In sum, a novel's ending necessarily engages readers in the search to create meaning out of the available signs and apparent indeterminacies of the text. Whether that search ends in satisfaction or frustration will be determined by the interaction of myriad factors. These include the particular manner in which the author has chosen to execute the concluding sequence, the variety of cognitive operations (*Gestalten*) put into play in the attempt to detect organizational patterns that are end-derived, and the extent to which the very concept of closure and its apprehension are governed by certain basic cultural assumptions that are part and parcel of the "social character of artistic structure."[11] The relationship of novel to life, of novel to reader, and of novel to other narrative texts and the laws governing their production are all in some way conditional upon the text's denouement. Precisely what form the ending takes can of course vary widely, even in the classically readerly vehicle of the nineteenth-century novel.

Henry James offers one possible response to the challenge that closure tenders the novelist. In one of his more famous statements on the genre, James wittily compared the novel to a kind of bountiful fictional repast, carefully prepared by authors and avidly hungered after by readers. Indeed, compared to the relatively spare turn-of-the-century fictions of Unamuno, Azorín, and Baroja, noticeably leaner in their use of naturalistic description and temporal concatenation, such extensive works as *Fortunata y Jacinta*, Clarín's *La Regenta*, or Pereda's *Peñas arriba* seem like high-calorie indulgences, larded with all the scenic detail and causal explanations characteristic of the mimetic impulse. As one critic gently gibes: "Faced with 'that tempting range of relevancies called the universe' (G. Eliot), the Realist's attitude is one of repressed gluttony."[12] What James objected to in his essay, however, was not the density and voracious appetite of realism but rather the insistence of readers upon a particularly clichéd kind of ending as the only dessert suitable to topping off the groaning board symbolized by the novel-banquet. Obviously, James was referring to the happy ending so prevalent in sentimental popular fiction, by means of which the hero or heroine's identity as unified self is confirmed and social norms are upheld or restored. According to such a conception, closure will only be deemed satisfactory when and if the morally deserving are rewarded for their labors while their persecutors receive their so-called just deserts.

Judgments regarding the strength and cohesiveness of narrative closure in *Fortunata y Jacinta* have often seemed predicated upon this same hunger for social justice and moral resolution; they have varied in direct proportion to critics' expectations regarding the culminating events of part 4, chapter 6. Do these events represent a tragic defeat of individual aspirations by the forces of biological and social determinism or, instead, exalt the spiritual triumph of conscience over the prevailing materialism of society? The question is a troubling one, for as Thomas Lewis points out, "the novel's closure retroactively problematizes the representation of the lower middle class in this text by subverting the narrative's structural premises of organic social synthesis and meliorative comic resolution."[13] In the highly conservative "distribution at the last of prizes, pensions, husbands, wives, babies, millions, appended paragraphs and cheerful remarks" that according to James so often signal a novel's end,[14] Stephen Gilman, for example, detects a seriously flawed novelistic design:

The way the novel ends makes Galdós appear to be a kind of toadying Estupiñá dedicated to providing the Santa Cruz fortune with an heir. When the enormous river of the novel reaches its delta, it seems to have been converted into a benediction of the bourgeois values and institutions it began by criticizing. Read as a treatise or "human document," *Fortunata y Jacinta* can teach us about social justice and class conflict in nineteenth-century Madrid, but read as a novel in which all parts join to form an organic whole, it is a failure. Because of its strongly emphasized and ostensibly counterrevolutionary ending, it cannot convert its historical and social raw material into a coherent work of art.[15]

Gilman, however, claims to be less disturbed by the novel's conclusion than are Marxist critics of *Fortunata y Jacinta* who, in Fortunata's final act of entrusting her son to the Santa Cruz family, see only the victory of an oppressive and hypocritical middle-class society. For Gilman, the ending of Galdós's text reveals a basic division between the social world and the sphere of individual action; the defeatist attitude that characterizes the one is counterbalanced by the note of hope that radiates from the other. Injustice "will continue to fester," but meanwhile the protagonist has achieved her own spiritual salvation, forgiving not just Jacinta but "Madrid and its history" (*Galdós and the Art* 244, 247).

Despite these oft-acknowledged contradictions at the level of ideology, other readers have also found the ending of *Fortunata y Jacinta* to be structurally justifiable and vigorously affirmative. Thus Sobejano writes in quite a different vein about the novel's final reprises and realignments, discovering personal redemption and continuity where some critics see only death and the crushing weight of social institutions:

> As opposed to the recurrent ending that characterizes the first three parts (search for Fortunata, encounter with Fortunata, new search for Fortunata), the last part is distinguished by its ending which is not mechanically reiterative and obstructive but rather generative and open: the defunct Moreno survives in Jacinta's memory; the dead Fortunata lives on in the blood of her son and the memory of Jacinta, Segismundo, and Maximiliano; the latter, locked up, lives in the freedom of his conscience: "I dwell among the stars."[16]

It is difficult to reconcile such disparate readings, for textual interpretation is inevitably mediated by the subjectivity of the reader. Statements made about *Fortunata y Jacinta*'s closure vary according to the particular critical discourse that the reader has adopted and the historical and ideological position that informs it. However, since thematic discrepancies and ambiguities not infrequently locate their counterparts in structural complexities, it ought to prove fruitful to reframe the discussion of *Fortunata*'s ending in terms of the novel's organizational model, the better to gauge how it respects (or violates) the parameters of literary realism.

Debates over the nature of *Fortunata y Jacinta*'s ending have addressed only in passing a closely related question—that of the novel's frame, which to be properly identified and interpreted requires an examination of both narrative overture and closure. As Gerald Prince has observed: "Narrative moves back and forth from a beginning to an end which condition each other and this movement constitutes a very powerful motor of narrativity."[17] Prince adds that "since—from the beginning—the beginning is oriented by the (idea of the) end, one could claim that the end comes at the beginning and before the beginning." As readers traverse the narrative middles of texts, a similar sort of bi-directional movement conditions their attempt to integrate at the semantic level what they have read so far and to anticipate what remains.

This quality of structural interconnectedness has already been observed in *La de Bringas*. The preceding chapter detailed how the description of the hair picture in the initial pages of that novel transforms the image of the empty tomb into an empty frame, offering an example of everything realism is not, or cannot be. The cenotaph, although still remaining the focus of the reader's attention, represents a tour de force not because of the relevance of its subject matter or the manual dexterity of its creator but rather because of the supremacy of the narrator's control over its display. In this critique of realist representation, meaning is displaced from the contents of the pictorial and narrative fields to the discourse of the duplicitous narrator, whose authority is incontrovertibly asserted by his interruptions into the story. Significantly, these interruptions occur not merely in this first chapter but also very prominently in the final one, where the full extent of his moral callousness is laid bare. The text is thus sealed off at several removes from reality, framed by a narrator who ultimately wields sole power over the configuration of meaning.

If, in fact, the opening of *La de Bringas* tacitly predicts the ending, then the closing frame of Galdós's monumental *Fortunata y Jacinta* may be said to effect a reversal of this process; reverberations of the text's conclusion can be traced retroactively through the entire novel, coloring our reading of it in equally significant fashion. Elements of the last chapter link up with tropologically similar ones in the beginning chapter to outline a frame-structure which, not unlike the one governing *La de Bringas*, is based on overt gestures of interpretive authority and which, moreover, offers a series of remarks, both evaluative and prescriptive, on the labors of composing and processing fiction. Such metacommentary at once englobes the narrative in its entirety yet is itself but a part of that whole, allowing for a complex play of boxes within boxes, stories within other stories, that is emphasized by *Fortunata y Jacinta*'s massive reliance upon internal framing strategies. That the end which is to come (after Fortunata's death, two of the more minor characters reflect upon the urge to tell her story) has in fact already arrived at the start (the narrator indeed tells the story of Fortunata and her rival Jacinta, a story that integrates that same pair of secondary characters into the action) invalidates neither the temporal and hierarchical progression of events in the novel nor the implementation of diverse temporal, spatial, and rhetorical conceits in order to achieve closure. What it suggests, however, is that just as the frame is at once interior and exterior to the text it frames, so, too, in Galdós's hands realism obliges—that is to say, accommodates, but requires also—the simultaneous naturalization and revelation of its own ruling narrative conventions.

In dealing with the problem of closure, it may be helpful to remember that the realist novel by definition presents a strip of human social activity explicitly delimited in time and space. The demarcation of that strip from the ongoing flow of events and experience and its enclosure within the borders of a work of fiction are acts that necessarily attribute to it a certain measure of importance for author, narrator, and reader alike. More often than not, it is an importance that resides, paradoxically, in the everyday, the unheroic, the mundane: an artistically undistinguished hair picture, an on again, off again love affair between an infantile *señorito* and an illiterate young woman of Madrid's teeming underclass, a crass moneylender's distress in the hour of his son's illness, to cite only examples from the novels examined here in chapters 1–3. In deeming the ordinary or the vulgar worthy of consideration, the reliance of realist representation upon synecdoche—the substitution of the framed part for the whole—is revealed to be consciously selective rather than merely arbitrary. The attention of readers is forcibly directed to the contents of the novel's "social pictures," as they were called by Spanish authors, who saw fit to equate these verbal forms with traditional painting and later, perhaps, with the newly invented art of photography. Such highlighted scenes and tableaus, even when pretending to the most Flaubertian extreme of deadpan presentation, obliquely prompt: "Look at this misery and infirmity, this exploitation and vice, this bad taste and banality." Mimesis thus entails a lesson in critical observation. The very placement of the frame tends to be a gesture tinged with didactic or moralizing overtones, either covertly, at the level of ideology, or more directly so, in the opinionated rhetoric of the narrator's discourse.

That a moral lesson or other general inference regarding the whole may be drawn inductively from a part thereof is evidence of the fact that realist novels presume to offer a legible model of the entire universe. Nonetheless, their plots often tend to be predicated upon the occurrence of individual, random episodes that defy meaningful explanation or justification. A novel's claims that the world is constructed upon a pattern that is possessed of significance, and that therefore is susceptible to interpretation, not infrequently are invalidated by the particular order and nature of events transpiring within its pages, characterized by ellipsis and aleatory juxtaposition. Addressing this seeming incongruity, Lotman offers a useful clarification when he affirms that "it is the mythologizing aspect of a text which is associated primarily with the frame, while the story aspect tries to destroy it." The symbolic functions and properties of that frame are dual, since the outermost narrative frame is composed of two distinct parts or segments: "The beginning of a text is in some degree associated with modeling the cause," whereas "the end activates the feature of the goal." [18]

The tensions generated by the incompatibilities between a text's mythologizing and anti-mythologizing tendencies, between frame and story or enframed contents, at times find their way to the surface in narratives whose conclusions appear to be incoherent, contradictory, or inconclusive. Of course not all indeterminate endings are perceived as disturbing. Certain narratives, such as the historical chronicle or the serial novel of indefinite extension, are unavoidably open-ended and accepted as such, just as others—Lotman identifies among them apocalyptic tracts and utopian writings—can only convey the weight of their moral or theological teachings through an exclusive emphasis on the story's final outcome.

By contrast, a closure of weak or uncertain status in a nineteenth-century realist text generally attracts attention to itself as something of an anomaly. From Henry James to the more recent Lukács, Jameson, and Barthes, critics have categorized the realist novel as an essentially conservative form that exhibits a marked distaste for ambiguity. Although not immune to challenges to its underlying political and aesthetic conservatism, as the examples of Balzac, Flaubert, and Galdós clearly suggest, realist fiction most often seems the embodiment of society's desire for containment: of illicit sexual relations, of political revolution, even of narrative itself, which threatens to proliferate ceaselessly. Undoubtedly linked to nineteenth-century notions about the transcendent, linear progression of political and natural history, what the varied endings of realist novels most frequently share is a predilection for closure that enforces such containment, that respects and maintains the integrity of the frame at the level of structure and characterization.

As a form of literature closely allied with bourgeois values, the realist novel tends toward endings and epilogues which reinforce the moral and social order, and in which protagonists either conform to the principles imposed by the social body or else succumb to the various unhappy fates visited upon those unwilling or unable to comply with its demands: alienation, passive renunciation, humiliation, madness, death. Such punishments are meted out as a warning to characters who indulge to excess their genius, knowledge, idealism, or desire, or who persist in their search for personal emancipation in the face of collective social restraints. Examples of nineteenth-century fiction that diverge from this regulatory pattern, either by allowing the ending to subvert these social controls or by calling undue attention to the frame that would secure them, are further evidence perhaps of the fact that realist fiction "is situated precisely at the threshold of the modern problematics of closure." [19] That is to say, the problematics of the modern novel whose ending, corresponding to a revised view of the physical universe and human history, favors fragmentation and discontinuity over order and closure; but also the problematics of closure as viewed through the critical lens of poststructuralism and related modern theories of textuality, which have attached new meaning to the qualities of literary openness and discord. Over and over in these readings, one finds demonstrations of how in even the most explicitly bounded work the intended closure may be denied or disrupted by the disseminative effects of language and desire.

In her review of such closural strategies as circularity, parallelism, incompletion, tangentiality, and linkage (although surely these are not the novelist's only possibilities), Marianna Torgovnick stresses that these patternings may be established through language, situation, and/or the grouping of characters. [20] Readings of *Fortunata y Jacinta*'s ending have dealt primarily with the latter two aspects. They emphasize the prominence in the last chapter of such features as circularity (Fortunata's return to her old address at #11 Cava San Miguel), interiorization (the transition from the streets outside to Fortunata's rented room and eventually to her and Maxi's mind), spatial reduction and convergence (the meeting of all the characters on the staircase of Fortunata's house or in her bedroom), and the play of thematic oppositions and reconciliations (passion/law, rivalry/ forgiveness, angelic conversion/demonic behavior, and so on). However, the role of language, of metaphor specifically, is equally deserving of consideration, for it is one of the principal means by which Galdós engineers the framing of his novel. Closure in *Fortunata y Jacinta* may be said to hinge on a series of rhetorical figures and conceits, reminiscent of James's comments on fictional endings, that liken the cultivation of the novel to the preparation of a dish of sweets and reading novels to indulging one's passions for the honeyed stuff of fiction. Metaphors of desserts, dining, and digestion are in fact equally as important as the novel's elaborate and oft-commented use of bird imagery, their "ironically modest nature" notwithstanding.[21]

Peter Goldman has explored the significance of this figural network as related to the manner in which the novel exposes conflicts between ideology and practice. In defining how Segismundo Ballester functions as the advocate in *Fortunata y Jacinta* for a dialectical system integrating opposing yet complementary values and life experiences, he seizes upon Galdós's felicitous metaphor of "el trabajo digestivo del espíritu" 'the digestive work of the spirit.'[22] Ingestion of new ideas, attitudes, and realities is followed by elimination of old ones, which are either rejected or forgotten, while the synthesized residue left behind feeds the soul. Goldman's discussion of the Hegelian posture that characterizes the humble pharmacist Ballester, focused as it is upon these images of alimentation and composting, is fitting indeed. Notions of production, consumption, and assimilation, all couched in terms relative to the eating process, inform not just the ideological and thematic horizons of the novel but its narrative operations as well. In the fusion of the discourses of corporeality and narrative poetics, writing itself is metaphorized as a process whereby a word, a concept, a text swallows up another. Both are transformed, but the residual traces of the ingested material are never successfully erased.[23]

The life of the body, and of the body in society, is a perennial topic in the *Novelas contemporáneas*, so it is not surprising that the members of upwardly mobile bourgeois society in *Fortunata y Jacinta* are defined through their approach to the pleasures afforded by contemporary gastronomy. Culinary metaphors as well as actual descriptions of food appear at frequent intervals in the text, as indicators of social status, symbolic overdeterminants of character, or simple props of the mimetic illusion. Suffice it to say that the many meals, all lavishly detailed, that function as events rather than mere interludes of description in the narrative (for instance, the Christmas feast of 5: 1/X, iii–vi, 132–40) as well as the abnormal relationship of the numerous characters to the act of eating (Feijoo's chronic indigestion, Nicolás Rubín's gluttony, Guillermina's abstinence, José Ido's meat-induced delirium, Mauricia *la Dura*'s inability to eat during her final illness and her previous hallucination of devouring the Eucharistic host) all attest to Galdós's interest in food and social eating practices as encoding structures of the narrative in *Fortunata y Jacinta*.[24] Above all, food imagery is pressed into service at the novel's formal borders. In *Fortunata y Jacinta*, the story of the eponymous wives is symmetrically demarcated by a critical discourse on the relationship of utterance (telling, writing) to reception (hearing, reading), of fictionalization to documentation, and of literature to life. The exact nature of these relationships is explained by means of commonplace analogies drawn from the everyday realm of cooking and eating.

In fact, *Fortunata y Jacinta* begins with a pork chop and ends several hundred pages later with a macedoine of fruits. At the very beginning of the novel the narrator cites the young Juanito Santa Cruz's aversion to book-learning as a strictly passive, fabricated experience. "Living is relating to others, enjoying and suffering, desiring, hating, and loving. Reading is an artificial, borrowed life," he insists (5: 1/I, i, 15). Juanito's platitudes are purely self-serving; they allow him to rationalize his antipathy to all forms of labor and intellectual commerce. Still, they manage to contain a small nugget of truth, as the narrator admits: "he [Juanito] would make a comparison that was not lacking in exactitude." The comparison between reality as it is lived and as it is recounted secondhand, between perception and its imaginative re-creation, is presented by Juanito as follows: "He used to say that between these two ways of living he observed the difference that exists between eating a chop yourself and being told how and when someone else has eaten it, making the story very lively, you understand: describing the face the person made, the pleasure that chewing gave him, the satisfaction with which he swallowed, and the tranquillity with which he digested" (5: 1/I, i, 16).

The privileged status accorded to life over fiction and to presence over representation in the novel's opening chapter appears to be counterbalanced, if not altogether reversed, in the novel's concluding chapter. On the way to the cemetery for Fortunata's burial, Segismundo Ballester begins to tell everything he knows about Fortunata's biography, with special emphasis on the events surrounding her final days: "[He related] everything he knew about Fortunata's story, which was not inconsiderable, without omitting the last part, which was undoubtedly the best" (5: 4/VI, xvi, 543). His friend Ponce discerns in this bare-bones account "elements for a play or a novel," that is, the suggestion of a literary text in embryonic form. Still missing are the "warps in the texture [of the fabric of fiction] that are absolutely necessary for the vulgarity of life to be converted into aesthetic material." For the critic Ponce, the unmediated reporting of observed people and events must give way to a mediated narrative in which active authorial intervention using strategies of narrative selectivity and reorganization are deployed to produce a more palatable work. Ponce insists that life may be incorporated into art only after long and deliberate reworking: "dressed, seasoned with fragrant spices, and then placed on the fire until thoroughly cooked." The Ponce-Ballester debate, once again hinging on a culinary metaphor, is suspended on a note of irresolution: "In the end it turned out that well-ripened raw fruit was very good, as were compotes, if the cook knew what he was doing" (5: 4/VI, xvi, 543). Plain, ripe fruit or fruit salad? Must one eat the chop, or can vicarious satisfaction be sufficient? [25]

The fact that the framing device of the food tropes initiates an inquiry into the form and functions of fiction is of twofold significance. Thematically, it serves as a reminder that whatever else they are portrayed as doing in the novel—seducing young women, performing charitable works, practicing usury, imitating their social or moral superiors—the characters in *Fortunata y Jacinta* are constantly engaged in telling stories to each other and themselves. The encyclopedic trove of political and social knowledge that undergirds *Fortunata y Jacinta* (everything from the role of women, family, and marriage to urbanization and class relations) cannot mask the fact that even realist narrative, with all its gestures toward the referential world, can be its own subject and reflect upon the processes of its own creation. Structurally, the frame constructed out of the food tropes is an "outwork," a literal and figurative "hors d'oeuvre" that stands outside the text yet is already contained within it, in the embedded narratives that the characters practice and perfect composing and interpreting. [26] For their part, these interior narrations are also metaphors: "metaphors for the act of reading, which traces an inexorable zigzag between the present moment of the reader (the reading) and the preterit tense of what is read (the story)." [27]

In some instances, the internal framing process, common to narratives of any sufficient length, is accomplished relying upon a strong spatial component; the resulting shifts in the angle of vision may respond to either naturalistic or symbolic purposes. *La de Bringas* begins with the near-sighted description of a framed art object and goes on to exploit a series of distorted, expressionistic perspectives that demarcate individual scenes. Incomplete or oddly positioned visual frames in *La de Bringas* suggest the defective vision of the monarchy and the middle class. Moreover, such framing lends a highly theatrical character to scenes already based on ceremony and spectacle, such as the Holy Thursday foot washing ritual performed by the royals. (These theatrical frames will be more fully discussed in chapter 4 on Galdós's *Tormento*.) Scenes viewed from great heights or through narrow apertures suggest a distanciation between observer and actor, subject and object, that is at once geographical and moral. Many similar examples of visually oriented interior framing can be found in *Fortunata y Jacinta*. Juanito first glimpses Fortunata standing silhouetted in the doorway of the poultry shop (5: 1/III, iv, 40). Fortunata sees the dead body of Mauricia *la Dura* through a crack in the bedroom door (5: 3/VI, ix, 394), and Ballester, contemplating Fortunata on her deathbed, sorrows over such a "pitiful scene" (5: 4/VI, xv, 540). The street fight between Maxi and Juanito is witnessed by Fortunata (or so she tells doña Lupe) from the window of her flat (5: 2/VIII, xii, 290) and the transformation of José Ido from docile salesman and hack novelist to raving, jealous husband strikes Jacinta as a "disagreeable spectacle" (5: 1/VIII, iv, 92).

More arresting for its structural implications is the continual recourse in *Fortunata y Jacinta* to subordinate narrators and their tales. The use of embedded narrations underscores the importance of narration generally in the world of the Santa Cruz and Rubín families.[28] Caught on the treadmill of the forces governing their society—biology, capitalism, social morality—Galdós's characters frequently resort to storytelling as an outlet which affords them some small measure of control, if not over their historical circumstances then at least over the management and flow of human experience. Storytelling has many goals in *Fortunata y Jacinta*. It encourages characters to give free rein to the expression of their imaginative faculties and rhetorical gifts. It allows them, when recounting their autobiographies, to manipulate the manner in which others perceive them. Finally, it serves as a kind of wish fulfillment, for as Juanito says of his wife: "Ah, women! They all have a novel in their heads, and when what they imagine doesn't come to pass in life, which is what commonly happens, they take out their little compositions" (5: 1/X, vi, 143).

The activity of narrating, and often of listening or reading as well, is experienced as a deep, visceral response of pleasure or pain, which confirms for the storyteller the vitality of fiction. For Estupiñá, storytelling is a "licor palabrero," that is, verbal spirits of intoxicating powers (5: 1/III, i, 35). During his illness in part one, the inveterate tale-bearer and conversationalist passes the time reading the only book in his room, the Ecclesiastical Bulletin of the Lugo Diocese. He sounds the syllables out loud and when he comes to more difficult passages he figuratively "sinks his teeth into them." The book is surely as dry as sawdust, but for him it becomes a food as savory as any he has relished: "He ended up acquiring a taste for such an insipid dish and read through certain paragraphs twice, chewing on the words with a smile" (5: 1/III, iv, 42). Estupiñá's gustatory delight in conversing and reading has as its obverse the honeymooning Juanito's drunken confession of his infidelities. Telling his wife of his past is an act comparable to the "physical vomiting produced by a very strong emetic" (5: 1/V, vii, 64). The inexperienced Maxi Rubín is especially predisposed to devouring the stories he hears; hence he believes Fortunata when she tells him that her life has turned out as it has owing to a run of bad luck. His aunt Lupe can scarcely contain her sarcasm: "Tienes buenas tragaderas" 'You'd fall for anything" (Span. *tragaderas* "gullet," "gullibility"). In fact, his propensity to idealize Fortunata enables him to swallow her explanations without question (5: 2/III, iv, 201). The continued use of a culinary lexicon and metaphors of hunger, eating, and satiety further reinforces the connection between inner and outer narrative frames.

The significance of embedded narratives for the work that encompasses them is relative to the functions they perform. Embedded narratives may have an actional, an explicative, or a thematic function; that is, they may further the plot, reveal information about events and personalities, or establish relations of analogy between the inner and the outer levels of the story.[29] In the embedded narratives of *Fortunata y Jacinta* there are examples of all three functions at work. Among Juanito's first words to Fortunata upon renewal of their ties in part two are precisely these: "We have so much to talk about! . . . What I've gone through, my dear! I'll tell you all about it . . . We have so much to tell each other" (5: 2/VII, vi, 276). Storytelling is an important motor for the advancement of the novel's plot, since Juanito renews the search for his former mistress on the strength of Villalonga's recounting of Fortunata's elegant reappearance in Madrid (5: 1/XI, i–iii, 150–57), in a chapter appropriately titled "The End Which Turns Out to Be the Beginning." Fortunata falls under the influence of Mauricia *la Dura* at the moment the latter tells the story of how she came to do penance at Las Micaelas (5: 2/VI, ii, 234–36). Even Feijoo and Fortunata owe their frank and practical relationship at least in part to the candid sharing of their life histories (5: 3/IV, iv, 334–36).

In many cases the novel can only proceed by relying upon an "informational polyphony."[30] The personalized narrator-observer in charge of communicating these "two stories of married women" often switches from omniscience to a position of limited knowledge and must defer to outside sources to fill in the gaps. Resultingly, the text is strewn with moments in which he confesses his dependence upon data obtained secondhand and of sometimes dubious worth:

> The earliest references I have to the person who goes by this name [Juanito Santa Cruz] were given to me by Jacinto María Villalonga. . . . (5: 1/I, i, 13)

> Villalonga recounts that years ago Casa-Muñoz used to speak in a ludicrous manner, and he insists having heard him say once, before he became a marquis, that "the doors were hermetically open"; but this hasn't yet been confirmed. (5: 1/VII, iii, 81)

> Jacinta has recently told me that one night her irritation was such . . . that she was on the verge of exploding and revealing herself. (5: 3/II, i, 308)

> Zalamero knows better than anyone everything referring to this renowned lady [Guillermina Pacheco]. (5: 1/VII, i, 510)

The narrator also is informed by Rafaela, Nicolás Rubín, and Fortunata herself. On occasion the principal narrator, rather than incorporating into his own discourse the knowledge that other characters have given him, instead cedes the responsibility for telling what happened next to an embedded (intradiegetic) narrator. Thus Juanito is the sole authority to testify to what transpired during his first liaison with Fortunata. "Once upon a time," his story begins, and continues at intervals, not unlike a serial novel (5: 1/V, i–ii, 47–52 and v–vii, 57–64; also 5: 1/X, vi–vii, 142–47, and finally 5: 3/II, ii–iii, 311–16). The description of Mauricia's death is exclusively doña Lupe's. Without her words, this dramatic scene would be missing altogether from the text (5: 3/VI, ix, 392–94).

As the novel's narrators multiply, the frequency and consistency with which they tell their tales begin to vary, often in inverse proportion to each other. As each internal narrator repeats his or her story, varying its style, duration, focalization, or narratee, the reader is confronted with several different repetitions of the same plot. Fortunata, for example, confesses her past first of all to Maxi, naming all the men she has been with since the death of her child but skimming over those details too painful for her to relive and for Rubín to accept: "And she rapidly continued disclosing that ugly page of her life . . . She made some cuts in the telling of her tale, surpressing not just words but paragraphs and entire chapters" (5: 2/II, ii, 175–76). Next, she is obliged to communicate her sins to Nicolás Rubín as part of the spiritual preparations preceding her marriage: "She told him about the business with Juanito Santa Cruz, feeling no little shame, and incoherently related her sad story" (5: 2/IV, iv, 214). The unfeeling priest scarcely heeds her words; he equates Fortunata's situation with the tribulations of fallen women everywhere and brusquely commands: "Be brief." [31] This scene is reenacted at the very end of part two, when she confesses her unfaithfulness to Maxi. On a third occasion it is Feijoo who will be asked to listen to Fortunata's disclosures, but only after having regaled her with the tales of his military expedition to Cuba and his love affairs of several continents. Unlike Juanito, Feijoo is an eminently trustworthy narrator—"he didn't even retouch his naturalistic scenes and portraits"—and Fortunata responds in kind: "Fortunata did the same when it was her turn to be the narrator, prompted by her protector to reveal some chapter of the story of her life, which, though brief, already offered adventures worthy of being recounted and even written down" (5: 3/IV, iv, 336).

As a narrator, Fortunata is entirely without guile, even at the cost of wounding the moral sensibilities of others. Explaining to Guillermina how she came to marry Maxi and why she considers herself more a wife to Juanito than the barren Jacinta could ever be, she states simply: "I'm telling you everything just as it happened" (5: 3/VII, ii, 404). In this she is the opposite of Santa Cruz, who is constantly honing his skills as storyteller by the use of judicious editing of details that are unflattering to his character. In fact, his seduction of Fortunata succeeds at least in part because of his ability to spin convincing fictions; he had somehow managed to convince her that he would marry her. Then, for Fortunata, as now, for Jacinta, embedded narratives are bedtime stories as well. The orality of storytelling leads in one direction toward metaphors of food and eating, in another direction toward eroticism and the expression of sexual desire, also described on occasion by metaphors of predatory consumption.

Another prominent example of multiple accounts of the same story is the inclusion in *Fortunata y Jacinta* of the several versions of the *Pitusín* episode, first invented by the hack novelist José Ido and propounded by the mercenary José Izquierdo. Juanito explains the story to Jacinta to disabuse her of her error: "What I'm about to tell you is the final paragraph of a story I've been telling you in installments. This will be the end. Case closed." Dispelling her illusions that she has located the child of her husband and his mistress, he warns: "Bid farewell to your novel, that great invention of those two geniuses, Ido del Sagrario and José Izquierdo" (5: 1/X, vi, 143–44). The swindle is also described by Mauricia to Fortunata (5: 2/VI, iii, 240) and by Juanito to Fortunata: "Did you hear what happened? Well, they really swindled him" (5: 2/VII, vii, 280).

As we have seen, the principal narrator of *Fortunata y Jacinta* frequently subcontracts the task of dispatching the story to a series of characters who act as ancillary narrators. At a level internal to the novel, these individual narrations may either recount facts (Fortunata's confession) or fictions (the *Pitusín* fable). The line between the real and the fabricated soon becomes blurred, however, as happens in Juanito's tale to Jacinta of his second breakup with Fortunata. Juanito's presentation of the story makes fine use of rhetoric to twist his vices into virtues, "retouching the entire story so that what was black and dishonorable . . . would appear white and even noble." Nonetheless, the facts of the story are substantially truthful; Juanito has left his mistress and wants only to return to his wife. Jacinta seems torn by what she hears, on the one hand thinking, "Was it all true or not? It was too well spun to be a lie," but on the other hand saying, "It seems to me that everything you've told me is too well composed. I don't trust you, I don't trust you, because there's no one like you who is so good at building triumphal arches of phrases and then passing through them, giving yourself airs" (5: 3/II, ii–iii, 313–16). It is a confusion worthy of Cervantes, and, indeed, the narrator compares Jacinta's double bind to the dilemma of Sancho Panza as posed by don Quijote's wild tale of Montesinos's cave.

It is also notable that whether they recall events already recorded in the novel as historical or fabricate unrealities instead, all the ancillary relations are spoken. None of the subordinate narrations are presented in the form of a letter, a diary, or a written text.[32] All this narrative activity takes place within the intensely oral, dialogic milieu of nineteenth-century Madrid and its temples of conversation: café, *tertulia*, shop counter, salon, and bedroom. A distinction is thus drawn between the principal narrator who presents a written text to an audience of real and implicitly imagined readers, and the characters who as raconteurs present narratives of stunning immediacy to an audience of avid listeners. But, as happens in works obeying conventions of realist *vraisemblance*, this distinction is soon submerged. Oral narrative is no more inherently truthful or reliable than written narrative. As John Kronik explains: "Writing, with the higher stature and the permanence that accrue to it from the heralded word, is not so easily denied as speech is. On the other hand, the act of narration is shown to fictionalize fact. There is no way to untangle the contradictory notions that writing embodies supreme authority and that fiction is a written lie." [33]

The many embedded narratives of *Fortunata y Jacinta* perform complementary novelistic functions. They emphasize the importance of storytelling in establishing intimacy and friendship and highlight the role of memory, imagination, and desire in the creation of stories. At times they may disrupt the linearity of the text; they substitute a more complex temporal pattern according to which events unfold and force the reader to abide by these detours and digressions. Many of the interior narrations are told incrementally, which has the effect of postponing future closure or undoing that which has already occurred. The narratee (or reader) thinks he has heard the last of a story, only to discover that more has happened or there is information still to be revealed, as the story is continued by the same or another narrator. When the embedded narratives present differing versions of the same story, each time varying the factual details or the narrative situation, the epistemological concerns of readers and characters are intensified. Did Feijoo really pursue doña Lupe the year after her husband died, as she claims, or did she make this story up, as Feijoo insists? How can readers know, if the embedded narratives are their only evidence? Constantly reframed by new perspectives or even contradicted outright, reality becomes mutable, unstable. The supposed transparency of reality and realism thickens, and knowledge of the real begins to appear foreordained to incompletion or dispute.

Finally, in their continual switching from principal to interior narrator, or from one interior narrator to another, the embedded stories in *Fortunata y Jacinta* call attention to the act of framing in a manner that is inimical to the professed aims of realism. As Marvin Minsky has observed of the cognitive process in general, "the more frequently our high-level agencies change their representations of reality, the harder it is for them to find significance in what they sense." In order to perceive reality as continuous and comprehensible, we must avail ourselves of an "immanence illusion" which masks or suppresses our experience of constant frame-shifts between successive, unconnected images and mental events. [34] The narrative cloisonnement of *Fortunata y Jacinta* cannot help but call attention to these frame-jumps. In so doing, it intimates to the reader that what is (or in potential might be) continuous is not so much reality but rather our representation of it. Such emphasis on the frame, as the marker of representation, undoes the immanence illusion that realism strives to sustain and stresses instead the fictionality at the core of the novel.

The status of the final chapter of *Fortunata y Jacinta* is greatly clarified by a consideration of the principles of framing and closure. Relative to the whole of Galdós's novel, it displays in microcosm the preoccupation with the dynamics of narrative creation and reception. Not unlike that part of the novel's frame that it enfolds, the final chapter relies upon a composite structure. Both storytelling and the internal framing that is the means by which this storytelling is inset into the text-continuum are prominently featured at novel's end. In this sense the conclusion is both a summary of and an expansion upon the theory of fiction outlined in the first and last chapters.

Of the many ways in which plot mechanisms are set into motion in *Fortunata y Jacinta* by narrative activity, the most catastrophic consequences of storytelling are to be found in the final chapter of book four. Fortunata complains to her former husband: "You want to kill me, and instead of shooting me you come to me with this story" (5: 4/VI, iv, 509). Maxi's bedside narration is a cruel and unrelenting documentation of Juanito's and Aurora's affair. It provokes Fortunata to engage her rival in a fight, after which she suffers the hemorrhage that leads to her death. Returned to her sickbed, she describes over and over her set-to with Aurora. The repetitiveness of her recitation acquires an incantatory tone: "But she kept going back over the episode with Aurora, giving it tragic proportions, and as soon as she finished she began to tell it again" (5: 4/VI, ix, 522). In this chapter, too, the reader can detect the still visible but ever-weakening contrast between factual narration or reporting (Maxi's revelation of Juanito's betrayal) and pure fiction and prevarication (Aurora's gossip that Jacinta has dishonored herself by becoming Moreno Isla's lover and that Segismundo is the true father of Fortunata's child).

In earlier moments of the novel, the narrator of the outer story frequently paused to allow other characters their say, then stepped in again to take the reins of interpretive control. In the last chapter this process is taken still further; the narrator's presence is in great measure effaced altogether, replaced by the mimetic and expressive language and the point of view of the characters themselves. More and more, the novel focuses on the psychological dimensions of the characters.[35] As a corollary to the progressive interiorization of space in book four and the shift away from the panoramic exploration of historical and social forces toward a more individualized treatment of human experience, the final chapter marks a significant reduction in the amount of intrusive metanarrative discourse imposed upon the story. The formal indicator of this reorientation of perspective is the replacement of other forms of speech by free indirect discourse and by the interior monologues of Estupiñá, Maxi, Jacinta, and Fortunata.[36]

This constant recourse in the concluding chapter to secondary narrators and supplementary narrations is in itself emblematic of the novel-compote that Ponce defends in the closing frame and that Galdós has constructed in *Fortunata y Jacinta.* Jean Rousset, examining the theoretical function of such narrative interventions, in fact seizes upon the very same metaphor as did Galdós in describing the resulting structure of the text: "The *author* allows a series of *narrators* to begin to speak instead of him and to substitute for his words a discourse that doesn't come from him. These insertions are, by their very nature, sporadic; the result is a fractioning of the text, a compote (Fr. 'macédoine') that is very far removed from the uniformity of style considered to be 'classical.'"[37] The text becomes a composite, an amalgam of voices, registers, styles, and values.

Nor does the final chapter indicate any lessening of the impulse to narrative. In fact, the last few pages of the novel present three additional fictions, three pathetic attempts at fiction-making that challenge the world of the real. The first of these pertains to Maxi Rubín. Severed from the world by physical infirmity, solitude, and his maniacal thirst for moral redemption, Maxi buries the image of the Fortunata he knew, preferring to venerate instead an unbesmirched Fortunata that he has imaginatively conceived: "I adore what is ideal and the eternal in her, and I see her, not as she was but exactly as I dreamed her and envisioned her in my soul . . . the disgusting elements of reality have disappeared, and I live with my idol in my mind" (5: 4/VI, xvi, 546). Maxi's life, or what is left of it by the time of his internment in Leganés, is solely sustained by the universe of fiction, for he rewrites Fortunata's text, her history, in the shape of a fairy tale: "The world, for Maxi, becomes literally the representation that he holds of it."[38]

Possessed by an idea as tenacious as any held by Fortunata, Jacinta launches a second valiant offensive to hold reality at bay. She daydreams a new scenario in which she is the biological mother of the infant Juan Evaristo Segismundo: "The lady entertained herself by building in her fantasy castles of smoke with towers made of air and cupolas that were more fragile still, because they were made of pure thought." Readers who have followed

Jacinta's marital tribulations and maternal ambitions over the course of the entire novel are not surprised to discover that "so powerful was her imagination that the putative mother finally became enraptured with the fabricated memory of having carried that precious son in her womb." Mentally she reorganizes her adopted baby's features. There will be no trace of resemblance to Fortunata; his face will look like hers, but also like Juanito's, or perhaps Moreno's. The manner in which she re-creates his face is again reminiscent of the recipe for turning raw fruit into fruit compote, reality into fiction: "She recomposed [Juan Evaristo Segismundo's] features, attributing to him her own, mixed and confused with those of an ideal being" (5: 4/VI, xvi, 543). Ironically, the melodramatic novel of the false *Pituso* has at last been transformed into reality; the narrator even refers to Fortunata at this juncture with the epithet *la Pitusa*. More ironically still, this reality is immediately converted back into fiction by the obsessively maternal Jacinta.

In the third example of storytelling, Ponce proposes to turn Fortunata's biography into a "drama or novel." In a perfect gesture of self-reflexivity, the linguistic construct in the text which goes by the name of Fortunata is naturalized according to the psychological and literary conventions governing the realist novel, to the point where she becomes an animate and independent character. Yet, having gained this autonomy, she passes once more into fiction in part four, chapter 6—specifically, into the novel *Fortunata y Jacinta* which we readers have just finished, but also, by extension, into other fictions derived from the incessant rewriting and rereading of her life, all of them composite in nature.

Fortunata y Jacinta's final chapter demonstrates that all raw material (history, biography, social relations) can be fictionalized, but not all fictions are infinitely productive or self-generative and self-sustaining. Those invented by Maxi, Jacinta, and Ponce may very possibly survive the end of the novel; they hurt no one but their authors and indeed give them life after a fashion. By contrast, fiction that is knowingly deceitful or injurious will eventually be forgotten, superseded by less blatantly engineered stories. Galdós structures his ending so that upon Fortunata's death these latter narrations grind to a halt. The internal narrators cease their activity and their listeners turn away.

Juanito is one of the more prolific and skilled taletellers of the novel, well-versed in the arts of digression, self-censure, and hyperbole, but when Fortunata dies he loses the subject of all of his stories to Jacinta. The circularity of the ending (Fortunata's return to her former domicile, Maxi's regression to a state of childlike impotence, the politically futile substitution of Restoration for revolution) implies no doubt that Juanito will have new love affairs in the future, following the already established pattern of his adulterous behavior with Fortunata in the past and currently with Aurora. Even so, it would be pointless for him to compose new stories, for by the novel's end Jacinta has declared her total indifference. She will no longer pay attention to Juanito's stories. As a result, Juanito is the only major character absent from the final chapter, having become a totally superfluous figure, a raconteur without an audience. Characterized by the sterile idleness of the bourgeois *señorito*, he now becomes no less unproductive in that one area in which he had previously shown himself to excel, the art of storytelling. The last time he is heard from in the novel, he is still trying to defend his actions toward his lover and his wife: "Some things he denied, and others, the most bitter ones, he sweetened and sugar-coated admirably" (5: 4/VI, xx, 542). No one in the family, least of all Jacinta, is listening to these cotton candy confections. The same fate awaits José Ido, who had conceived the outlandish tale of Juanito's illegitimate child so eagerly accepted by Jacinta. The latter now has a real, flesh and blood child and can dispense with Ido's extravagant fictions.

The lessons of the ending in *Fortunata y Jacinta* are threefold. Everything can, in potential, be fictionalized; not all fictions can continue indefinitely; and composing and reading fictional texts is akin to cooking and dining. Narration, like food, can truly sustain life, merely feign the appearance of health, or even mete out death. Nourishment or poison: these are the images consistently selected by the author to explicate the workings of fiction in both its moral and its aesthetic dimensions. Novels may prove to be the true sustenance of discerning writers and readers, for as Galdós, in his *Memorias de un desmemoriado*, says of his own literary apprenticeship to Balzac, "With my reading of that little book, *Eugenia Grandet*, I breakfasted upon the great French novelist" (6: 1431).[39] On the other hand, they may be ruinous. Consumers of popular fiction ill-advisedly "regale their stomachs with the indigestible novels that some newspaper editors invent," he warns in *Crónicas de Madrid* (6: 1338). The cluster of alimentary metaphors in *Fortunata y Jacinta* describing the making and consuming of fiction undoubtedly has naturalist overtones, suggesting the inevitable sway of physical impulses, the crudeness of the digestive function, the hunger of the lower classes contrasted with the dietary surfeit of the Santa Cruz household, even Fortunata's inability to nurse. Nonetheless, Galdós's use of the pork chop–compote equivalence to narrative transcends the constraints of naturalism as a quasi-scientific and methodical relationship between text and referent in which narrator and reader have little to add. Instead, it postulates a much more active and internalized role to be played by narrators (as structuring agents of texts) and readers (as creators of meaning in those same texts). By turning narrative into a bibliophageous process, Galdós enlarges upon his contemporaries' definition of realism as observation and mimetic transcription of the referent. Food does not pass through the digestive tract as does water through a conduit; eating entails ingestion, absorption, assimilation, elimination, and synthesis. So, too, the exercise of realism in literature does not stop for Galdós with the notion of specular reproduction. Also required is the intervention of the imagination. Reality is not something to be corresponded to but rather to be re-created narratively and experientially. Pure idealism exhibiting no connection to the concerns of the accidental, material world may be unacceptable; such is the lesson of Maxi's flight into fantasy. At the same time, if there is no recourse to the imagination, a purely representational image of that same world is no better than a stenographic transcription. Galdós moves in *Fortunata y Jacinta* toward striking a balance between these two extremes. This reconciliatory gesture is best symbolized by the unexpected and rather poignant friendship of Ponce and Ballester that develops amid so much death and dissolution in the novel's last chapter, despite their antithetical positions as literary critics: "If you could only see the affection Ponce feels for me! We have long discussions on realist art and the ideal and aesthetic emotions" (5: 4/VI, i, 502).

Last but not least, *Fortunata y Jacinta* illustrates how narrative is generated in precisely that tension between disequilibrium and equilibrium, repetition and variation, hunger and satiety. Regardless of how much fresh fruit (Ballester's "vulgarity of life") or fruit compote (Ponce's "aesthetic material") is served up, the partakers of the novelistic feast will eventually have to sit down and start over again with another full-course meal. Individual narratives must necessarily conclude, but the invention and re-reading of fiction itself is a never-ceasing process. Outwardly, *Fortunata y Jacinta* would appear to rely upon two of the most traditional conventions used in the novel to convey a simulacrum or, in E. M. Forster's terms, a "faking" of closure: death and the concomitant transfer of property, here symbolized by Fortunata's bequest of her newborn son to Jacinta and the deeding over of her stocks to Guillermina Pacheco. Yet Ponce's suggested transformation of Fortunata's life into the substance of a novel signifies more precisely a refusal of closure, in that the ending of *Fortunata y Jacinta* projects us back to the beginning, to a rereading of the novel. Such a process has already been initiated, in the sense that the narrator's recovery of the multiple, embedded stories already constitutes a kind of internal Galdosian rereading of the text.

The forging of Fortunata's persona—what Sherman Eoff called the emergence of her "adjustive personality" and Gilman the surfacing of her "consciousness"—is certainly the crux of *Fortunata y Jacinta*. But it should not be forgotten that the problematic self-definition of the protagonist's identity also carries implicitly within it a meditation on the art of making novels. Who Fortunata is and what she has become: while this is the principal subject of the novel's four volumes, the endpoint of the novel is furnished by the discussion about how this human trajectory can best be cast into literary form. That form, logically, is the compote (from the Latin *composita*), that is, the socially and narratively dense, multivoiced artifice of novelistic fiction whose composition (also from the Latin *compositiō, -ōnis*) is both subject and object of *Fortunata y Jacinta*.

The interrelationship of part and whole, of internal and external frames resolutely confirms that the nature of the artistic text is inevitably a compound one.[40] But in moving from the textual to the supratextual level, at which the *Novelas contemporáneas* are treated as a single, integrated body of work, it becomes apparent that *Fortunata y Jacinta* consolidates two of the author's lifelong preoccupations whose integration into the novel will require antithetical modes of presentation: investigation of the motor-principles of Spanish society and analysis of the generative mechanisms and inner workings of narrative transactions. To accomplish the first in versimilitudinous fashion, Galdós avails himself of all the techniques in mimesis' arsenal. To carry out the second, he necessarily lays bare those same devices to expose the novel's fictionality. What he does is construct both a frame and an ending to *Fortunata y Jacinta* that alternate between closure and nonclosure, code and message, sign and signifier. In so doing, Galdós successfully challenges the limits set by realist representation; he manages to have his cake and eat it, too.

Young soldier, where are you going?—Lamennais,

Paroles d'un croyant

On other occasions he began by quoting "Young
soldier, where are you going?" And finally, after a
good deal of vexation, the reader was left not know-
ing where the soldier boy was going, unless all of them, including the author and
his public, were going to the lunatic asylum at Leganés.—Galdós, Torquemada
en la hoguera

In structural terms, Galdós's *Torquemada en la hoguera* (1889) follows
a pattern that has already been examined in *La de Bringas*, for both
novels open with an intrusive metanarrative commentary. In the case
of *La de Bringas*, the narrator's interposition between the story and the
reader might perhaps be considered minimal, grammatically speaking.
The novel's lengthy first paragraph extends a seemingly impersonal, omniscient vision of Francisco's cenotaph, which is interrupted only once by the
"I" of the narrator. Nonetheless, the latter's rhetorical question ("How shall
I describe it?"), uttered in a tone that falls somewhere between mockery
and genuine perplexity, proves to be the fulcrum upon which hinges the
ironic interpretation of the follies of Francisco and Rosalía Bringas, their
ousted sovereign, and the pseudorevolutionary bureaucrats who replace
her. *Fortunata y Jacinta*, too, is recounted by a narrator who discreetly
inserts himself into the first section of the opening chapter, then abjures
the use of the first-person pronoun for long stretches at a time, although
his perspective and value judgments are never far from the surface of the
narrative. By comparison, the initial discursive frame of *Torquemada en la*

hoguera is both protracted and considerably more overt, although no less deceptive:

> I am going to tell how the inhuman fiend, who consumed by fire so many unhappy lives, went to the stake; some he skewered through the liver with a glowing iron; others he stuffed, well larded, into cauldrons, and the rest he grilled part by part, over a slow fire, with diligent, methodical anger. I am going to tell how the ruthless executioner became a victim; how the hatred he provoked turned to sympathy, and clouds of curses rained pity upon him; a pathetic case, a very exemplary case, ladies and gentlemen, worthy of being recounted for the instruction of all, a warning to offenders and an admonition to inquisitors. (5: 904)

Much of what the narrator promises to tell, however, is belied by the rest of the story. This modern-day incarnation of the inquisitor Torquemada, *el Peor*, indeed inflicts tortures upon his hapless victims, but the abuse is emotional, not physical. More space is dedicated to his own suffering than to his crimes, and despite the abstract character he attributes to this exemplary tale, the story takes place in the realm of the everyday rather than that of the symbolic. As Urey rightly notes, the novel "has less to do with constructing a perfect moral *exemplum* than with identifying the conventions of reading which govern the texts of novel, society, self."[1]

The narrative situation set in place at the beginning of the text is made all the more ironic by the fact that the narrator's exordium is modeled upon the proem of the *romance de ciegos*, a class of texts that presents tragedy under the guise of the grotesque. As Pierre Ullman suggests, this borrowing is doubly significant. It implies that Francisco Torquemada, although he feels deeply the adversity he suffers, has no self-awareness of his grotesqueness. Moreover, it lulls readers into believing they will witness Torquemada's fall from a certain distance and with little emotional involvement, as they might watch a puppet show, and then subtly draws them into feeling for the "inhuman fiend" who turns out to be all too human.[2]

We have seen how *Fortunata y Jacinta*, Galdós's longest work, is built up out of myriad embedded narratives and enframing structures. Given its brevity, *Torquemada en la hoguera* might scarcely be expected to accommodate the presence of so many voices and internal partitionings. Yet from the very first paragraph, readers discover that other texts and other genres have been subsumed by Galdós's tale. The didactic oration, the religious sermon, and the *romance de ciegos* all manage to coexist in the first paragraph. Therefore it should come as no surprise to readers when they encounter yet another alien piece of writing, whose incrustation in the story is made all the more prominent by its physical disposition on the page, centered between left- and right-hand margins and, in the *Complete Works* edition, set off in a typeface considerably smaller than that employed in the rest of the text. Moreover, whereas the textual insets of *Fortunata* consist of characters telling stories, this particular embedded textual fragment in *Torquemada en la hoguera* can be seen, even upon first reading, as sententious, certainly (melo)dramatic, possibly even lyrical—anything but narrative. Taken at face value, the framed segment purports to be a direct citation by the narrator of representative writings by one José Bailón, a relatively minor figure whose intervention in the action of the novel is minimal. Yet as will soon become evident, Bailón's rambling prose bears within it the traces of an anterior text whose stylistic eccentricities and extravagant semantic content have managed to contaminate both his thinking and his writing. Hence, in *Torquemada* the frame's boundaries are supplied by an unwritten but implicit set of quotation marks surrounding a highly visible intertext.

Quotation, in the words of Edward Said, "is a constant reminder that writing is a form of displacement."[3] In terms of its rhetorical functions, "quotation can serve to accommodate, to incorporate, to falsify (when wrongly or even rightly paraphrased), to accumulate, to defend, or to conquer—but always, even when in the form of a passing allusion, it is a reminder that other writing serves to displace present writing, to a greater or lesser extent, from its absolute, central, proper place." Inevitably, this raises questions of originality and authority. The invocation of parody, fundamental to *Torquemada*, engages with this idea of displacement; by creating a text that repeats or closely imitates another with the aim of burlesquing it, the meaning of the first is detoured. As a "turning away" from literal meaning, parody may be viewed as a trope that serves to frame the intertext in *Torquemada* no less effectively than the food tropes mark off the opening and closing scenes of *Fortunata y Jacinta*.[4] With one important difference: the framing of the intertext in Galdós's novel moves beyond the purely cognitive act of perception to encompass a social and political dimension. It is not just that intertexuality, like social life itself, operates on the basis of reevaluation and transformation (of texts, in the former case; of experiences, in the latter). Rather, the choice of intertext, the manner of its transposition to the host-text, and the degree to which readers' attention is called to the act of transposition, are all framed from the outset by cultural presuppositions. When one text is overtaken by another, "it no longer speaks, it is spoken. It no longer denotes. It connotes." [5] The switch from transitivity to intransitivity marks the exercise of a narrative authority at a level superior to the intertext, and authority, by definition, makes its statements in the service of some historical or ideological discourse.

The ex-theologian Bailón, whose writings have been absorbed into the narrator's tale of Torquemada, strikes readers as a singularly unattractive creation. Among the repertoire of marginal figures—servants, indigents, family members—who flesh out the background in Galdós's parable of avarice, Bailón shines by virtue of his extravagance. Indeed, he is an outlandish character who makes his sole appearance in this brief installment of the multivolume *Torquemada* saga.[6] Perhaps because his is a noncyclical figure that quickly passes out of the *Novelas contemporáneas*, perhaps because he is an open target of the narrator's derision, Galdós's purveyor of the theory of "el gran Conjunto" 'the great Whole' has only infrequently been an object of inquiry. Of course Bailón is easily recognized as an exemplar of bourgeois mediocrity and intellectual bankruptcy in Restoration society, a dubious distinction he shares with such other inhabitants of the *Torquemada* series as doña Lupe *la de los Pavos*, Zárate, and Morentín. He has also been singled out as the initial one in a line of mentors and advisors who dazzle Francisco de Torquemada with their command of rhetoric (Donoso, *Torquemada en la cruz*), their social skills (Cruz del Aguila, *Torquemada en el purgatorio*), or even their powers of intercession with the Divinity (Gamborena, *Torquemada y San Pedro*).[7] In his repeated efforts to console and convert Torquemada to his own brand of theology, Bailón becomes the miser's earliest spiritual director, the first of many who attempt to reform the crass moneylender Torquemada into a socially, if not morally, acceptable individual. As such, Bailón has been perceived as a key element in a particular narrative patterning, the antinomy of change versus constancy, which by its very repetition establishes the thematic intelligibility and unity of all four of the *Torquemada* novels.[8]

On occasion, critics have sought to broaden the definition of Bailón's role in the novel by attributing to him both allegorical and aesthetic functions. Thus he has alternately been viewed as representative of a spiritual malaise occurring nationwide, one of many such instances in Galdós's works in which the trajectory of an individual's biography recapitulates the movements of the collective forces of history; as exaggerated personification of clerical abuses; or as exemplification of a literary program dubbed the "bourgeois grotesque."[9] In fact, most commentators agree that the caricaturesque Bailón is a symbolic embodiment of the zeitgeist. Nonetheless, Bailón has undergone so many religious and professional transformations, all of them mutually exclusive—Catholic priest, revolutionary, freethinker, Protestant, anticlerical pamphleteer, and eventually moneylender—that it is no simple task to halt the chain of narrative signifiers bound up in the Bailón character and assign to it a singular and definitive meaning. Conversely, defending infinitely plural readings of Bailón's role in the novel produces such generalized statements as the claim that "Bailón represents the face of a faceless cultural evil."[10] Although perhaps ironically reminiscent in its hyperbole of the very pamphlets it condemns, this and similar judgments indicate the very central place that Bailón's writings occupy in Galdós's novel.

In fact, the issue of Bailón's pamphlets is more relevant to the novel than earlier critics may have realized. The basic premise of *Torquemada en la hoguera*, namely, the protagonist's inability to comprehend the concepts of charity, salvation, and death except in terms of personal profit or loss, is communicated by means of multiple narrative strategies. These include the equivocal use of a religious vocabulary (Galdós is forever punning upon Torquemada's use of the words "cross," "inquisitor," "stake," "martyr," "purgatory," and the final "conversion"), as well as the reiterated punctuation of novelistic dialogue with such profane interjections as "¡biblias pasteleras!" and "¡rebiblias!", and the subversion of all manner of Christian symbols and objects within a secular context.[11] Bailón's pseudo-philosophical tracts, cast in a style that yokes traditional evangelical fervor with a distinctly nonorthodox theological content, appear to be yet another example of the constant intersection of religious and purely materialistic motifs in the novel.

This "nonsense written in biblical style," as the narrator uncharitably designates Bailón's compositions, are very much part of what has been described as a system of "humorous 're-inscriptions' of the novella's relation to the Scripture."[12] But Bailón's pamphlets do not necessarily embody a direct or univocal correspondence with sacred texts. On the contrary, it can be shown that their satirical impact is derived from the often literal dependence of Galdós's novel upon a particular class of mediatory texts: French romantic manifestos of utopian socialist thought. In the 1830s and 1840s, in the writings of such social theorists as Pierre Leroux, Étienne Cabet, and the disciples of Fourier, the content and characteristic style of the Scriptures are borrowed for quite a different purpose: the incitement to radical social reform, rather than the promotion of conformity to religious dogma. Believing that early Christianity was essentially democratic in spirit, these utopian socialists interpreted the promises of fraternity and justice in the Gospels as a fierce critique of prevailing political and economic realities (monarchy and industrial capitalism), thus linking religious belief with the defense of revolution.

Decades later, when the hypocritical Bailón, for very different reasons, espouses as his own these early nineteenth-century religious socialist notions, the relationship between Galdós's text and the Scriptures shifts from secondary to tertiary. As the number of channels of interference multiplies between the scriptural source texts and the site of their reinscription in Bailón's opuscules, so, too, the distortion surrounding their original meaning grows as well. They are framed, and then reframed, in a manner that grows ever less innocent. Moreover, the repetition of fragments of a romantic work within Galdós's realist novel emphasizes differences rather than identity with respect to the reactions and evaluations of various sets of readers, both past and present, internal or external to the *Torquemada* novels, as they encounter these same (or similar) text fragments now set in an alien literary environment. This examination of resemblance and difference carried out by the reader is an analytical rather than a synthetic operation. It does not lead to a naturalization of the conventions of the source text; instead, it implies a critical posture that in effect sabotages the original, as "the dominance of the parodist's own *vraisemblance* is temporarily asserted" over that of the prior text.[13] Galdós is cannily able to demonstrate that indeed no work is identical even with itself; the process of writing, as exemplified by the imitation of early nineteenth-century religious utopian tracts in Bailón's broadsides, is always inevitably a process of rewriting, mediation, interpretation, and reinterpretation. In this light, *Torquemada en la hoguera* can be seen as a highly overcoded literary edifice built upon intertextual operations that accrue full meaning for the reader only when the provenance of Bailón's pamphlets is taken into account.

Here it is important to state that the discovery of a model for Bailón's writing should not be complacently viewed as an end in itself, as the end of the story. Rather, it must mark the starting point for an examination of the structural relations and transformations that couple these two texts in the form of what Genette calls a "palimpsest" and, beyond that, an inquiry into the manner in which all texts are rendered intelligible by virtue of their belonging to a general discursive space of culture. To proceed otherwise would be to fall prey to a narrow and not overly useful notion of literary borrowing.

An orthodox reading of Barthes or Kristeva, for instance, would very likely disqualify this identification of a direct textual source for Galdós's novel as antithetical to the concept of intertextuality. For these two critics, intertextual relations are infinite, and the sources of the conventions and signifying practices that are the conditions of meaning cannot properly be traced to any nameable origins. As Roland Barthes posits: "Every text, being itself the intertext of another text, belongs to the intertextual, which must not be confused with a text's origin: to search for the 'sources of' and 'influence upon' a work is to satisfy the myth of filiation. The quotations from which a text is constructed are anonymous, irrecoverable, and yet *already read:* they are quotations without quotation marks."[14]

Nonetheless, the fact is that in contemporary critical practice the application of the concept of intertextuality more often than not is identified precisely with the activity of identifying specific precursor texts that, once decoded, determine the reader's understanding of successive texts that through the process of citation feed parasitically upon them. In speaking about the intertext of *Torquemada en la hoguera* one is therefore forced to recognize a certain contingency of meaning that can only be resolved if the paternity of the intertext is elucidated as well and, again, only if the intertext is subsequently examined in light of other possible intertextual models and the pertinent discourses of nineteenth-century culture.[15]

In the past, conflicting claims have been advanced regarding the literary paternity of Bailón's pamphlets. Everything ranging from Krausism to Feuerbach's *The Essence of Christianity* has been proposed as possible inspiration for what Bailón writes. When no direct textual antecedent could be found, some critics assumed that the excerpts included in *Torquemada en la hoguera* were a stylistic pastiche manufactured by Galdós himself. In fact, the incendiary leaflets read by the gullible and uncultured Torquemada can be directly traced to a literary pre-text. They consist of selections either lifted verbatim or else thinly paraphrased by Galdós from one of the most clamorous works of the nineteenth century: the *Paroles d'un croyant* (1834) by the abbé Hugues-Félicité Robert de Lamennais. Not just Lamennais's *Paroles* but also his *Le livre du peuple* (1837), both in Parisian editions dated 1866, could be found in Galdós's library in Santander.[16] That Galdós was familiar with Mennaisian thought and had recourse to quoting from his works is not unduly surprising. Because of its potentially explosive combination of Catholic thought and provocation to social and political upheaval, the *Paroles* was noisily received throughout Europe. Evoking both admiration and hostility, it spawned a series of parodies and critical responses to the revolutionary democratic ideals contained in the book; in fact, the invention of the Bailón character hardly represents the first occasion on which Lamennais's writings were lampooned.[17] Hundreds of thousands of copies of the *Paroles* were sold, despite (perhaps because of) its condemnation by Gregory XVI in the papal encyclical *Singulari nos*, and within two months of publication it had been translated into several major European languages.

Spanish readers had at their disposal several translations of the *Paroles* into Castilian: one each published in Marseilles and Bordeaux in 1834; another two published a year later in Cáceres and Seville.[18] In September of 1836 the editorial house of Repullés supervised the publication of still another translation, this one the work of Mariano José de Larra, who also included a prologue ("Cuatro palabras del traductor") explaining his reasons for presenting such a doctrinally controversial work to the predominantly conservative Spanish reading public.[19] Successive editions continued to appear in the intervening years between Larra and Galdós. Almost two decades after the appearance of Larra's translation, an announcement in *Las Novedades* of July 25, 1855, stated that the *Palabras* and also Lamennais's *El libro del pueblo* were among the works included in volume 1 of *El eco de los folletines*, currently on sale in the offices of *Las Novedades* in Madrid. Both works had previously been serialized in the paper sometime between 1854 and 1855. Still another edition of the *Paroles*, translated by one J. Landa, appears in Barcelona in 1868. The reissue of Lamennais's book at these three particular moments of Spanish history—shortly after the death of the absolutist Fernando VII, subsequent to the lifting of censorship during the liberal *bienio* of 1854–56, and again in 1868 in the shadow of the Revolution—is indicative of Spaniards' close association of Lamennais's program with progressive and revolutionary politics.

Despite the fact that the inventory of Galdós's library includes copies of Lamennais's works in the original French, it seems indisputable that don Benito also had recourse to one of the various Spanish-language translations while writing *Torquemada*. Upon examination, one finds that although there are similarities to Larra's frequently reedited version, Bailón's pamphlets most closely mimic the Landa translation, *Las palabras de un creyente*, significantly subtitled "La regeneración de la humanidad" 'The regeneration of humanity'—a subtitle not appearing in the French work, but obviously germane to the motif of "God is Humanity" in *Torquemada*. Undoubtedly the September Revolution served to revive interest in Lamennais's writings; it is certainly not mere coincidence that Landa's edition was published in Barcelona by the Imprenta de los Hijos de Domenech during the politically turbulent year of 1868 under the rubric "Biblioteca del hombre libre" 'Library of the free man.'

A comparison between key portions of Landa's translation of Lamennais and the narrator's recounting of Bailón's perorations reveals that the citations take various forms.[20] A few are admittedly rather generalized, as is the case with the opening line of the *Paroles* ("Glory to God on high . . ."), repeated by Bailón, but also found in the Gospels and the initial line of the *Gloria in excelsis Deo* doxology. Some of the citations, given the confluence of stylistic features and ideological content, demonstrate clearly convincing parallels; still others—most notably the query of "Young soldier, where are you going?", a direct reference to the most widely commented and satirized chapter of the *Paroles*—are sure signs of *imitatio* in Galdós's text. As a comparison of Bailón's words to the French author's reveals, the Mennaisian contamination is not limited solely to don José's published pamphlets but also pervades both the phrasing and the spirit of the sermons he preaches to Torquemada in an attempt to counsel the moneylender in his anguish over the sudden, devastating illness that afflicts his son Valentín.

> "Glory to God on high, and peace . . ."
>
> "The times are approaching, times of redemption, when the Son of Man will be master of the earth."
>
> "Eighteen centuries ago, the Word sowed the divine seed. It bore fruit during a shadowy night. Behold its flowers."
>
> "What are they called? The rights of the people."
>
> "Here is the tyrant. May he be cursed!"
>
> "Lend me your ear and tell me from whence comes that vague, confused, strange sound."
>
> "Place your hand on the earth and tell me why it has trembled."
>
> "The Son of Man approaches, determined to recover his primogeniture."
>
> "Why does the tyrant's face pale? Ah! The tyrant sees his hours are numbered. . . ." (5: 911)
>
> "Young soldier, where are you going?" (5: 911)

Behold how man vacillates and becomes confused in the face of the great problem. What is good? What is evil? My son, open your ears to the truth and your eyes to the light. Good is loving our fellow men. Let us love, and we will know what good is; let us hate and we

will know evil. Let us do good unto those who abhor us, and thorns
will be transformed into flowers. This is what the Just Man said, this
is what I say . . . Wisdom of wisdom, and knowledge of knowledge.
(5: 921)

Courage, my friend, courage. In these cases we recognize strong
souls. Remember that great Philosopher who expired on the cross,
having consecrated the principles of Humanity. (5: 932)

The similarities between Lamennais's tract and the textual fragments
that Galdós has included in *Torquemada* are indeed striking. Moreover,
a strong case can be made for the fact that Galdós did not simply make
a mechanical transcription of portions of the *Paroles* and attribute them
to his character. Rather, he evidently was well-informed about the often
contradictory circumstances of Lamennais's life and the errant fortunes of
his book, and incorporated this information in an ironically inverted manner into the framework of the José Bailón figure. So that here the notions
of intertextuality and parody become dependent in turn upon another one
of the dominant features of Galdós's narratives: the process of noveliza-
tion of history, the transmutation of biography into fiction, which is itself
historically determined and ideologically motivated. What makes Galdós's
calculated choice of progenitor text so interesting is the fact that Lamennais
is a complex figure whose oeuvre defies any easy taxonomic classification.
Rather, he overlaps several categories in his capacity as theologian, social
reformer, philosopher, and writer. On the one hand, he stands at the point
of intersection of Church and state, and his uneasy movement between
these two spheres is undoubtedly of enormous concern to Galdós who, as
early as 1870, had sensed the difficulty in reconciling social morality and
political exigencies with religious norms, stating:

What stands out in the first place is the religious problem, which un-
settles households and offers frightening contradictions . . . At the
same time, one observes with horror the ravages of adultery, that vice
that disorganizes the essence of family life, and one doubts if this
ought to be remedied by a religious solution, by pure morality, or
simply a civil reform. We know that it is not the novelist who will
decide directly these grave matters, but he is indeed charged with
the mission of reflecting this deep disorder, this incessant struggle
between principles and facts that comprises the extraordinary drama
of present-day life.[21]

But while Lamennais stands poised on the borders of Church and society, he simultaneously takes up a position on the intersecting frontiers of literature and the social sciences, both practiced under the aegis of romanticism. Often referred to as a poet who in the *Paroles* gives free rein to his lyrical gifts, he is no less a literary stylist than he is a historical and political theoretician. This conflation of issues and interests personified in Lamennais must have seemed especially compelling to Galdós, simultaneously engaged in *Torquemada en la hoguera* in "the literary project of a fictional representation of society, with a concentration on the middle class" as well as "the ideological project of a search for a way to renovate that society."[22]

A brief historical excursus may help to clarify the generative relationship between Lamennais's *Paroles* and Galdós's reframing of them in *Torquemada*. Lamennais (1782–1854), born into the *petite noblesse* just prior to the French Revolution, began his career together with Louis de Bonald and Joseph de Maistre as a leading exponent of ultramontane thought. When his father's business foundered owing to the continental blockade brought about by the Napoleonic Wars, he turned to journalism to earn his livelihood and began publishing brief pamphlets and brochures. A brief flight to England during the Hundred Days of Napoleon was later followed in 1816 by his ordination as a priest. Throughout the Bourbon Restoration, in works such as the highly popular *Essai sur l'indifférence en matière de religion* (1817–1823), Lamennais was known as a noted Catholic apologist who defended the truth of religious dogma as vital to the health of society, as well as the rights of the Church to exert its sovereignty over the temporal order.

At the outbreak of the July 1830 revolution, Lamennais's constant preoccupation with the socially regenerative potential of Christianity slowly began to undermine his earlier allegiance to the theocratic principle of government. Instead, he began to envision an alliance between an enlightened Catholicism and the doctrines of liberalism. At La Chênaie (1823–1833) he founded a community of disciples and supporters, including Gerbet, Lacordaire, Maurice de Guérin, and Montalembert (he also counted among his friends Hugo, Sainte-Beuve, Vigny, and Lamartine), and edited the daily journal *Avenir* (1830–1831) under the slogan "God and liberty." The *Avenir* program, later condemned by papal encyclical (*Mirari vos*, 1832), espoused freedom of religion, press, and education as well as universal suffrage, on the assumption that the fulfillment of the promise of Christian progress would of necessity result in the establishment of a liberal regime. By the publication of the *Paroles* in 1834, Lamennais's thinking had undergone a 180 degree turnaround. Breaking ranks with the papacy, Lamennais presented in the *Paroles* a new scenario: a bitterly oppressed proletariat, brutalized by the capitalist labor system and equally tyrannized by secular despots and a corrupted institutional Church, would eventually live to watch its enemies laid low and see ushered in a new age based on Christ's original message of peace, fraternity, and social justice.

Regarding Lamennais's hopes for society, Sainte-Beuve remarked that "it can be seen that his goal remained the same: to spiritualize, to heal, to moralize by Christian means a society that has passed from material-ism to indifference."[23] And indeed, one can point to certain aspects of Lamennais's early thought which presage his later position vis-à-vis the interrelationship of religion and politics. For instance, already in the *Essai sur l'indifférence* he sets forth as a demonstration of religion the so-called doctrine of "common sense," an anticipation of his later validation of the *vox populi* as the source of all truth. Similarly, when after the July Revo-lution the control of education in France was turned over to Victor Cousin and the eclectic philosophers—all hostile to Catholicism—Lamennais es-poused the Church's right to teach as it saw fit, and this struggle over freedom of education eventually became extended to the other freedoms and civil liberties associated with the democratic-socialist political plat-form. Even Lamennais's ultramontanism, by locating the seat of religious authority within the papacy rather than the state, prepares the way for his later statement that the voice of religion is superior to (and critical of) the political establishment.

Nonetheless, the method that Lamennais in his *Paroles* perceived as necessary to achieve this desired healing of society is vastly removed from his previous ultramontane beliefs and consequent support of the ultraroyal-ist political faction in France. In fact, what disturbed so many critics of the *Paroles* was Lamennais's association of popular emancipation with the figure of Christ and his advocacy of popular rebellion in situations where rulers contravened the tenets of divine law. By suggesting that the meek might inherit the earth in this world rather than in the next, Lamennais earned for himself the title of "priest wearing the red cap of revolution."[24] Echoing such opprobrium, one Spanish commentator for whom the publi-cation of the *Paroles* signified the "shipwreck" or "fall of a great writer," transformed from "a vehement and eloquent defender of Christianity" into an unbeliever, angrily asked: "But didn't he [Lamennais] see that such a book was a crime against religion and society? . . . The *Palabras de un creyente* was the red cap of revolution placed on Jesus Christ's cross."[25] The Vatican promptly condemned the *Paroles* as heretical. Lamennais, although never officially excommunicated, chose the path of apostasy over submission to papal authority. By the 1840s Lamennais appears to have rejected, according to one ecclesiastical historian, "the hypothesis of a supernatural order" and disavowed the concepts of miracles, revelation, arbitrary divine intervention, and expiation of sin.[26] Instead, he turned to the issue of pauperism, whose resolution he saw as crucial to humanity's future.

Soon enough, the initial furor over the *Paroles* died away, and oblivion overtook both the book and its author. In Spain, one reliable witness' testimony to this obscurity which engulfed Lamennais is that of Marcelino Menéndez y Pelayo. Addressing himself to the doctrinal and stylistic metamorphoses that Lamennais experienced during his lifetime, he writes in the *Historia de ideas estéticas en España*:

> Among critics, orthodox as well as heterodox ones, the belief is fairly common that Lamennais's ideas as well as his style deteriorated noticeably after his apostasy . . . And it is true that while the *Ensayo sobre la indiferencia*, despite its deplorable metaphysics, today continues to be read and studied by unbelievers and believers . . . only one of the books from Lamennais's second period, that strange and eloquent apocalypse he titled *Palabras de un Creyente*, still finds readers, although its revolutionary value is expended.
>
> Certainly, this shadow of indifference, disdain, and oblivion, weighing more heavily every day upon his person and his writings, was for Lamennais a punishment from Providence.[27]

Menéndez y Pelayo's observations are noteworthy in that they highlight the two constitutive features that establish the analogical relationship between Lamennais and Bailón (defection from the Church hierarchy; rapid fall from celebrity into anonymity). Additionally, his comments indicate that the *Paroles* did continue to circulate, such knowledge of the book being necessary if the parody generated by this text's repetition within Galdós's novel was to be appreciated by the reader. If only Torquemada takes Bailón seriously as a political theoretician and religious philosopher, it is because he is a "man who scarcely reads" (5: 911), and evidently remains unaware of the reception history of either his friend's pamphlets or the Mennaisian texts that serve as precedent for them.

Lamennais's passage in France through the Empire, the Restoration, and the July Revolution finds its equivalent in Bailón's own charting of the waters of Spain's Revolution of 1868, the short-lived republic, and ensuing Alfonsine Restoration. Allowing for the shift in the temporal frame, there is a startling, almost perverse proximity with which the events of Bailón's life as portrayed by Galdós in *Torquemada en la hoguera* imitate those of Lamennais's. The basic chord of similitude is struck when the narrator informs the reader: "This señor Bailón is a priest who hung up his habit in '69, in Málaga, throwing himself with such raging ardor into a career as a revolutionary and freethinker that he could no longer return to the fold, nor would he have been accepted even had he wanted to" (5: 910). Not only is Torquemada's companion a defrocked priest as was Lamennais; in times of economic hardship he, too, generates an income by writing incendiary political pamphlets and working for a newspaper. The reader learns that "he ended up in the editorial office of a very radical little newspaper whose mission was to lob firecrackers at all the authorities: the priests, the bishops, and the pope himself. This happened in '73, and from that period can be dated the political tracts on contemporary problems that the ex-priest published in the newspaper and of which he had reprints made . . . and which, unbelievably, enjoyed brief periods of success" (5: 910). Later comes Bailón's sojourn abroad, for reasons dictated by the inhospitable political temper of the Restoration: "But all that passed, the revolutionary fever and the leaflets, and Bailón had to hide, shaving off his beard to disguise himself and be able to flee abroad" (5: 910). After a two-year absence, Bailón returns to Spain, only to land in El Saladero prison, on suspicion of carrying messages from the political émigrés. Finally, Bailón, not unlike his prototype, passes out of the collective memory of history, losing all his readers and disciples save the benighted Torquemada, "the only mortal who was still reading Bailón's tracts ten years after their publication; it was a literature that was obsolete almost at the time of its birth, and whose fleeting success can't be understood unless we remember that a form of sentimental democracy in the style of Jeremiah also had its day" (5: 911).[28]

It would, of course, be misleading to imply that the narrative patterning of Bailón after Lamennais is carried through to the letter. Significant differences in their characters serve to throw into even sharper relief the critical eye with which Galdós's narrator surveys the reemergence of Mennaisian thought in *Torquemada*. The most obvious of these differences is the fact that not just Torquemada, ascending the social ladder to senator and marquis, but also Bailón, with his flock of goats, his she-donkey milking establishment, and his investments managed by *el Peor*, is a propertied Spaniard. Bailón readily confesses that "he no longer felt like participating in conspiracies, since his daily bread was assured and he didn't wish to risk his hide to facilitate the ambitions of a few troublemakers" (5: 911). So much so, that in one breath he counsels resignation to the distraught Torquemada ("Before Nature, before the sublime Whole, we are pieces of atoms that know nothing") and in the very next tries to recruit his friend's help in expanding and exploiting the production potential of his small commercial establishment ("setting up a large, modern milk business, with prompt home delivery, fixed prices, an elegant retail outlet, telephone, etc.") (5: 921). As for Torquemada, he is the man who wholeheartedly endorses the ideas propounded by his friend Donoso, as he states in *Torquemada en la cruz*: "the rich man who lives in misery, among ignorant and ordinary people, sins gravely, yes sir, but against Society. The latter needs to build up its strength in order to resist the attacks of the envious proletariat" (5: 956). That either of these two characters, faithful to their respective credos of political expediency and "positivist usury," would knowingly espouse the Mennaisian vindication of revolution, popular sovereignty, and redistribution of worldly goods is absurd indeed.

Furthermore, one of the principal messages of the *Paroles* is that "Justice is life; and charity is also life, a sweeter and more abundant life." Charity and justice, conjoined as the foundation of society, are the guarantors of human liberty. By contrast, in *Torquemada en la hoguera* Galdós details the miser's several abortive attempts at performing acts of charity, conceived as part of a celestial bargain to save the life of his dying son Valentín: the donation of the old cape rather than the new one, the supposedly interest-free loan to Isidora in exchange for Martín's paintings, the gift of a pearl for the icon of the Virgin, the offer of his mattress to *la tía Roma*, and the feeble gestures of munificence toward his tenants. By the closing sentence of *Torquemada*—" 'Whatever mercy I may have from now on, damn it, let them throw it right back in my face' " (5: 934)—the presence of the *Paroles* in Galdós's novel has been reduced to that faint echo that remains after the evisceration of Lamennais's most basic notions regarding pauperism, social inequity, and the role of religion in redressing these two maladies.

Of course Bailón's pursuit of material gain and his befriending of the miserly Torquemada is not the sole point of contrast between Lamennais and Galdós's ecclesiastical renegade. As opposed to the author of the *Paroles* who, even after his abrogation of faith and separation from the

Church, continued to lead an exemplary, retiring existence, Bailón throws off his vows not just of poverty but of chastity as well, for a time winding up, as the narrator puns, "in biblical fashion, living in concubinage with a rich widow" (5: 910). Similar verbal assaults throughout the novel are evidence of the narrator's overt dismay at Bailón's literal expropriation of the Mennaisian line of thought and the seductive hold it exercises over Torquemada. The narrator's full measure of disdain is distilled in the epithets he uses to describe Bailón's writings; they are "nonsense," "idiocies," "gibberish," "a joke on Humanity," "farrago," and "wordplay," just as the character himself is variously ridiculed as an "ex-priest," an "apostate priest," and a "diabolical author." This abrupt dismissal of the rhetoric and ideology of the *Paroles* recurs even after Bailón has disappeared from the novel. The Mennaisian theme developed in Bailón's pamphlets surfaces again in *Torquemada en el purgatorio*, in a conversation between Zárate and the protagonist, spitefully recalled by the narrator:

> They went on to another matter, which must have had something to do with socialism and collectivism, for on the following day, when Torquemada went out into the streets, he had become an expert on those subjects. He found *points of contact* between certain doctrines and the evangelical principle, and wrapped his nonsense in phrases that he hit upon by chance and used with dubious opportunity. (5: 1064)

Clearly Bailón's repetition of Lamennais's writings can in no way represent a neutral reprise of the earlier text. The fundamental incompatibility between Mennaisian ideals and their literal resurrection by Bailón, resulting in the apparent disparagement of the Lamennais intertext, is partially a function of their chronological dislocation. In the context of bourgeois, postrevolutionary Spain, even a sincere attempt to carry out as praxis the social program extolled in the *Paroles* was likely to meet with no greater success than don Quijote's effort to reenact the medieval chivalresque ideal in seventeenth-century Castile: it represents a profoundly inappropriate, ahistorical endeavor. At best, if Bailón were writing his pamphlets in earnest, he would provide one more example of a pathetic Galdós character mistakenly laboring under the still to be dispelled topoï of romanticism.[29] This, however, is hardly the case; Bailón's theories, a distorted mélange of socialism, positivism, and reincarnation, are knowingly co-opted from other sources in response to the ex-curate's desire to impress Torquemada with his pseudoerudition. While Lamennais was, by all reports, "an absolute and extreme soul during the first as well as the second period of his philosophical and religious life, . . . disposed toward oratory and emphasis, but sincere even in the midst of the most absurd discourse," [30] Bailón is a mere poseur, a charlatan who "used to speak in a very different style from the way he wrote" (5: 921). Like Manuel Pez of *La de Bringas* and the bureaucrat Pantoja of *Miau*, Bailón shifts allegiances in response to prevailing political winds: vociferous revolutionary until 1874, thereafter a comfortably entrenched defender of the status quo whose motto is not utopia but rather opportunity.

The radical disjunction that can be observed between the original meaning and the mood of the *Paroles* and its discredited status in Galdós's novel is indicative of the manner in which the intertextual process operates. The inclusion of the Mennaisian text is not just a case of recurrence but rather of inscription by means of which Galdós's novel not only repeats the source text but also "places it in quotation marks, makes it conditional." [31] The fragments of Lamennais's work placed in quotations and attributed to Bailón function as a signifier whose primary signification is substantially altered by the text surrounding it. In such instances, Todorov explains, "the external text is not a simple model which can be imitated or mocked, it provokes or modifies the present discourse; the formula is that of the question/answer pair, and we habitually designate this relation as a concealed polemic." [32]

By citing Lamennais's *Paroles d'un croyant* in *Torquemada en la hoguera*, Galdós effectively problematizes Bailón's and Torquemada's relation to Scripture, as well as to the many correlatives evoked by the Mennaisian text: romantic literature, the political movement of utopian socialism, the redemptive possibilities, personal and collective, of religion itself. Not only does this reinscriptive stratagem play actual readers' foreknowledge and recognition of Lamennais's *Paroles* against the characters' ignorance, with the consequent production of parody, it also permits Galdós to posit anew the entire issue of social decay and regeneration confronting late nineteenth-century Spanish society.

For the most part, the *Torquemada* series is cast in the negative, in that it offers a critique of those ideological alternatives that Galdós believes will not effect the required transformation of society. Neither Rafael's impossible longing to return to a precapitalist, aristocratic milieu, nor Gamborena's attempted reclamation of souls for the greater glory of a materialistically oriented Church, can serve as the catalyst for moral and social regeneration; yet neither can the worship of a religion of humanity and the vindication of popular sovereignty as preached by Bailón in imitation of Lamennais. As Miguel Artola notes: "The interest of pre-Marxist or utopian socialism resides more in its criticism of the consequences for the working class that result from a system of economic freedom than in the theoretical or practical value of the solutions that it proposes or on occasion attempts to implement."[33] The antagonism expressed in *Torquemada en la hoguera* toward the Mennaisian agenda and its untimely revival has its most likely explanation in two facets of Galdós's thought that can be traced through most of his novelistic production: his repeated condemnation of the pernicious effects of an anachronistic attachment to the vestiges of romantic thought, as well as his embittered reaction to the recent example of the failure of the September Revolution.

One might also add that the brunt of Galdós's sarcasm may have been directed less at the spirit and intent of Lamennais's *Paroles* (that is, the censure of all those institutions, monarchy and Church included, that have made possible and even acceptable the ruling system of social inequity) than at Bailón's blatantly insincere manipulation of them as a means of gaining a certain philosophical or moral ascendancy over the unlearned Torquemada. In fact, the reader can detect in some of Galdós's late works written after the turn of the century—a period when the author became increasingly attracted to republican socialism and more radicalized political platforms—a decidedly more urgent tone to his calls for reform. In *Casandra* (1905) Galdós openly advocates a solution predicated on violence to arbitrate a dispute regarding economic and social injustice, while in *El caballero encantado* (1909) several of the characters proffer revolutionary statements taken from certain lesser-known patristic texts of Saint Augustine, Saint Gregory, Saint John Chrysostom, and others regarding the abuses of ownership of property and the search for distributive justice. As to how Galdós came by his knowledge of these writings which he anthologizes in *El caballero encantado*, Rodolfo Cardona shrewdly speculates that it was Galdós's readings of Lamennais that provided the vital connection.[34]

It needs to be stressed that the highly problematic inclusion of Mennaisian writings in *Torquemada en la hoguera* also opens up an inquiry into the nature of the historical process, an inquiry which is consonant with Galdós's own career-long preoccupation with his century's historical dynamics and the sources of historical knowledge.[35] As Linda Hutcheon and others (notably the Russian formalists and Bakhtin) have pointed out, parody revives a dialogue, however critical or ironic, with the past, and in that sense extends not just a formalist gesture through the imitation of models (that is, an interart discourse) but also a link between art or text and the world.[36] In this instance, the search for a better understanding of Spain's present and for a way to remedy its most egregious defects of social and political organization leads readers back to the past: the more remote past of inquisitorial intolerance, evoked by the protagonist's surname, which has distorted the original message of the Church and the Scriptures, and the more recent past of political oppression of the individual and the national subject that served as provocation for the social upheaval fomented by European romanticism and such documents as Lamennais's *Paroles* (in yet another return to the Scriptures).

Disconcertingly, however, what *Torquemada* reveals is that the retrieval of the past can never be more than an approximation. Historical knowledge appears to consist solely of the accretion of layer upon layer of text: fragments of Church writings, fragments of Lamennais, and now, fragments of Bailón's pamphlets which, significantly, are never transcribed in their totality but instead are presented piecemeal to the reader by the narrator, whose tale about the miser is also told in bits and pieces by other "unpublished historians" (5: 1338). As historical origins recede ambiguously behind a horizon of infinite regress, the task of ascertaining prime causes becomes futile, no less so than Torquemada's efforts to fathom the workings of divine providence, and is supplanted by the multiple revisions and rewritings of the already written as exemplified by the intertextual process. Signs refer to other signs; they can no longer be correlated directly with signifieds whose stability is unassailable. History, therefore, can no longer lay claim to a privileged status. It becomes, in effect, another form of discourse, ultimately to be annexed by fiction. The parody of Bailón's almost-forgotten tracts reiterates Galdós's general distrust of politicians who traffic not in ideas but idle words that in the final analysis are rendered nonsensical by virtue of their self-reflexivity: one thinks of the example of José María Manso in *El amigo Manso*, an aspiring candidate to the Rampant Democracy Party, who announces that "things fall on the side toward which they are leaning" (4: 1222). Beyond that, the Mennaisian parody of *Torquemada en la hoguera* functions as a warning that while to understand the present it is necessary to study the past, studying the past consists primarily in reading about it; and reading as Galdós portrays it is frequently a devastatingly ironic process that cannot be relied upon to summon up an unchallenged vision of reality.[37] It would seem that whichever way one positions the frame of reference in *Torquemada*, one can never fix within its borders the dream of historical or epistemological certainty cherished by the realist author. Within the frame, all is literature, fiction.

Beyond the semantic coincidences of Bailón's and Lamennais's writings, Galdós employs other, broader methods to invoke satirically the Mennaisian intertext. One specific reason for the notoriety of the *Paroles* during the nineteenth century was the novelty of its style. Galdós's highly opinionated and intrusive narrator comments that "Bailón used to write those absurdities in very short paragraphs, and sometimes broke into Holy Writ" (5: 911). In point of fact, Lamennais's prose, divided into chapters and verses independent of linear plotting, is a lexical and compositional imitation of liturgical texts, characterized by a colloidal mixture of invective and lyricism. Depending upon their political allegiances and religious convictions, contemporary critics either praised the eloquent simplicity and poetry of the book (what one of Lamennais's correspondents called "a new, sublime, and holy language, easily intelligible to the people"), or else ridiculed it as an indulgence in bloated imagery and melodrama masquerading in the guise of parable or mystic exercise ("an impure alliance of radicalism, Saint-Simonism, and Catholicism, with images that were sometimes bloody or horrific, sometimes sombre, despairing, sardonic, and insulting," according to another reviewer).[38] As one contemporary Spanish opponent of the *Paroles* concurred, Lamennais "made use of the fallacious resources of the imagination, fictions and phantasms, parabolic forms, and all kinds of illusory means . . . creating and sending around the world a tract entitled *Palabras de un Creyente*," a work, he claims, "in which nothing is examined or discussed, a work in which dreaming has replaced reasoning, which concludes and prophesies instead of testing."[39] Pardo Bazán, writing with a half-century's distance and noting— not unlike Galdós does in *Torquemada*—the superannuated agenda of the *Paroles*, also comments on its unusually compelling style:

> I have just read this little book, also called the *Apocalypse of the Devil*, and I confess: from the distance which now separates us from the era in which it first appeared and reached such a prodigious number of editions, and was translated into all the languages of the world, it seems to me one of those obsolete machines of war that are preserved for curiosity's sake in museums. Because of its lively coloring and its poetic exaltation, the *Palabras* is purely romantic. What undoubtedly lent force to this tract—besides its circumstances—was the strangeness of its style, divided into chapter and verse and artfully copying the Old and New Testament.[40]

For his part, Menéndez y Pelayo discounted Lamennais's politics as hopelessly extravagant, locating instead what redeeming value he could find in
the *Palabras* in its powerful rhetoric. The French priest's "prophetic daydreams," he wrote, "ought to be valued only as magnificent prose elegies,
in which the heart played a greater role than the intellect."[41]

Both camps noted that the *Paroles* is distinguished by its reliance upon
figurative language used to heighten the visionary impact of its prose. It
is a work filled with prophetic dicta and forebodings of the coming apocalypse, of landscapes characterized by trembling mountains, roiling seas,
and livid clouds that serve as backdrop for the waging of mortal combat
between the hosts of Satan and the newly risen Christ. In Lamennais's
eschatology, "everything that happens in the world has a sign that precedes it." Hence his emphasis on dreams and mystical transports in which,
through the privilege of divine revelation, select individuals foresee the
impending natural and social cataclysms which must purge the earth and
humankind before the millennium can be instituted.

Once again, the reader of Galdós is obliged to read *Torquemada en la
hoguera* against a grid of references supplied contextually by Lamennais's
Paroles. For in fact, Galdós integrates into his novel these same motifs of
otherworldly divination and imminent earthly destruction, while simultaneously negating their validity. Here, the book of the world has become
suddenly garbled; the reading of its signs becomes a misreading, con-
ducive only to error and self-deception. *Torquemada en la hoguera* is filled
with prophets and apocalyptic premonitions, but these self-styled prophets
merely have foreknowledge of material concerns, and the majority of the
novel's predictions turn out to be thoroughly inaccurate. Lamennais had
written that the powerful are inevitably surrounded by a populous ret-
inue of hangers-on including "the rich and the flatterers who covet wealth,
the fallen women, the infamous ministers of their secret pleasures, the
hypocrites, the buffoons who lead their consciences astray, and the false
prophets who guide them."[42] Capitalizing upon the motif of the false
prophet, the first volume of the *Torquemada* series apprises the reader that
Bailón "is the living image of the sybil of Cumae, painted by Michelan-
gelo, along with the other sibyls and prophets, upon the marvelous ceiling
of the Sistine Chapel" and also that "listening to him, don Francisco was
thoroughly charmed, and in all matters of a lofty nature held him to be an
oracle" (5: 911).

The hollow ring to the repeated use of the two epithets "sibyl" and
"oracle" in the novel reverberates off the various dire prognostications
for humanity which ultimately never come to pass. In chapter 4, when

Torquemada, fearing he may lose Valentín, relents in his persecution of the tenants on rent collection day, the word begins to circulate: "Don Francisco with humanity! That's why that star with a tail comes out in the sky every night. The fact is that the world is coming to an end" (5: 916). Torquemada, however, sheds his humanitarian posture shortly after his son's death. Likewise, the blazing comet hailed by the tenants is no more a portent of the end of days than the death of Valentín, though his father mistakenly assumes that the passing of his Christlike son will cause the very structure of the cosmos to come unglued: "What a terrible case that was! So many hopes dashed! . . . It was enough to drive one mad. The unhinging of the universe would have been more natural than the death of the prodigious child who had come to earth to illuminate it with the light of his talent" (5: 917).

Galdós renders nonfunctional the visionary elements stemming from Lamennais's *Paroles* by showing how his characters' expectations are consistently undermined. Much like the revolution, demoted to the status of nonevent by the mercenary conduct of Bailón, Valentín dies but the world goes on. Later, the coming of the new redeemer is announced (Valentín II) but he is born a congenital idiot. Worse still, Torquemada is accepted into polite society yet catastrophe does not rain down as had been predicted by his brother-in-law. In the positivistic universe inhabited by Torquemada, where life follows a course dictated by economic and biological forces, there is no apocalyptic cleansing, no divine intervention to punish or set accounts straight. Torquemada's society is a self-regulatory and self-contained system, a kind of perpetual motion machine whose laws admit no tampering. Within this world, the prophecies made by oracles and sibyls, given their spurious nature, are desacralized to the extent that the threatened apocalypse never materializes. Instead, as is suggested in *Torquemada en la cruz* by the figure of Cándido Valiente, who uses gunpowder to make pretty fireworks rather than dynamite for anarchist rallies, virtually all the moments of crisis in the novel represent a kind of pseudo-apocalypse occurring not with a bang but a whimper. In answer to Wolfgang Iser's query of "when is the end not the end?", surely we may reply: in the *Torquemada* series, where the deaths of Valentín I and of don Francisco himself at the respective conclusions of the first and the fourth volumes of the tetralogy (the end) most emphatically do not entail the imminent "unhinging of the spheres," the breakdown of the universe (the End).[43]

Yet it is also true that the betrayal of expectations is one of the chief characteristics of literature of the apocalypse. If the anticipated upheaval is not forthcoming, then the fiction of the end is not dismantled but rather revised, the better to accommodate changing historical circumstances. In this sense, it is most fitting that Galdós chooses to conclude *Torquemada en la hoguera* with a variation on the paradigmatic structure of apocalypse harking back to Lamennais's tract. For *Torquemada en la hoguera*, similar to most apocalyptic literature, is nothing other than a vast fiction of adjustment and adaptation, personified by Torquemada over the course of the tetralogy and emblematically portrayed by Bailón in the first volume. Personal and textual identity, however, are both imperiled by this same process of adjustment. *Torquemada en la hoguera* simultaneously registers the efforts of individuals to conform to changing social conditions while still defending their identity, and of texts to inhere in other texts while also preserving their autonomy of the signified, with only partial success in either instance. In the case of the *Paroles*, especially, accommodation to Galdós's novel via the process of reinscription is achieved only at the cost of ironic dissociation from Mennaisian utopian ideology. The narrator's parodic framing of Bailón's rewriting of Lamennais ultimately evacuates all purpose from the contents within that frame.[44]

The motif of false apocalypse in *Torquemada en la hoguera* reminds us that closure, as already noted in the example of *Fortunata y Jacinta*, does not always automatically ensue in a realist text. Structural and psychological closure is deferred as don Francisco continues his self-transformation in the three novels that follow. What *is* closed off is the possibility of resurrecting Bailón's (and by association, Lamennais's) discourse as an instrument of political and social redemption. In this example of intertextuality, the author "repeats in order to encircle, to enclose within another discourse, thus rendered more powerful. He speaks in order to obliterate, to cancel."[45] Here, textual enclosure and ideological closure become synonymous.

With this enclosure or enfolding of Mennaisian thought and expression into the novel, curious parallels begin to emerge between the role of intertexts in *Torquemada en la hoguera* and the functioning of embedded narratives as epitomized in *Fortunata y Jacinta*. Interior narrations tend to disrupt the temporal sequence of the outer story; in skipping from one voice and perspective to another, they place the framing process in the spotlight, thereby diminishing the illusion of narrative continuity. Similarly, intertextuality may disrupt the linearity of a text, especially when the intruding material is as overtly identifiable by visual and stylistic criteria as it is in this work. The reader, upon reaching the intertext, must choose either to continue uninterruptedly on the path of the main story, or detour and follow the intertext to someplace beyond and anterior to what is being read. Comparable to interior narrations, intertexts and intertextuality represent a framing of the second order. Literary realism, too, is a doubly hierarchical system, a representation of a representation, although it must obscure rather than reveal this fact in order to safeguard its effectiveness as an aesthetic and an ideological program. When realist fiction such as *Torquemada en la hoguera* openly parades its referent, defining it not as the world but as still more text, that effectiveness is compromised.

Both embedded stories and intertextual networks are a perennial compositional feature of Galdós's novels, as indeed they are of narrative generally. The pervasive presence of Cervantes in the *Novelas contemporáneas* and the *Episodios*, or the structural dependence of *Tormento* upon the genre of serial novels (see chapter 4 herein), are typical of the intricate horizontal and vertical relations that govern his fictions. Although at times the complexity of *Torquemada en la hoguera* has been downplayed (it is in fact the shortest and most rapidly narrated of Galdós's works, with correspondingly little space in which to elaborate a detailed universe of description), surely an examination of intertextual framing in the novel dispels this assumption. The story of the miserly don Francisco is presented by the narrator as a moral exemplum; the integration and disintegration of Mennaisian thought in *Torquemada* is no less exemplary of the complexity of narrative structure and textual politics that characterize the realist novel.

TWO

Cultural

Frames

*

The play was well prepared for when the occasion might arise to perform it.—Galdós, La de Bringas

The deciphering process that occurs during the act of reading is made possible largely by the application of frames to texts. Readers construct these frames based upon models already known to them from their own perceptions and experiences as well as from their previous encounters with literature. Equipped with an understanding and command of language, they must depend upon several other sources of information—a mastery of logical operations, a familiarity with interpretive conventions, a general knowledge of the world—to make sense out of what the text says.[1] Readers frequently approach narrative prose, for instance, using temporal models to explain the distribution and (non-)sequentiality of events in the story. In the case of realist novels, readers additionally draw upon their acquaintance with the organization of social life that such texts pretend to emulate and with the interpretive norms (symbolism, connotation, and so forth) that fiction so frequently presses into service. Nonetheless, given the dynamic nature of the reading process, a single set of frames may not prevail from start to finish. Changing information provided by the text may force readers to revise their initial frames or switch to different ones altogether. Texts that seem to accommodate multiple, antithetical frames or that call attention to frame-shifts may strike readers as especially challenging, distinguished by a peculiar hesitancy or ambiguity.

Such frame vacillation is characteristic of Galdós's *Tormento* (1884), which might best be described as a novel predicated upon moral and psychological equivocation. On the threshold of marriage to a respectable businessman, the eponymous heroine must decide whether or not to confess her earlier tryst with the priest Pedro Polo, an infraction which the text's own hermeneutic code insinuates but refuses to name or confirm outright. All around her, not so very unlike the novel's narrator, who obscures the facts with his textual mutism, others in her circle prevaricate upon matters of conscience, desire, and ambition. Whether they are social innocents or consummate hypocrites, the novel's principal characters recognize themselves in thrall to a bourgeois society that demands slavish conformity to appearances, placing special emphasis on the display of material wealth and the obedience of rigid codes governing social conduct. Consequently, everything about them—their manner of dress, style of speech, preferred modes of social intercourse—is geared to maintaining the illusion of economic prosperity and sexual propriety. Their success in this venture, however, is at best intermittent. The impression they make upon their fellow characters and upon readers is inconsistent, varying with the level and skill of their performance.

Typically in *Tormento*, true vocation is eclipsed by meaningless pomp and circumstance, just as genuine feeling is clouded by affectation and literature seems to overtake life. The net result is a basic instability at the novel's core: not simply a political instability, although in fact the novel is set in 1867 and early 1868, only months before the outbreak of the September Revolution, but an ontological instability as well. Names and identities fluctuate or collapse outright; a character's seeming class affiliation or show of moral rectitude is often contradicted from one moment to the next. Thus the Rosalía Bringas who attends public functions, elegantly attired in a manner that befits a woman who claims to be on personal terms with Isabel II, must be reconciled with that other Rosalía who, bedecked in an old bathrobe as she tends to household chores, might have been taken for "a landlady of the most humble means" (4: 1523). The relationship between Rosalía and Amparo Sánchez Emperador likewise involves the muddling of class distinctions and the overlap of several levels of social interaction, for Rosalía is at once a despotic employer, a friend, and a distant relative of the young woman. The narrator notes this difficulty in determining the rank occupied in the Bringas household by "Amparo, la Amparo, Amparito, señorita Amparo, since she was called by all these four names" (4: 1480), and stresses that a similar ambivalence governs her current relationship with Polo, in which she appears by turns subservient or independent. Eating at Polo's table, Amparo, known to her former lover by the sensationalistic name Tormento, "was now a dinner companion, now a servant" (4: 1513).

One of the more outspoken condemnations of this confusion of identities, appearances, and values issues from Amparo's future husband. Agustín Caballero, who earned his fortune in the New World before returning to his native Spain, describes his experience of life in Texas as a disgusting mix of linguistic and racial identities and sexual customs: "And what a confusion of interests, what moral and social disorder! Americans, French, Indians, Mexicans, men and women of all castes, all mixed up together . . . There, concubinage, polygamy, and polandry were the order of the day" (4: 1494). His return home is motivated by a desperate search for legal order and inviolable standards of behavior; the American experience represents for him only "fraudes de género y sentimiento" 'fraudulent trade and bogus sentiment.'

In its complexity of semantic associations, the phrase "fraudes de género" is wholly emblematic of this novel of counterfeit emotions and multiple, substitute identities. Since *género* signifies "merchandise," "goods," no doubt Caballero is remembering the shady transactions and dishonest business practices he encountered during his years on the Mexican-American frontier. Alternately, "fraudes de género" may be a play on the meaning of *género* as "genus," "species." Having just disparaged the frequency with which the locals used to engage in promiscuous relations that cut across racial lines, Caballero may also have in mind these ambiguous and extralegal sexual couplings of the human animal, of which he wants no part. Then, too, only a few sentences later, he makes an explicit connection between *género* "property" and the female sex, reckoning that it will be easier to find a suitable wife in Madrid because "where such merchandise abounds (pardon my commercial language), it's easy to find the genuine article." In this context, it is not inconceivable that "fraudes de género" may refer to acts of deception perpetrated in word or deed by women upon men in general. As such, it would represent one of the more ostentatious examples of ironic foreshadowing in the novel, for even in the traditional Spain that he reveres as a bastion of law, Agustín falls victim to Amparo's misrepresentation of herself as a poor but honorable woman, an image that is no less fraudulent for its having been fostered without malicious intent.[2]

In addition to this cluster of potential meanings bound up in Caballero's words, the reader is certainly aware that *género* also signifies "genre," "literary kind," and, indeed, there is a further sort of trickery or manipulation that governs the novel's composition. *Tormento* is built up out of thematic elements and formal markers belonging to several different genres—the traditional realist novel, nineteenth-century popular fiction (which most often takes the form of the serial novel and is therefore a subset of the novel proper), and the drama—all of whose seams are clearly visible in the completed text. The equivocal nature of *Tormento*'s generic identity thus not only reenacts at the level of the novel's structure (where it is applauded) the thematic syntagm of illicit fusion and combination (where it is censured). It also immediately raises questions regarding the nature of the reading process: how it is activated by the conventions governing realist fiction or thwarted when such conventions are parodied or supplanted altogether by those belonging to nonnovelistic genres. It is at this juncture that the interdependent concepts of frame and intertextuality, now joined by that of genre, once again can be seen as paramount in exploring the anatomy of realist representation as handled by Galdós in his novels.[3]

The preceding chapter examined the status of intertextuality in *Torquemada en la hoguera* as a special kind of framing that is context-bound and ideologically motivated. The use of intertextual framing in this brief novel—the modification or "translation" of one text into another—foregrounds the signifying quality of the representation.[4] It makes readers aware of both the author's contentious dialogue with the past in his reformulation of the precursor text and of the interpretive procedures they themselves must employ in sifting through these various layers and accretions of meaning. Such practices cannot help but weaken the illusionism that mimesis seeks to promote, for the fixation upon the intertext in *Torquemada*, even down to its graphic layout on the page, destroys the notions of perceptual continuity and textual autonomy propounded by realist representation. Intertextuality lodges itself between language and the world by insisting that one cannot proceed directly to an actual historical referent but, instead, must first excavate layer upon layer of text.

It is important to remember, however, that the intertext that inhabits José Bailón's pamphlets in *Torquemada* can be specifically traced to the writings of a single author. Galdós's recourse to the *Paroles d'un croyant*, while also introducing other discourses whose borders are broader and more diffuse (romanticism, utopian socialism, political rhetoric, religion and the Scriptures), still offers a clear case of citation, of intertextual relations *in praesentia*. Equally as common are examples of allusion, that is, of intertextual relations in absentia, in which no single precursor text is quoted directly. Instead, the intertextual process must be inferred from the exploitation of general thematic coincidences or the recurrence of stylistic and organizational features that may in fact characterize an entire class of texts. This set of norms and features, along with the code governing their usage—what we call genre—comprises a separate text which may itself be subjected to the intertextual mechanisms of assimilation and contestation of form and meaning: "A genre is a text, . . . a text of texts, and as such possesses a discursive existence apart from that of the works it brings together . . . The formal and thematic constraints which define it, and which are inscribed in critical discourse, constitute a text in their own right."[5]

That the intertext in *Tormento* is constituted by several genres in competition with the traditional realist novel obliges readers to reconsider the entire matter of generic criticism, which, with some recent exceptions of note, has been relegated to the margins of literary studies ever since the overthrow of eighteenth-century neoclassical poetics. Nineteenth-century romanticism rejected the prescriptive rules of genre as restrictive of individual genius, and sought instead the synthesis of the variously demarcated genres into "the literary absolute."[6] Croce's *Estetica* (1902) intensified this dismissal of genre; in his view, a theory of literary kinds, each distinguished by fixed traits and unchanging laws, was incompatible with the realm of the aesthetic, in which works of art are distinguished by their creative singularity rather than by their similitude to others. Genre theory fares little better in certain poststructuralist circles, albeit for reasons having nothing to do with the earlier defense of authorial genius. To the contrary, if the text is not a defined object but rather a production of plural meanings, a network of infinite relations, and an open field of signifiers, it can scarcely be contained or explicated by the tidily arranged classes of generic taxonomy: "The Text does not come to a stop with (good) literature; it cannot be apprehended as part of a hierarchy or even a simple division of genres. What constitutes the Text is, on the contrary (or precisely), its subversive force with regard to old classifications."[7]

Nonetheless, critics ranging across a wide spectrum of reading positions have concluded that while readers and writers may well chafe at the normative strictures that genre categories imply, and, indeed, often propose to violate or supersede them, it is well nigh impossible to speak about literary works without having recourse to the sort of classificatory system of experience that genre represents. Pace Hernadi, it is not at all clear that literature and its readers can ever get "beyond genre."[8] We are reminded over and again that there is no frameless activity in human life, that only through framing, as a means of hierarchical organization, is meaning created. This is precisely the role of genre: it is "a set of recognized 'frames' or 'fixes' upon the world," one of a series of competence models or schemata that are inevitably applied, either historically or theoretically, when studying the interrelatedness of structure and content, author and audience, literary text and cultural context.[9] Yet it is also acknowledged that genre frames, in mediating between what in a text is individual (markers of difference and novelty) and what it shares in common with other texts of a similarly designated class (markers of repetition and recognition), are necessarily constructed and then imposed upon groups of literary works, rather than being found naturally occurring within them. Genres, as Adena Rosmarin asserts, "are designed to serve the explanatory purpose of critical thought, not the other way around."[10] This definition of genre as avowedly rhetorical, pragmatic, and institutionalized, in no way detracts from its usefulness as an interpretive tool. Genres do not inevitably constrict; rather, they expand the opportunities for literary talk and are, indeed, the very conditions of possibility of such talk. In their capacity as frames, they may deservedly be called, in Genette's words, "blank windows," but as he notes, "the blank window may, under the circumstances, shed true light."[11]

In discussing the instances of generic hybridism in *Tormento*, I will be focusing for the most part on the encroachment upon the novelistic host text by attributes drawn from the generic repertoire of drama.[12] In this, I part company with those who have analyzed *Tormento* solely in terms of the intertext provided by the serial novel, a subgenre that stands today, as it did in the Spain of Galdós and his "Observaciones sobre la novela contemporánea en España" (1870), in an antagonistic relationship to the realist novel. This is not to deny the importance or validity of such an approach. It is immediately evident that both serial pulp fiction and the drama make their presence felt in *Tormento* through themes and formal devices. Both these literary institutions are woven into the fabric of the characters' daily activities, receiving their share of praise and blame. While the Bringas family attends the theater, Agustín forswears the purchase of season tickets as "immorality, the negation of the home" (4: 1541). Similarly, José Ido writes pulp fiction, which is subsequently read and commented upon, with varying degrees of admiration or scorn, by Ido's friend Felipe Centeno, by Amparo, her sister Refugio, and Rosalía and Francisco Bringas as well. As Frank Durand has noted, the novel within the novel that Ido is writing "introduces the plot, parallels the main action, enhances suspense, and forms an integral part of the structure through its part in both maintenance and revelation of the secret."[13]

One would have to add to this the role of the confrontation of two opposing versions of the Amparo-Polo-Caballero triangle—one viewed through the lens of realism, the other bathed in maudlin sentimentality—in demolishing by means of parody the time-honored conventions and topics of popular fiction: poverty, orphanhood, charity and the Church, love, honor, marriage, chastity, and happiness—in other words, the entire moral code sustaining the serial novel, along with its clichéd use of time and space.[14] Moreover, because the *folletín* is often directed at a female reading public, the study of its uneasy incorporation into *Tormento* also lends itself to scrutiny of the status of women, culture, and politics in late Isabeline and post-revolutionary Spain.[15] And, in portraying the ironic results that ensue when the activities of reading and writing become so obsessive as to break open the frame of the universe of literary discourse, thereby allowing it to invade real life, *Tormento* uses the parody of serialized fiction to evoke still another intertextual dialogue with corresponding parables of literary excess in Cervantes.

In truth, a discussion of the intertextual linkages between realist novel and drama in *Tormento* does not automatically exclude the serial novel from its purview, insofar as the latter shares many attributes with the theatrical genre of the melodrama, another important form of popular entertainment in the nineteenth century. The motifs, values, and devices of the feuilleton that are ironized or inverted in *Tormento* can surely be found in the melodramatic aesthetic that flourished during the Romantic period and later in the plays of Echegaray, Sellés, and Cano: the reliance upon convoluted plots and last-minute reverses of fate; the electrification of the text by intense emotionalism, suspense, and fast-moving peripety; the deployment of stereotyped characters based on the confrontation of moral opposites, symbolizing the persecution of virtue by vice. Using a rhetoric of gesture, sign, and what Leo Levy calls "emotional gigantism" and Peter Brooks an "aesthetics of astonishment," melodrama in both its theatrical and narrative incarnations provides a means of organizing moral experience; it offers the assurance that evil will ultimately be defeated by good.[16] Both these critics confirm that, for all its hyperbole, melodrama fulfills an important function in dramatizing affective responses to pressing ethical dilemmas. In the wake of the French Revolution, with its destruction of tragedy and replacement of the transcendental by the secular, melodrama pretends to uncover a "moral occult" still functioning at the center of human life, even if only on personal terms.[17] Melodrama's revelation of this moral core and the rot that may afflict it finds its way into many of the novels of Balzac, Henry James, and the Galdós of the *Novelas de primera época*. By contrast, in the later *Novelas españolas contemporáneas* such a clear-cut conception of life's moral dimension will appear infrequently, and then only in parodic guise, as in José Ido's overblown romances. If melodramas and serial fiction pretend to tell all and judge all, the mature realist novel of Galdós as represented by *Tormento* reinstates ambiguity as its governing principle.

Mary Ann Caws suggests that "in some measure the art of framing is itself a will to the mixing of genres," although she notes that the more usual procedure is to inset a play into a play, a painting into a painting, and so forth: "Narrators and narratees, explicit and implied, present or putative, abound, but the kind of reading competence necessary is of one kind only."[18] *Tormento* demands that its readers be unusually versatile in their manipulation of competence models, for it introduces a novel within a drama within a novel. Bits and pieces of José Ido's absurd *folletín* are presented in theatrical scenes (especially chapter 1), which are then subsumed by the novel as a whole. Exploring the intertextual dimension to the relationship between readers and spectators, novel and drama (or melodrama), bares the many ways in which framing contributes in *Tormento* to the definition of the realist aesthetic and its deficiencies of signification.

The theater is founded upon a very special instance of framing, in which lines are drawn between stage and audience, written text and live enactment, performance make-believe and reality. The crossing of these boundaries inevitably engenders a series of ontological paradoxes. Footlights, curtains, and the walls of the stage sets are merely the physical reminders of the pact that actors and theatergoers have established: to accept that, for the duration of the performance, what is taking place on stage is real. When the curtains and lights go down, when the audience laughs at an actor's missteps, when applause breaks out in mid-act for the performers (not the characters they are portraying), the frame is abrogated: "Whatever had been portrayed onstage is now seen as not the real thing at all but only a representation, one made benignly to provide vicarious involvement for the onlooker."[19] Even when dramatic illusionism is not imperiled in this manner, the typical exchanges of the social world that are reproduced within a play appear as if within quotation marks, reinscribed within the theatrical context. When these instances of theatrical framing are inserted within *Tormento*, the novel's own status as signifier, as secondhand framing of the real, is foregrounded as well.

By its annexing of dramatic structure and techniques to the matrix of the novel, *Tormento* internalizes the interrelated concepts of theater and theatricality. The result of this generic inclusionism is not simply a program for the expansion of realist fiction beyond its limited confines, but also a proposal for the renovation of Spanish bourgeois theater, inasmuch as the failed performances of Polo, Caballero, and Tormento are in many ways equivalent to the failures of dramaturgy and stagecraft in late nineteenth-century Spain. The abuse of rhetoric, the falsified dramatic situations, the impoverished language, and superficial social concerns that exemplify the interaction and confrontation of the characters in *Tormento* are the same defects that weaken the plays being produced contemporaneously on the stages of the Príncipe, the Español, and the Comedia. As each of the two frames, theatrical performance and generic purity, is dissolved, social reality (the text's outside) and literary illusion (the text's inside) bleed together.

To understand more fully what is at stake in Galdós's merger of genres, it may prove useful to profile briefly his theoretical writings and professional experience with respect to the Spanish stage. What immediately becomes evident is that the prolific character of Galdós's novelistic enterprise has tended to eclipse his other literary activities, including the interest he displayed in the theater throughout his career. For many years, there was scant recognition of Galdós's predisposition to the use of dramatic form. What little commentary existed on the subject was confined to biographical notes and summary descriptions of his writings for the theater. These latter often emphasized that whatever limited success he may have achieved in his day as a dramatist was more a result of his unleashing of the explosive energies that fueled contemporary ideological polemics than of any intrinsically superior construction of the works themselves. The case of critical and public reaction to the debut of his *Electra* (1901) was not infrequently exhibited as evidence of the appeal made by his dramaturgy to such extra-aesthetic concerns.[20]

Many manuals of Spanish literary history imply that although the young author declared early and enthusiastically his inclination toward the theatrical vocation (his juvenilia in fact include various stage writings), his twenty-four plays, appearing as they did in print between 1892 and 1918, constitute somewhat of a postscript to his lifelong cultivation of the novel. Cleaving to a variant of the *post hoc ergo propter hoc* fallacy, critics have sometimes argued that the very order in which his works were published suggests that the dramatic arts, capturing Galdós's attention only belatedly in his career, were dimmed stars of secondary magnitude in the firmament of Galdós's literary creativity. This argument was based on an apparently irrefutable chronology; the author's publication of various traditionally structured novels was later followed by a series of innovative novelistic texts in dialogic format, beginning with *Realidad*, which in turn was succeeded by that group of works properly titled "dramas" or "plays."

By virtue of this diachronic viewing of Galdós's literary production in terms of a simple, linear progression, it became a critical commonplace to state that his plays lacked independent motivation. Never conceived as works in their own right, they were said to be primarily the lackluster result of quantitative transformations performed on his novels. This process was accomplished by a quadripartite strategy: the elimination of certain incidental scenes, the abbreviation of the cast of characters, the pruning away of subthemes, and the compression of time and space. As evidence, many nineteenth-century critics pointed out that Galdós himself had averred in his prologue to *El abuelo* (1897) that the theater signified above all "the condensation and coupling of everything that constitutes actions and characters in the modern novel" (6: 11).

In this manner, those who criticized Galdós's dramatic efforts suggested that although he may very well have intuited the requisite synthetic nature of theatrical works, what he finally brought to the stage were simply transpositions of his novels into abridged, oral form: "Pérez Galdós, a novelist above all else, has wanted to write for the theater and until today has done nothing but put on stage, more or less transformed, *novelistic* ideas, outlines of novels."[21] Critics characterized his plays as hybrid works that sacrificed the most notable features of his novels—the lush use of descriptive detail and the profound psychological exploration of individuals at their most introspective—while contributing to the confusion of two unmistakably distinct literary genres. For these critics, the resounding failure of the plays *Los condenados* (1894), *Voluntad* (1895), and *La fiera* (1896) was an indication that Galdós had erred in choosing to pursue the more elusive fame of playwright rather than continuing to devote all his energies to the novel. In this endeavor, of course, Galdós was not alone. Valera, Pardo Bazán, and Alas were all involved at some point in their careers with dramaturgy. In fact, across nineteenth-century Europe, novelists including Balzac, Flaubert, Zola, the Goncourt brothers, Eugène Sue, George Sand, and Henry James were writing plays or staging versions of their novels.[22]

The persistent image of Galdós as an unsuccessful dramatist, one who falters precisely because he is unable to rid himself of his habits of novelistic construction, is somewhat misleading. In the first place, Galdós himself fails to understand why his work as a novelist should keep him from entering the world of the theater and public performance. "Don't speak to us of incompatibility between the art of constructing dramas or plays and other, more or less similar forms," he insists in the prologue to *Los condenados*. "It is very well to state that a certain author was more successful in the novel, or in poetry, or in the didactic genre than in the theater. But to want to erect barriers to human endeavor, to go so far as to affirm that the gifts of the novelist or the poet hamper knowledge of the complicated dramatic framework, seems to me unspeakably foolish" (6: 706). The author neither admits nor agrees that cultivation of the one genre necessarily and by definition excludes the felicitous cultivation of the other. The use of certain novelistic techniques in the elaboration of a dramatic work is always potentially admissible; inversely, there is no objection in principle to the application of elements of theatrical construction to the novel.

On the contrary, the admixture of genres that characterizes much of Galdós's literary production can only be understood as an effect deliberately sought by the writer. Thus, he declares in the introduction to *Casandra*, subtitled a "Novel in five acts" (1905): "The times demand that the theater not completely disavow the analytical process, and that the novel be less sluggish in its developments and be carried away by the active concision with which the art of the stage presents human deeds" (6: 116). Accordingly, references abound to what Galdós called "subgenres" or "products of generic crossing." *Realidad* (1889) is a novel presented entirely in dialogue and divided not into chapters but rather into acts; along with *El abuelo* (1897) and *Casandra* (1905) Galdós labels it an "intensive Novel or extensive Drama" (6: 116). *La razón de la sinrazón* (1915) is a "completely unbelievable theatrical fable," while the first version of *La loca de la casa* (1892), although traditionally included in the series of *Novelas españolas contemporáneas*, actually bears the subtitle of "play in four acts."

And just as there are novels that by virtue of their subject matter easily lend themselves to dramatization—among them, several by Galdós himself[23]—so one can cite the case of dramas that for reasons of their great length, complicated exposition, or frequent change of scene become difficult or impossible to stage. Some of Shakespeare's plays resemble "spoken novels"; the *Celestina* might best be categorized as a kind of "ideal theater" meant to be read but not performed (6: 11). Undoubtedly, Galdós considered the maintenance of the formal integrity of the genres a secondary concern, especially if, by fusing them, he could help put a halt to the ever more conspicuous deterioration of the Spanish theater which he denounced in essays such as "Decadencia" in the collection *Nuestro teatro*.[24] The regeneration of national theater was a topic that evoked passionate partisanship on Galdós's part, and it was his firm belief that the possibility for such regeneration lay in a fertilization of the drama by the novel. The reasons for this are clear. The theater is intended to reflect back to the public an essentially recognizable image of itself and its historical and moral crises, and of all the literary genres, it is the novel that in the nineteenth century has proven to be "the most attuned to the status and problems of bourgeois society."[25]

At the same time that Galdós was explicitly endorsing a rapprochement of drama and novel in a campaign to shore up the credibility of the former, he was also engaged in a complementary attempt to broaden the narrative possibilities of the latter, once again by incorporating features from an alien genre. Manuel Alvar, in an astutely argued essay, is one of the first critics to have suggested that the process and terms of the contagion ought to be reversed: "The theater is the technique Galdós transplants into his novels, not the other way around. His novels are viewed with the fixed and inevitable scheme of the theater: exposition, climax, denouement . . . and dialogue."[26] Galdós's *Tormento* is an especially apt novel with which to test Alvar's speculations regarding the confluence of novel and drama. While one can point to a proliferation of studies on the theatricality inherent in such early melodramas as *Doña Perfecta* or on the dramatic disposition of form in the dialogue-novels, there are many fewer critical explorations of the theatrical content and construction of the *Novelas contemporáneas*, perhaps because these have been classified as the novels of Galdós that most clearly exhibit a realist aesthetic, a naturalist vocabulary, and an unambiguous generic status.[27]

Tormento presents the story of the indecisive Amparo Sánchez Emperador, unable to choose between her ardent wish, on the one hand, to find true love and social legitimization by marrying the wealthy *indiano* Agustín Caballero, and the moral obligation she feels, on the other, to confess the truth of her tainted past. As in many of Galdós's narratives, *Tormento* demonstrates the "living and permanent lesson of the superiority of Nature" over "the artificial labyrinth of societies," a lesson equally prominent in *Lo prohibido* and *Fortunata y Jacinta*.

One of the most notable elements of that artificial social labyrinth, as we have seen, is the serial novel, fanatically cultivated by José Ido and parodically incorporated into *Tormento* so as to establish an intertextual dialogue between the conflicting codes of imagination and reality, originality and plagiarism, moral order and disorder.[28] But if the *folletín* represents a sort of countertext, a literary venue whose insertion provokes a collision and questioning of its values (honor, chastity, sentiment) and techniques of novelistic presentation (formulaic characters, extreme conceptions of good and evil, suspense, unequivocal narrative closure), the interweaving of drama and novel creates an oppositional relationship, this time not between discrete variants of the same novel form but rather between two disparate literary modes characterized by their differing emphasis on mimetic values. *Tormento*'s structure and its central thematic concerns thus involve a subtle meditation in the novel upon the closely coupled concepts of theater and theatricality.

In view of its unusual construction, mixing dialogue with narration, leisurely description with telegraphically relayed stage directions, gestures with words, and summary with scene, *Tormento* is located at the crossroads of the novel and the play. On the one hand, it displays the features of a work which, given its length, is intended for private and solitary reading, a work, furthermore, in which a narrator is always present and whose task it is to re-create an entire world on the basis of protracted interludes of description and the expansive analysis of human conduct. On the other hand, it also exhibits many of the features that characterize a work intended for the stage and its collective audience: the absence of a narrator; the direct presentation of characters through their speech; the recourse to simultaneous, multiple perspectives; the compression of time, space, and cast of characters. Ironically, Galdós relies upon the power of dramatic form to infuse his novel with the effect of an augmented realism that was precisely the aim of nineteenth-century fiction. Realism seeks above all to create the impression of the text's autonomy, independent of a creator who inhabits some world external to the boundaries of fiction. The search for this correspondence between exterior world and literary word is what inclines realist novelists toward the technique of narrative objectivity and makes the achievement of verisimilitude the touchstone of their success. In this regard, the use of techniques adapted or borrowed from the drama are in large measure responsible for the fact that at certain moments in *Tormento* "we see and hear, without external mediation, the event and its actors, and more easily forget the hidden artist who offers us a clever imitation of nature" (6: 11). Angel Tarrío reformulates Galdós's agenda in semiotic terms, noting that what the author sensed was the demand placed on realist discourse to achieve the "maximal elimination of authorial omniscience" and the resulting tendency of realism to "take refuge in the theater."[29]

At the same time, *Tormento* makes ample use of the concept of theatricality, defined by Elizabeth Burns as "the double relationship between the theatre and social life."[30] Theatricality presupposes the contrived or fabricated nature of human conduct, whether of actors or real-life individuals, which is best explored through the analysis of conventions. In social situations, as in actual stage settings, behavior is scripted according to norms that are necessarily intelligible to all participants; otherwise, communication could not take place. This notion of role-playing, as important as it is to the actors' learning of their parts and their assumption of different characters or personalities, is no less vital to the domain of everyday life. Sociologists who have studied the function of role-playing in the socialization process which organizes human behavior emphasize that it leads to the creation of a consciousness of the coexistence in individuals of a genuine and a performed self. The conventions governing everyday behavior are generally naturalized to the point that they are accepted as informal and spontaneous, only becoming visible on ceremonial or ritualistic occasions (weddings, funerals, religious services, lectures, and so forth). Likewise, the agreement between audience and actors is such that a frame is placed around the theatrical event, leading to "a suspension of belief in the reality of the world and events external to the occasion so framed" (*Theatricality* 19). Only when frame-breaks occur do people become aware that the supposedly real action taking place on stage is only an illusion, or that behavior in real life is sometimes inappropriately "theatrical," composed. As Goffman notes, "when we say pejoratively of a person that he has given a 'real performance,' we mean that he has taken more than usual care and employed more than usual design and continuity in the presentation of what is ostensibly not a performance at all" (*Frame Analysis* 127).

This quality of theatricality, which in turn indicates the significance of the theater as a public institution and frame of social knowledge with its own history and conventions, is omnipresent in *Tormento*. Virtually all the characters are well acquainted with the theater as a historical and cultural phenomenon. The arrival of theater tickets in the first chapter for Amparo and her sister sets the novel's plot in motion. Two entire chapters (6 and 8) are devoted to describing Rosalía and Francisco Bringas's preparations for an outing to the famous Teatro del Príncipe. The account of what those attending the play that evening think, do, and say offers a treatise on the stratification of nineteenth-century society as observed in the theatergoing public on a microcosmic scale. Yet the characters in *Tormento* do not simply watch the play; they cross over the imaginary frontier separating audience from stage and live their lives as theater. In an ironic manipulation of the venerable topic of the "gran teatro del mundo" 'the theater of the world,' the protagonists in this novel inhabit a society in which life consists of a vast sign system built upon masks and false appearances.[31]

Many are the characters in *Tormento* who seem to live their lives in conformity with a dramatic script, from Rosalía Bringas, a conscientious defender of bourgeois decorum, to the three main characters of the novel. Nonetheless, while Rosalía is a master at the art of the social comedy, those caught up in the central triangle are unable to comply with the sanctions of custom or law. Trapped in the *theatrum mundi*, unable to integrate their many selves, they indulge in melodramatic behavior only to criticize their histrionics during moments of dawning self-awareness. Such self-conscious dramatizations are metafictional in nature; they signal frame-breaks that unseat the ontological certainty that realism feigns to communicate. Pedro Polo, for instance, is the man of nature ("savage," "beast," "brute," "monster," "dragon") who comes ill prepared to undertake his religious role. As a priest without a vocation, characterized by passionate rages incompatible with the clerical state, he soon loses his school, his chaplainship, and his ecclesiastical licenses. Following his sacrilegious liaison with Amparo, he is effectively divorced from the church and abandoned by his sister Marcelina. The explanation for this moral degeneration can be found in his obvious lack of temperamental adaptation to the role imposed upon him by his choice of profession, a choice that had been dictated by monetary concerns. Polo senses the need to wipe away the great error he has committed: "to have placed myself where I wasn't called and to have deceived Society and God, donning a mask to frighten people" (4: 1515). In his daydreams, he imagines himself a hardened imperial warrior or a rustic lord and paterfamilias, insinuations of alternative roles in life he might have essayed with greater success. These flights of fancy pass before his eyes much like the changes in scenery that occur onstage, so that "letting himself be carried away, he discovered his fantasy lay elsewhere. It was a change that seemed like something out of the theater" (57).

For don Pedro, the priesthood signifies an obligation to carry out "the theatrical mimicry of the pulpit" and pronounce "swollen and empty sermons" (4: 1511).[32] In his own words, he has been a "hypocritical, religious actor" who only came to believe in God after tearing away his "careta," his mask (4: 1552). When Amparo visits him during his illness, she notices the outward physical signs of his emotional deterioration, the discontinuity between his authentic and feigned selves. What impresses her is the contrast between "his rough, yellowish face, the color of bile, the color of tragedy, and his comedic laughter and the childish joy that filled him" (4: 1513). Alternating between tragedy and farce, Polo no longer belongs to himself but rather to the clerical role he can never hope to perform adequately. Consequently, his personal redemption can only be achieved by an exercise of will: the removal of his clerical costume and his departure for a foreign post, far away from the temptation ("tormento") that Amparo represents. At bottom of Father Nones's campaign for Polo's spiritual regeneration lies his intuition that the former chaplain and pedagogue "was a man who could no longer continue the falsification of his being and was dashing headlong toward . . . carrying out a revolution of the self, and overthrowing and destroying everything artificial and inauthentic in himself" (4:1511).

Eamonn Rodgers makes the point that Nones's plan is part of an appearance-reality dichotomy, the conceit of equivocation around which the novel is structured. Emigrating to the Philippines and continuing there in the priesthood scarcely seems a measure designed to promote Polo's spiritual transformation; on the contrary, it would assuredly expose him to new temptations. Rodgers indicates that "for Nones, the 'salvation' of Polo does not mean ensuring that he should be happy and fulfill whatever potentialities he possesses, but that he should be tidied away into a predetermined compartment of life. He is concerned, in fact, with maintaining an appearance of regularity even at the sacrifice of the inner worth of the person." [33] The kindly Nones condemns Polo to continue the performance; the actor may not withdraw from the stage because the public will not permit it. Galdós's priest emerges from a society whose order is predicated upon imposture and whose theater reproduces, as in a mirror image, this same falsification of gesture and word. Galdós, in his essay "Decadencia," explains this relationship between theater, theatricality, and society as satirized in *Tormento*: "The bourgeois, home-centered public that has dominated the last generation has had no small part in the decadence of the theater. It is responsible for the predominance of that stage morality that informs contemporary works, a morality destined exclusively to adorn dramatic literature. It is a morality that is entirely artificial and circumstantial, that of a society that lives upon fictions and conventionalisms." [34]

Agustín Caballero, the millionaire weaned on the anarchy of the New World, is yet another victim of theater transformed into life. Hoping to turn his back on the primitiveness and chaos that characterized his thirty years in America, he determines to live an exemplary existence founded upon the values of legality, religious orthodoxy, and moral decency. His is the modest dream of every middle-class Spaniard of the final decades of the nineteenth century: a peaceful home, a discreet wife, a comfortable income. By his own choice, Caballero sets out to comply with what the narrator ironically calls "the austere role of an irreproachably law-abiding person, a perfect, spotless, and smooth-running wheel in the triple mechanism of State, Religion, and Family" (4: 1536). Yet lacking the necessary refinement of speech and demeanor, he fails utterly in his dealings with Amparo. What few words he manages to stammer in her presence, in imitation of the gallantries spoken by the leading man in a play to his lady (or by an orator before parliament, in the theater of political life), had been previously rehearsed. At the solemn moment of the declaration of his love, he forgets his lines altogether. Recognition of his failure brings further embarrassment: "His unconventionality was not so great that he could view with indifference the ridicule that befell him on occasion" (4: 1484).

The discovery of Amparo's dishonor smashes his dreams of decorous living, and over the course of four days he gives vent to his disillusionment in a rambling monologue that is transcribed fragmentarily in chapters 37–39. The narrator, in a moment of self-conscious irony, claims that "if such a speech were heard, the public would (as they say) be throwing stones," given the inadequate manner in which Caballero delivers his speech. Only at the end of the novel does he acknowledge his ignorance of the social fictions necessary for his survival. Following one of the few courses of action remaining to him, he sheds "this falsified and counterfeit self" and leaves for France with Amparo, whom he takes for his mistress but for not his wife, exhorting the coming revolution to sweep away the artificial world of gestures and poses to which he has never managed to assimilate.

Amparo, the third member of the triangle of amorous melodrama, is an unskilled actress, no better equipped than Caballero or Polo to carry off her double role. The equivocal nature of her identity is symbolized by the alternation of her names; she is both Amparo, the faithful and demure bride-to-be, and Tormento, the former lover of a priest. Unlike the two male protagonists, however, she stays within character less out of conscious choice than out of simple indecisiveness. She can neither make up her mind to confess to the one, nor end all dealings with the other. In her attempts to persuade the brutish Polo to leave Spain, she reveals her histrionic talents to narrator and reader. At the moment of her second interview with him, she persuades herself: "If you don't get flustered, you'll vanquish the monster, because you're the only being on earth who has the power to do so. But you need to study your role" (4: 1550). In her apprenticeship to the conventions of social theater, she makes use of a growing "actress's knowledge" in order to placate Polo's jealousy. She tells him comforting lies "with her mouth and her head, energetically, like children do during their first rehearsals in the human farce" (4: 1552).

Unfortunately, an accumulation of incriminating evidence—the letters in Marcelina's possession, the slander of her character that Rosalía, Refugio, and Ido might unleash at any moment—makes her continued representation of the chaste Amparo an impossibility. Seeing her hopes of love and marriage evaporate, Amparo plans to take her own life, thereby putting an end to an existence of "scenes and sketches." Nonetheless, she has become so inured to the mask of her fictional self that the sincerity of her actions is again overwhelmed by theatricality: "So then, is her death perchance a play?" (4: 1571). In fact, her death is a moment of pure farce, for Felipe Centeno has switched the poison she plans to take with a sleeping draught. Instead of suffering a spectacular death that could not have failed to move Agustín, she awakens and flees to France to live with him as his lover, in an arrangement that will allow both of them a certain measure of happiness but neither legal nor social sanctification of their union.

When the characters in this triangle allow life to be upstaged by a series of prescribed conventions, they seal their dismal fate. Contradicting one's natural instincts, breeding, and circumstances, *Tormento* suggests, is akin to donning a costume and indulging in bad play-acting; it signifies the cheapening of life by false sentiment, petulance, and empty rhetoric. In the "theater of the world" of the medieval and Renaissance periods, it was God who judged the efficacy with which the actors had portrayed their respective roles. In the middle-class theater of actions of the nineteenth century, this theological judgment is replaced by the choral voice of society, and the eye of the divine spectator is for its part exchanged for the critical perspective of the novel's implied author. The framing of social life as it is reproduced in the theater, authenticated and naturalized by rhetorical conventions, is thus turned inside out in *Tormento*, where self-dramatizations, monologues, soliloquies, and asides are used in combination to heighten the fictive nature of ostensibly natural, everyday behavior. At the same time, this very behavior may well have been reinforced by the Spanish theater of the day, for "drama in performance is both formed by and helps to re-form and so conserve or change the values and norms of the society which supports it as against the alternative realities which lie outside the currency of any particular social reality" (*Theatricality* 4). The end result is a novel whose structure is derived from that of the theater and whose melodramatic tone imitates those same exaggerations and defects in the construction and production of plays that depressed the quality of the Spanish stage from 1870 to 1900.

In discussing the key role of the actors in authenticating the drama taking place upon the stage, Burns observes what is, paradoxically, the deceptive nature of their task:

> In both dimensions, performance and interpretation, the actor, as man or woman *in propria persona*, is first and foremost an interloper. He intervenes between the playwright and the audience so as to make the fictive world, *signified* by the first, a set of *signifiers* for the social reality of the latter. He acts—enacts—the rhetoric of the text by working upon 'the common stock of attitudes, of samples and convention, of truisms, and commonplaces' in the enthymemic system mentioned earlier. In a quite real sense, he is working a confidence trick, but one in which deceit is neutralised—'earthed'—by the visibly theatrical frame in which it is worked. (*Theatricality* 146)

In effect, Burns is describing the *fraude de género* upon which successful theatrical performances are based. Galdós moves one step beyond this. Although he establishes in *Tormento* the fraudulent nature—the theatricality—of the norms of social conduct of the late Isabeline period, he simultaneously appropriates techniques of the drama in composing his novel. *Tormento*'s structure resultingly calls attention to its very heterogeneity.

The instances of theatrical conception of the novel's action and setting are numerous indeed. Chapters are formulated as scenes in an act of a play; they begin and end with the ringing of the doorbell and the entrance of new characters (chapters 3 and 9), flourishes of dialogue and the departure or (pseudo)death of characters (5, 6, 34), or the arrival of the mailman bearing a letter whose contents will change the course of the story (24, 27). Dramatic lighting effects underscore the symbolic significance of the appearance of various characters at critical junctures in the action. Returning home and turning up the dining room lamp, Rosalía is surprised to find Agustín who, unbeknownst to her, has just asked Amparo for her hand in marriage: "One always meets you emerging from the darkness, like a weasel" (4: 1525). Backlighting frames the unexpected appearance of Padre Nones during the colloquy between Amparo and Polo in his dim, cramped flat, surrounding him with a nimbus of moral respectability: "Suddenly there appeared in the doorway a very tall, venerable figure, sheathed in black, with white hair and a luminous gaze" (4: 1561). In fact, entire scenes are contrived with a mind to their quality as spectacle. In chapter 10 Bringas bids good evening to Amparo, unable to give her the small sum of cash he normally does to supplement her meager income: "Don Francisco was adjusting his glasses with his right hand, and with the left held open the curtain to his study door. Through the small aperture that was formed, Amparo, as she was leaving, saw señor Caballero seated in an armchair and more attentive to the scene just described than to the newspaper he held in his hand" (4: 1496). Caballero, who has more than just a passing interest in the welfare of the young woman, watches intently this little drama of penury and subservience being played out before him, visually framed by the curtains at the doorway of Francisco Bringas's office. The businessman returned from America watches Amparo and Bringas, Amparo observes him in turn, and the narrator surveys the entire proceedings from an all-encompassing viewpoint, thus placing himself and the reader in the position of spectators witnessing a small but eminently theatrical moment.

Especially striking in *Tormento* is the use of modes of dramatic writing to effect a generic cross with the novel. The central portion of the narrative (chapters 2–40) is framed at the beginning and the end by two chapters entirely cast in dialogue (chapters 1 and 41). The reader is confronted with what appears to be the text of a play: there is no narrator present, only the dialogue itself, the indications of who by turns is speaking, and the descriptions of the gestures and expressions that the speakers employ. The body of the novel is further punctuated by a series of chapters that contain lengthy fragments of monologue, labeled as such by the narrator (chapters 9, 37, 39), one chapter filled with stage directions (18), and still another mixing traditional narration and direct reporting of dramatic dialogue (chapter 38). The embedding of dialogue throughout the narrative and the predominance of free indirect style similarly work to create scenes of increasingly dramatic character. In relying upon these structures, Galdós is shown experimenting with ways to import the mimetic values of theater into narrative prose, in the belief that only in this manner can realism carry out its charge to display the autonomy of the real. As he writes in the prologue to *El abuelo*: "The author's words, narrating and describing, don't have, in general terms, that much efficacy, nor do they give the impression of spiritual truth in such a direct fashion. They are always a reference, something like History, which recounts events and draws portraits and scenes for us" (6: 11).

Yet *Tormento* is not a play but rather a novel, and the continual shifting from mediated to unmediated forms of narrative presentation heightens rather than veils the reader's awareness of the artistic manipulation of the text as text, rather than reality "speaking itself." The narrator may at times seem to disappear, but standing behind him is another entity, the implied author and master framer, who selects certain scenes and outlines them by means of a textual format that differs noticeably from the rest of the novel.

The use of the scripted dialogue-frame bordering *Tormento* is particularly important in alternately strengthening and undermining the project of realist representation. Positioned at the extreme limits of the narrative, the frame is occupied by characters who are actually marginal to the central enterprise of Polo, Caballero, and Amparo.[35] The initial chapter of *Tormento*, a conversation between José Ido and Felipe Centeno about the serial novel, picks up where a similar conversation left off in the final chapter of *El doctor Centeno*, the novel that immediately precedes it. The final chapter of *Tormento* completes the frame, albeit in a nonsymmetrical fashion, for the identity of the speakers has changed. This time the discussion, about Caballero's conduct and Amparo's misconduct, is between Rosalía and Francisco Bringas, thus suggesting the links between this novel and *La de Bringas*, the next work Galdós publishes. Viewed in this light, the frame chapters provide a sense of continuity among several member texts in a single novelistic universe. Although the train departing for France signals the end of a particular stage in the relationship of Caballero and Amparo, *Tormento* ends on a note of openness. In response to the final conversation in chapter 41, the reader is primed to hear much more about the Bringas household in Galdós's subsequent novel.

At the same time, the dramatic frames of the first and last chapters offer the vision of a reality shattered into numerous conflicting perspectives which, left unreconciled by a suprapersonal narrator, inevitably thwart the possibility of novelistic closure. When Rosalía angrily denounces the "atrocious immorality" of her cousin Agustín's behavior as symptomatic of a contagious social gangrene, the reader must compare this posture with that held by Agustín himself. For the former, the novel's denouement represents an attack upon sacred conventions; for the latter, it is an opportunity to unmask hypocrisy and live a life of greater authenticity. Both these interpretations stand in contrast to José Ido's rewriting of the ending, offered in the brief dramatic scene included in chapter 38. Ido proposes an exaggeratedly sentimental treatment of the story of his friends: Amparo will become a nun, the subject of a novel titled *From the Brothel to the Cloister*; death will perhaps be her "poetic end" (4: 1581). The counterpoint established between the core narration and the dramatized scenes played out between Ido-Centeno and Rosalía-Francisco and the irreconcilable existence of three disparate explanations of the outcome—virtue triumphant (Ido), failed suicide and flight (the narrator), moral indignation (the Bringas family)—leaves the ending unresolved for the reader. Amid this multiplicity of perspectives, the text cannot coalesce. Reality is not monovalent, Galdós appears to postulate; the production of the world by language implies a continuous repositioning of the frame.

Tormento uses the many resources of drama as marks of rupture. Theater is interrupted by novelistic text, while the novel is divided into theatrical scenes. The smooth surfaces of representation are fractured by the contrast of opposing genres and the breaking of the reader's frame of expectation. Rosalie Colie has affirmed that "if the [literary] kinds metaphorize and mythicize their subjects, they are themselves subject to the same process, and can be used as metaphor and myth."[36] In *Tormento*, drama and novel are united, paradoxically, to create a metaphor for disunity and discontinuity, a metaphor which proposes the demythification of the realist frame *as* frame. Galdós himself writes in his discourse to the Real Academia that when the ideas and sentiments of a society are rigidly demarcated in very determinate categories, the result is that artists fall back upon practices, attitudes, and customs that have been mutually agreed upon and which serve as an institutionalized set of rules: "It seems that social characters come to the region of Art already contaminated by a certain affectation or conventionalism." He concludes, metaphorically: "The fact is that when these categories break down, suddenly the masks fall, and faces appear in their unvarnished truth."[37] Together, the complex acts of framing and the yoking together of antithetical genres in *Tormento* effectively tear the mask from the face of realist representation.

5

The

Museum as

Metaframe in

the *Novelas*

contempor-

áneas

*There is no greater calamity than being the friend
of collectors.*—*Galdós*, Fortunata y Jacinta

From "palace of the muses" to "cemetery," the
epithets that describe the role of the museum
in modern society all imply somehow its unique
status as a place apart from the bustle and ba-
nality of everyday life. We have examined how in *Tormento* the curtains,
the proscenium arch, the costumes, and actors' protocols serve to parti-
tion the theater into the opposing spaces of the real and the performative
or representational. That other social institution of the nineteenth century,
the museum, is structured upon similar principles. The museum's walls
act as a framing device dividing outside from inside, noise from silence,
utility from art, mediocrity from masterpiece, the naturally occurring from
the man-made. The frequent payment of an admission fee becomes the
gesture by which patrons acknowledge their passage into the privileged
domain that is physically and intellectually circumscribed by the building
or cluster of buildings the museum inhabits, buildings whose own architecture may underscore the grand designs harbored for the collections they
contain. Once inside, the distinctive nature of visitors' experience is reinforced by "the policed control over entry, the obligatoriness of the circuit
of the galleries, the imposition of frontiers established for the viewing of
the work."[1] Indeed, the rigidity of the separation between subject and
object, exponent and recipient of culture appears inviolable, all the more
so because the museum is a metaframe of cultural and social knowledge,
an expository model based on still other framed models. And yet a nagging
question insinuates itself. What becomes of the status of this knowledge if
the frame can be shown to be more fictitious than real, if it cannot achieve
closure but is perennially riddled with gaps? This is the dilemma raised by

a reading of the *Novelas españolas contemporáneas*. It is a dilemma at once epistemological and narrative, for these same Galdós texts that speak of museums are themselves products of realism's curatorial aesthetic.

"Therefore, I would like to examine briefly this model, speaking in pictorial terms, that surrounds us; it tells us, even demands, that we paint it, asking us . . . for its portrait in order to take delight in it, or to reproach the artist with harsh criticism." So Galdós in his address to the Real Academia spoke of the social milieu as the force responsible for the generation of the literary work.[2] Though his choice of imagery on this occasion may seem to correspond to a purely conventional defense of the mimetic impulse in the novel, the preoccupation with the visual arts as they relate to literature is actually a constant in Galdós's oeuvre, attested to by the many critics who have studied Galdós's reliance upon techniques borrowed from painting, photography, sculpture, and architecture. J. J. Alfieri, in his "El arte pictórico en las novelas de Galdós," offered an initial exploration of Galdós's use of religious iconography, his recourse to the popular nineteenth-century genres of portraiture and historical painting, and his evident knowledge of art and artists as incorporated into the lives of his characters.[3] Peter Bly has since expanded this discussion by analyzing the manner in which the pictorial arts not only determine the action of many of Galdós's novels but also deliver an object lesson, warning the reader against a trusting acceptance of reality as a visually transparent, truthful phenomenon that may be captured upon simple surface examination.[4] Abundant metaphors of blindness or optical illusions and the use of startingly elongated or foreshortened perspectives permit the author to deform and defamiliarize, thus calling attention to the physical and moral disorder inscribed in the commonplace scenes of Restoration life that he presents. Galdós's painterly manipulation of passages of novelistic description, as well as the careful spatial composition of many of his scenes, remind the reader of his aspirations to an aesthetic which, while labeled realist, is neither ethically value-neutral nor stylistically free of traces of the manipulative hand of its creator.

Yet, tempting as it may seem, establishing interart analogies or precise correspondences between nineteenth-century pictorial styles and Galdós's narrative techniques is at best a tentative enterprise. The sometimes debatable conclusions of Mario Praz in *Mnemosyne*, Jean Hagstrum in *The Sister Arts*, or Helmut Hatzfeld in *Literature through Art* suggest that in attempting to locate immediate parallels between specific novels and manifestations of the plastic arts (say, an *Episodio* and schools of European historical painting), critics run the risk of inventing overly simplified analogies and artificial or subjectively defined categories of period styles.[5] Relationships between the arts may indeed be familial, but whether the appearance of certain stylistic traits in an author's work is the result of currents characterizing the historical period or merely of individual expression is difficult to discern. Moreover, it seems entirely possible to reverse the usual order of the terms of the comparison and make a valid case for the priority of literature over the visual arts, since systems of images, whether rendered in stone, paint, or photographic film, posses signifieds whose very intelligibility is dependent upon the linguistic medium. It was this realization that provoked Barthes to assert that "the image—grasped immediately by an inner metalanguage, language itself—in actual fact has no denoted state, is immersed for its very social existence in at least an initial layer of connotation, that of the categories of language."[6] René Wellek and others continue to urge caution regarding what Alistair Fowler has called "the soft atmosphere of whimsy [that] still envelops the field of interart comparison."[7]

Rather than try to elucidate the influence of nineteenth-century pictorial conventions and genres upon Galdós's compositional practices, it might prove more fruitful to examine the author's attitude toward the official status of the plastic arts in his society as expressed in his writings. Here we find that Galdós draws consistently upon the institutional refuge of art and culture, the museum. Galdós records museum-going as one of his principal activities in the autobiographical *Memorias de un desmemoriado*, recounting in detail his visits to the Louvre, the British Museum, the Uffizi Gallery, the Vatican, and the outstanding museums of Cologne, Berlin, Copenhagen, Amsterdam, the Hague, Venice, Rome, and Naples. Early in his career Galdós contributed pieces dealing with the Spanish art scene to *La Nación*, *La Revista del Movimiento Intelectual de Europa*, *La Prensa*, and the *Revista de España*, and in a group of essays gathered together under the title "Las bellas artes en España" he offers an evaluation of painting, music, and literature in contemporary Spain.[8]

The most insistent use of the museum, however, is reserved for his fiction, although the emblematic nature of the museological project in the *Novelas españolas contemporáneas* series has heretofore elicited surprisingly little commentary. In these novels, the museum figures as a privileged agency of judgment and taste, assigning what is contained within its walls to a specially demarcated realm of value that is consonant with the position of the arts and culture in early industrial capitalist society. Ordering and exhibiting a diverse spread of material objects, the museum recounts in fact a history of materialism. As a classificatory apparatus, it proffers an institutionalized framework for systematizing the real and proclaims the possibility of historical knowledge, for through its inventory of objects the museum implicitly presumes to reconstruct an unbroken chain (temporal, stylistic) of causality. In Galdós's fiction, the museum delineates a unique public space, often imitated and domesticated in private quarters, where citizens go to see art or, more accurately, go to see themselves see art. The space of representation that the museum frames is thus notoriously reduplicative: the reader observes the characters observing themselves observing the most prized monuments of art and the finest and costliest examples of craftsmanship, or their *cursi* simulations. Such inscribed and enframed scenes, in which Galdós's characters self-consciously reflect upon the acts of seeing and knowing, lead the reader to reexamine the social and epistemological validity of the museum as a framework both for human experience and for the novel that would re-create this experience.

Historically speaking, the museum as we know it today underwent its principal phase of definition and expansion during the previous century, when it acquired its fame as storage depot of civilization, a place to warehouse works of art whose original cult or ritual value had been replaced by their nonutilitarian display value.[9] The nineteenth-century rise of the museum, moreover, reflected the economic shifts and changing class structures being implemented throughout Europe. In response to market forces, the art work became a commodity like any other whose uniqueness carried with it a price tag. At the same time, members of the newly ascendant middle class, well supplied with capital and eager to increase their prestige, purchased art objects to decorate their homes and pretended to cultivate their tastes by casually perusing the collections of their national galleries on weekend outings. The notion of the pleasure to be had from seeing art in museums consequently often became secondary to pedagogical motives. Obviously, museums were, in Hugh Kenner's words, "part of the nineteenth-century assumption that a wholly new enterprise, the acculturation of the middle classes, was thinkable; furthermore, that it was best conducted in a sort of orderly attic where things (1) difficult to do, (2) no longer done and (3) utterly useless were arranged in some graspable sequence (and No Smoking!)."[10]

Kenner's tart observation alludes to other important facets of the nineteenth-century conception of the museum. For one, the fiction of the museum's transcendence was sustained by the foolhardy belief that human experience could be ordered and then representationally embraced via the display of the museum's collections. In the 1800s, the walls of Spanish galleries were usually covered from floor to ceiling with canvases. Similarly, display cases in institutes of natural history bulged with objects, on the assumption that the museum functioned analogously to Noah's ark; by containing at least one of everything, it could illusorily reflect back to the viewers a comprehensive image of the universe they inhabited. Then, too, there is the matter of the contradictory nature of the basic philosophy underlying the modern museum's creation, that at one and the same time it could enshrine art as an elitist product and yet function as a tool for the democratic education of a newly created mass audience. In France, expansion of the Louvre during the Revolution and later under Napoleon was carried out by means of the systematic confiscation of art works, ostensibly so that they could be enjoyed not solely by the aristocrats and churchmen who had been their previous owners but by ordinary citizens as well. Madrid's Museo Nacional de la Trinidad, opened in 1838 under the auspices of the Real Academia de Bellas Artes de San Fernando, was specifically created to house the treasures of Spanish painting that became the property of the state after the suppression of convents and monasteries in 1836 and 1837 by order of the laws of disentailment. But could average visitors to the Louvre or the Prado, deficient in education and exposure to the fine arts, seriously be expected to worship the sacred symbols of culture spread before them? Finally, there is the ultimately funereal character of museums to contend with. As a hallowed repository for the ashes of culture, the museum—what Adorno referred to as "the family sepulchres of works of art"—was a place where lifeless artifacts that no longer had a home in modern society could be given a properly respectful burial.[11]

That the entire museum project often ended in dismal failure is a fact recorded in the pages of novels as well as in the annals of art history, as may be judged by the description of a visit to the Louvre made by the wedding party following the nuptials of Gervaise and Coupeau in Zola's *L'Assommoir*. M. Madinier, a cardboard maker, first suggests the expedition for its edifying potential: "There are antiques, pictures, paintings, a lot of things. It's very instructive . . . Oh, it's something to see, at least once."[12] Unfortunately, the aesthetic impact of the visit on the group is nil. The guests find the Assyrian statuary "very ugly." In the multitudinous painting galleries they mostly fix their attention on the gold leaf frames and the highly polished floors. The bridegroom thinks the Mona Lisa resembles one of his aunts and the other men titter over the Rubenesque nudes. More than the paintings themselves, what catches the party's attention are the copyists at their easels, busily painting replicas of the masterpieces. By the time they stumble into the drawings section they are literally and figuratively lost, overwhelmed by the quantity and unfamiliarity of the objects on exhibit. In a final irony, having managed to emerge once again into daylight, the entire group pretends to be very happy to have seen such a comprehensive display. No one has seen any practical purpose either to the collection or their visit, but good form dictates that they all express their satisfaction in imitation of their bourgeois confrères. In a similar account of Spanish origin, this one in an entirely more jocular vein, a first-time visitor to the Prado, when asked by a friend what he most enjoyed seeing, is said to have replied: "Well . . . the height of the ceiling." [13]

Nineteenth-century Spain, whose past monarchs (including Carlos V, Felipe II, and Felipe IV) had always evinced strong interest in building collections of antiquities and art and had sponsored artists under the patronage system, proved to be no exception to the course of evolution of the modern museum. The Prado was established by royal mandate of Fernando VII in 1818, the Biblioteca Nacional y Museo by Isabel II in 1867; and the post-1868 periodical press was filled with reviews of the art featured at international expositions in Spain, France, and elsewhere. [14] The very word *museum*, currently defined by the dictionary of the Real Academia as a "non-profit institution, open to the public, whose purpose consists of the acquisition, conservation, study, and exhibition of those objects that best illustrate the activities of humankind or are culturally important to the development of human knowledge," came to acquire other connotations, the most notable being a miscellaneous collection of short fiction or articles.

The titles of such series as the *Museo de las hermosas: Colección de las más escogidas e interesantes novelitas que se publican en el extranjero* (Madrid, 1845, 4 vols.), the *Museo de los niños: Colección de leyendas y apuntes históricos y morales* (Madrid, 1848–50, 4 vols.), and the *Museo de novelas históricas* (Cádiz, 1842?, 5 vols.) are typical examples of nineteenth-century usage of the word to connote an anthological assemblage of literary pieces. Between 1824 and 1826 José Joaquín de Mora published his newspaper the *Museo Universal de Ciencias y Artes* from exile in London, while the entire first part of Espronceda's *El estudiante de Salamanca* was reproduced in the *Museo Artístico y Literario* of 1837. From 1843 to 1871 the *Museo de las Familias: Periódico Mensual* was published in Madrid and a similarly titled periodical, *El Museo de las Familias o Revista Universal*, appeared in Barcelona at irregular intervals during the

1830s and 1840s. Even in the latter portion of the century, Clarín relied upon the broadened significance of the term in editing one of his collections of critical essays, the 1890 *Museum (Mi revista)*, explaining: "As for the way it is named, Museum refers to the variety of its contents." The title represents a catch-all for him, and he promises to name other volumes in the same fashion if no better title occurs to him.[15]

Historical patterns of usage also reveal that *museum* as a word denoting any heterogeneous and plentiful assortment of goods was plainly understood in a nonliterary or nonartistic context. In part one of *Fortunata y Jacinta*, Barbarita Santa Cruz and Plácido Estupiñá ring up a marketing bill of eight or nine hundred *reales* in the Casa de Pla, "that universal museum of provisions" (5: 74). In what may constitute one of the earliest mentions of the topic by the author, the narrator of Galdós's second novel *La sombra* (1870) dismisses the well-worn clothing of the eccentric protagonist don Anselmo, noting: "His dress attracted no attention here, where there is a museum of absurdities on permanent exhibition in the streets" (4: 197). Apparently exhibitionism and vulgarity are traits that define Madrid itself as one enormous museum without walls and certain of its citizens as exemplars of its tasteless collection.

Given the ubiquitous nature of the institution, it is not surprising that Galdós repeatedly thematizes the metaphor of the museum in those novels most directly concerned with the observation, recording, and analysis of the society in which he lived and wrote. At times the incorporation of the museum motif is both direct and literal, particularly in the earlier *Novelas contemporáneas*, where it not only demonstrates the growing importance of the museum in the cultural life of Madrid but also plays a major role in the definition of the protagonists' characters. The integration of the museum motif is accomplished neither causally nor chronologically (that is, metonymically) but rather metaphorically. Often the scene featuring the museum becomes a sort of *tableau vivant* or set-piece. It does not advance the novel's action per se but eventually becomes integrated at the syntagmatic level of narrative, summing up the chief conflict or tension that is in fact the generative motor of the story. Borrowing the vocabulary of the visual suggested by the world of art objects themselves, one might posit that the scenes in which Galdós's characters take their leisure in Madrid's museums are not unlike small narrative cartouches. Within their framed expanses are inlaid patterns that may at first glance appear merely ornamental in nature, but that acquire a larger significance when viewed in relation to the whole of pictorial or, in this case, narrative space.

The first example of such a scene is found in the earliest of those works belonging to Galdós's "second style," *La desheredada* (1881), a novel in which the cognitive activities associated with perception are uppermost and in which family portraits, lithographs, caricatures, mirror reflections, and imaginative representations are key terms in the unfolding of the plot. The narrator offers a description of Isidora Rufete's visit to the Prado one Sunday in the company of Augusto Miquis:

> In the Museum, the impressions of that singular young woman were very different, and her ideas, taking flight, reached loftier regions than she usually frequented . . . Without ever having acquired a notion of true art through her readings nor ever having seen anything but junk, she understood the superiority of all that presented itself to her gaze. With silent admiration, her gaze passed from painting to painting, finding them all (or nearly all) so accomplished and perfect that she promised herself to go often to the Prado to savor that ineffable pleasure which until now had been unknown to her. (4: 1007)

Isidora's unlettered appreciation of what she views reflects her intelligence and native artistic sensibilities. Unfortunately, these qualities will not save her from the nobiliary obsession that rules her life and that can be detected in her pretensions to bar the access of the lower classes to such temples of culture as the museum: "She asked Miquis if in that place designated to house the sublime they also let the common people enter, and as the student answered yes, she was greatly astonished." This elitist wish to exclude the plebeian members of society is an early symptom of Isidora's inability to distinguish between her self-created, apocryphal life as the unrecognized granddaughter of the Marquesa de Aransis and her considerably more sordid real life in the poorer quarters of Madrid. That the woman who will ultimately be jailed as a "falsificadora" 'forger' contemplates in the museum the purest symbols of authenticity—for paintings to hang in the Prado they must be genuine originals, not fakes—allows Galdós to introduce in epigrammatic form the confrontation between reality and delusion, substance and surface that characterizes her life. In the manuscript of *La desheredada*, a passage subsequently deleted in the published version places Isidora before Velázquez: "Isidora laughed before los Borrachos, not managing to understand the truth of that artistic fiction."[16] This is precisely Isidora's failing. She can neither appreciate the truth contained in fiction, nor discern, for that matter, the truth that Velázquez's painting, or the novels she reads, or her claims to nobility, *are* fiction.

El amigo Manso, published in 1882, picks up these same themes and integrates them into a novelistic meditation on education and its role in the formation of the citizen. The Krausist-inspired course of instruction that Máximo Manso devises for his disciple Manolo Peña in fact includes regular visits to the museum as part of a program of peripatetic instruction intended to stimulate the imaginative faculties of the mentally undisciplined young man and inculcate in him a love of the fine arts, poetry, writing, and philosophy. Although Manolo is most frequently compared to a block of unchiseled marble, it is clear that his is a generous and intelligent temperament that only awaits the hand of a master sculptor to awaken and reveal his responsiveness to the principles of aesthetics. This Manso accomplishes not by using textbook reproductions of famous art works but instead by bringing him to study the paintings themselves in situ. The professor reminisces:

> On Sundays we used to go to the Prado Museum, and there we would become enraptured looking at so many marvels. At first I noted a certain bewilderment in my disciple's way of evaluating. But very soon his judgment acquired a startling clarity, and the taste for the plastic arts developed powerfully in him . . . He used to say to me: "Before, I had come to the Museum many times; but I had never seen it until now. (4: 1194)

The trips to the museum become an important training exercise for Manolo, for although he had spent many an idle hour there, only now can he truly see. It is a lesson well learned, for the student soon outstrips his teacher in this quality of acuity of sight, developing a pragmatics of vision that will guarantee his success in society. In this regard, the fact that Manolo's education in the arts also imparts a certain veneer of culture is not an inconsequential one. It soon becomes clear that his talents lie not in the field of speculative philosophy but rather in the practice of his oratorical gifts; unlike Manso, he is well suited for public life and public speaking. But in the middle-class society depicted by Galdós, predicated upon a cult of appearances, it is not easy for the son of a butcher to make his way into the living rooms of the wealthy or the corridors of government, and to that end the external trappings of style and refinement acquired in part from his museological training serve Manolo doubly well.

In *El doctor Centeno* (1883), Alejandro Miquis's occasional expeditions to the Prado together with his servant, the young *Aristóteles*, fulfill a similar function of character delineation. In charting the course of the latter's progressive personal and social development, Galdós significantly transports him from the impoverished world of rural Socartes to the august halls of the capital's leading shrine to art. Felipe's reactions to the treasures of the Prado illustrate not simply his naïveté but also his essentially sound capacity for assimilating new experiences and making value judgments:

> Sometimes they went to the Museum. Felipe would contemplate, open-mouthed, those very handsome figures, and had an intimation of the great worth of all of them. In the presence of artistic perfection, no individual, no matter how uneducated, cannot feel at the very least some secret pride in his affinity with the divine essence that inspired such beauty and his physical relationship to the hands that made it.
> —A man made this?—Felipe would ask in the height of candor.
> —Yes; Murillo.
> —And those angels, he made them up in his head?
> —See for yourself. (4: 1411)

The reader surely detects a lingering resonance of the romantic belief in the lyrical and artistic aptitudes of primitive peoples (*Volksgeist*) in Centeno's uneducated but spontaneous enthusiasm for the fine arts. At the same time, it should be noted that what surprises him most is not a portrait, *bodegón*, or other scene imitative of human activity. Rather, he marvels at Murillo's ability to conjure up images of angels from his imagination. As much as he may admire Murillo or, for that matter, his master's play *El grande Osuna*, Felipe will never lose sight of the immediate present and its demands: not for him the illusorily fantastic world of Golden Age theater and painting in which Miquis has immersed himself. It is often alleged that *El doctor Centeno* is characterized by a dearth of narrative action and that Felipe's principal activities over the course of the novel consist simply in observing and learning. Clearly, the museum scene, depicting as it does the slow illumination that dawns upon the young protagonist regarding the awesome and possibly treacherous power of art, later borne out in Alejandro's tragic death, once again represents in microcosm the trajectory of the entire novel.

In the later *Novelas contemporáneas*, rather than place his characters in the museum, Galdós has them erect their own. The notion of the museum is introduced by means of characters driven by an overwhelming impulse to reenact within the confines of their own four walls the same kind of operations carried out by public museums and academies on a much grander scale: acquisition, assemblage, framing, exhibition. These characters' exaggerated predilection for collecting provides not only insight into their dominant psychological traits (avarice, vanity, compulsion, and fetishism), but also specific information regarding the aesthetic and moral values they hold, values which are in great part determined by the ideological forces governing their membership in Spanish middle-class society. Often these characters are burlesque descendants of the Renaissance humanist tradition of wealthy private collectors who, by virtue of their strict adherence to archaeological criteria and their discriminating tastes, were able to amass collections of significant historical and artistic value.[17]

One such example is perhaps found in *Lo prohibido* (1884–1885), in Eloísa's efforts to furnish the palatial Carrillo home. Eloísa regularly acquires such valuable art objects as Imari vases, French tapestries, Wedgewood china, Parisian bronzes, antique furniture, statuettes, paintings, and watercolors. The effect, according to the narrator, José María Bueno de Guzmán, is quite grandiose. However, it is a collection that can only be sustained and increased at the expense of others, entailing very immediate dangers to the stability of Eloísa's domestic economy and to José María's own financial solvency. Bueno de Guzmán flatly asks Eloísa "how much that beginning of a museum had cost her" (4: 1717). A short time later he confesses his own role in encouraging his cousin's acquisitive mania: "But my costliest impulses were for Eloísa, to whom I was constantly giving surprises, adding diverse objects to her collections, sometimes a little picture with a famous signature, other times a whimsical piece of furniture, a valuable antique, or an exquisite and fashionable jewel" (4: 1728).

More striking than the collection itself is Eloísa's uncontrollable passion for ownership, which similarly afflicts so many other bourgeois in these novels. It is, in fact, as much a malady—a mental disorder presenting physical symptoms—as her recurrent obsession that there is a feather lodged in her throat which she can neither swallow nor expel. For Eloísa, the act of possession is accompanied by feverish enthusiasm; privation induces delirium in alternation with depression. The pattern of manic highs and doleful lows is established during her early childhood, when she collected all sorts of knicknacks which she kept under lock and key: "When her heart was set upon owning some trinket and we didn't give it to her, she spent the evening ranting" (4: 1692). Little has changed for the adult Eloísa, whose acquisitive ambitions far outstrip her pocketbook: "I've spent cruel nights, delirious over a Chinese tapestry, a little bronze enameled chest, a collection of Majolica ware" (4: 1719). Oriental textiles and lacquer boxes are the fetishes and fantasies that fill her dreams and incite her sexual desires. To combat such a disease, José María can find only one material remedy: "It was necessary to calm this exaltation with the only effective medicine: the purchase of the confounded object" (4: 1728). It comes as no small irony that at precisely that moment in the text when the adulterous affair is about to be initiated between the two cousins, Bueno de Guzmán finds Eloísa in the salon, her back to him, "perusing a collection of prints in a voluminous portfolio" (4: 1726).

The pathological drive to collect, one of her many psychological aberrations, finally destroys Eloísa's standard for selectivity. When she can no longer afford real antiques or the costly interior furnishings she covets, she buys fakes instead, and her house soon begins to resemble some baroquely overstuffed warehouse. It is only with a goodly dose of self-deception that Eloísa manages to keep alive the dream and the fiction of her home as a showplace of novelty, variety, and luxury. She convinces herself that her mediocre paintings are by Velázquez and her imitation tapestries from the royal palace. Eloísa's confession reveals the full extent of her addictive behavior: "And in this way I deceive myself, in this way I entertain myself, in this way I narcotize my vice . . . , yes, vice. Why give it any other name?" (4: 1719). Even José María temporarily loses sight of what he calls "the august laws of Arithmetic" and fantasizes buying for his lover "those chasubles from cathedrals that will end up as chair upholstery, and those vellum books whose leaves are turned into fans, and golden boxes, and ivory statues of Christ like Rothschild has, and Fortuny's urn, and Bernardo's sword, and Mary Stuart's Bible, and Napoleon's silver cup" (4: 1732). As can be seen in the abuse of polysyndeton, accumulation here even invades syntax.

José María is somewhat unusual in that he purchases for Eloísa "the most sublime art, the most skilled craftsmanship, and objects of historical value." With rather greater frequency, Galdós portrays characters who in their enthusiasm to search out unusual and costly artifacts fall prey to dilettantism and reveal their penchant for kitsch or *cursilería*.[18] Carlos Cisneros of *La incógnita* (1889) possesses a substantial collection of armor, antiquities, and fifteenth-century painted panels. However, his hardheaded godson, Manolo Infante, is admittedly not one of those who "pretend to go into ecstasy before some rusty piece of junk or faded and grimy rag." He describes Cisneros's treasures in the following letter to a friend: "If you're not careful, he'll have you believing with his demonstrations and exaggerations that the Kensington in London, compared to what he owns, is a stall in the Rastro. Undoubtedly, the collection is very large, and, in my opinion, just between us, not very select" (5: 688). Just as Cisneros's gallery fails to measure up to the standards of the museum because of the unequal quality of its contents, so, too, the unity of don Lope Garrido's collection in *Tristana* (1892) is undermined by its eclectic mixture of fine antiques and trivial erotica. Moreover, much as Eloísa overextends herself, don Lope is almost forced into bankruptcy by Josefina de Reluz's manias and must de-accession most of his holdings:

> Don Lope again had to dip into his depleted fortune, sacrificing that part of his property he loved most, his collection of antique and modern weapons, assembled with such great zeal and the intimate pleasures of an intelligent researcher . . . Now all that remained was his collection of portraits of beautiful women, which included everything from the delicate miniature to the modern photograph in which truth replaces art. It was a museum of the history of his amorous combats. (5: 1540)

Real museums feature permanent collections and libraries usually have noncirculating core collections, but this air of fixity is nowhere to be found in Galdós's universe of fictional collectors and collections. Instead, an initial moment of expansion is usually followed by a larger one of contraction; gain is supplanted by loss, and signs of transitoriness and flux are everywhere. Indeed, the moneylender Torquemada, by seizing the goods of his clients when they default on their payments, amasses a "museum of impossible luxury, of waste," as it is called in *La de Bringas* (4: 1666), precisely because of this circular economic movement. No wonder Galdós was led to remark that the activity of collecting always leads its enthusiasts to the auction block, since the heirs to great fortunes can scarcely afford to hold on to wealth that produces no income. As a result, "the State ultimately absorbs it all, and private collectors are, unconsciously, the worker ants of official museums."[19] The unmaking of fortunes and the dissolution of collections mark virtually all the *Novelas contemporáneas* and are symptomatic of a more general tendency toward the breakdown of known political and social structures and the obfuscation of historical origins. In the cyclical process of formation and reformation of collections, normally valuable data including the birthplace and paternity of the individual art work may be obscured or supplanted altogether by information on the chain of hands and circumstances through which it has passed. And as this chain of owners is multiplied, the objects that form the nucleus of the collection increasingly become the protagonists of extravagant accounts of their alleged antiquity or celebrity. As an attempted recovery of lost origins, this fictionalization of the antecedents of the collectible is seen as markedly unhealthy: "The mania of attributing histories to objects may cause mental disorders."[20] Collections are thus clearly linked to the sometimes aberrant activity of storytelling. Not only do collectors spin out fantastic stories about the genealogy of their prized possessions, but the collections themselves represent an attempt, in visual or symbolic terms, to structure the world's contents, to frame the knowledge they contain and engineer a coherent narrative that explains their existence and purpose. In neither case can there be certainty or unchallenged reliability. The narrative of the collection is simply one story among many, not a master narrative endowed with absolute finality and truth value.[21]

Certainly the most systematic transference of the institutional structure of the museum to an individual scale is Torquemada's project, chronicled over the length of Galdós's novelistic tetralogy. During the early stages of the miser's career, his accumulation of goods is marked by pure eclecticism, an absence of any selective hierarchy. Secure only in the power of his money and still suffering from the death of his son Valentín, Torquemada compensates for this emotional loss with the purchase of material goods, stockpiling them in his home and indiscriminately mixing objects of widely varying manufacture, styles, and value: "The rest of his lair was filled to capacity with furniture, tapestries, and other precious commodities acquired at public auction or bought for a song from debtors who were very pressed for cash." The inharmonious results may be judged by the fact that his rooms are furnished with "una heterogeneidad chabacana" 'a tasteless confusion' that mixes fine pieces from the days of his marriage to doña Silvia with recently acquired ones that are worthless and broken down (*Torquemada en la cruz* 5: 950). Nonetheless, *Torquemada y San Pedro* finds the now-respectable moneylender and his second wife comfortably installed in the Gravelinas palace where, having acquired Carlos Cisneros's entire collection of paintings and armor, they proceed to create an establishment equaled only by the world's finest galleries:

> Cruz had lavished the greatest possible care on the arrangement of such jewels, taking the advice of experts in order to give each object its due importance and appropriate lighting. The result was a museum that could easily rival the famous Roman galleries of Doria Pamphili and Borghese. At last, after seeing all that and noticing the crush of foreign and Spanish visitors who were asking permission to admire so many marvels, the great miser Torquemada ended up celebrating his having kept the palace. (5: 1121)

The only ecstasy that this treasure hoard produces in Torquemada is fiduciary. The art restorers and museum aficionados determine for him the probable worth of the Masaccios, Memlings, and Zurbaráns in his collection, and Torquemada crudely delights in this knowledge of their resale value, leaving the unprofitable and incomprehensible business of art appreciation to the discretion of others. Torquemada himself is both impervious to aesthetics and cynically unrepentant of his obtuseness; for him the museum is simply another investment.

Eventually, as Galdós makes his way down the social ladder to the lower middle class, the occasional lapses in taste displayed by the aforementioned protagonists become instead the general rule. The haphazard installation of bric-a-brac in the household of Máximo Manso's brother and sister-in-law is a case in point: "The dozens of gloves, the boxes of engraved paper, the bibelots, the fans, the artificial flowers, the little étuis, the painted fire shovels, lampshades, and crystal and porcelain novelties on top of the living room tables and consoles gave the ensemble an aspect of fantasy. Frankly, I thought they were going to open a store" (4: 1206).[22] Likewise, the houses decorated with the hideous religious articles that in *Miau* Víctor's brother Ildefonso Cabrera clandestinely imports from France ("objects of gilded brass, all of them fake, fragile, cheap, and tasteless") and the falsity of the decor in Isidora Rufete's apartments on the Calle Hortaleza (base metal passing for bronze, plasterboard for fine wood) are all signs of the museum perverted and ultimately doomed by the idiosyncratic tendencies and encyclopedic aspirations of its curators. Galdós notes that Isidora's domicile, although not badly decorated, was dominated by "heterogeneity and a great lack of order and symmetry. The absence of proportion indicated that the home had been set up hurriedly and by piling things together, not with the scrupulous juxtaposition of the true domestic household" (4: 1084). Some of the finer pieces were acquired through liquidations of the estates of the nobility, while the rest of her furnishings came from auctions and junk stores and were "veneered, fake, vulgar, and not very durable." Galdós offers no defense of such kitsch, not even on sentimental grounds.[23]

At the very bottom end of the scale, the complete degeneration of the museum occurs in *La de Bringas* (1884), the novel in which Galdós is most concerned with contrasting the vices of profligacy and miserliness, ostentation and voyeurism in Spanish society. Elsewhere the author wrote of a potentially pernicious monomania that had overcome many in the lower and recently empowered middle classes, laying the blame squarely on the museological aesthetic: "The creation of museums, an entirely modern phenomenon, has undoubtedly brought with it the taste for small, private museums, be they for stamps, matchboxes, or buttons." Unlike the wealthy aristocrats and burghers of the past, who collected paintings and armor, today it is the poor who are stricken by "the obsession to save and classify any sort of rubbish." Galdós saw a certain logic and value in the preservation of great works of art, but he confessed: "What is not so clear is the usefulness of those who spend their lives rummaging in the stalls of the Rastro to collect book covers, buttons, horseshoes, shoe soles, and other knicknacks."[24] In a story titled "Coleccionista," Pardo Bazán elaborates upon this image of the collector as a framer of life's inanities and trivialities. Her elderly and impoverished protagonist, la Urraca, picks up what others have lost in the streets, storing everything in hundreds of little wooden tobacco boxes, "prior to the most minute labor of classification ever performed upon the debris and castoffs of life in a capital city." Upon her death, the neighbors discover her hodgepodge of hairpins, combs, artificial flowers, handkerchiefs, coin-purses, medicinal flasks, books, love letters, bills, broken watches, and rings. Pardo Bazán's narrator is led to speculate that the "selfish and silent pleasure of gathering what nobody sees and what is of no use to us" is an almost visceral pleasure that la Urraca would never have given up.[25]

La de Bringas embodies the inevitable outcome of such activity carried to the extreme. Tirelessly, pointlessly, the members of the Bringas family accumulate and classify the series of objects that metonymically represent aspects of their sterile lives: dresses for Rosalía, gold and bank notes for Francisco, odds and ends including matchboxes, perfume bottle labels, cigar bands, French engravings of the Sacred Heart, and all the detritus of nineteenth-century popular culture for their offspring. Isabelita Bringas, especially, suffers from the collector's malady. Galdós wryly indicates that she is happiest when she can "poke through her treasure, and order and distribute the objects, which were extraordinarily varied and, for the most part, utterly useless" (4: 1663).[26] Of course it has already been observed in chapter 1 that Bringas enjoys this sort of classificatory activity as well. Repeatedly handling and counting the coins and bills locked in his false-bottomed box, the miserly Bringas provides a literal illustration of Marx's definition of capital as fetish object. The cenotaph that he is assembling is another fetishistic collectible that Pez somewhat derisively says "ought to go to a museum." Occasionally Francisco tears himself away from the hair picture to play with Isabelita. Father and daughter sit on the floor of the Gasparini salon, "without witnesses," and begin sorting and rearranging her prized possessions: apricot pits, bone and metal buttons, artificial flowers, postage stamps, whistles, screws, old gloves, and so on. In *La de Bringas*, quite evidently, the logic of the museum as a place of ordered and purposeful display of art and history is thoroughly discredited.

By carefully inventorying the contents of the households of Manso, Rufete, Bringas, and others and describing the disposition of these contents, Galdós draws attention to the multiple functions of the modern museum as repository, shrine, and classroom for an anxious middle class. At the same time, a comparison between the collectibles amassed by so many of Galdós's protagonists (clothing, cheap lithographs, hair pictures, gaudy imitations of pieces of decorative art) and the legitimate holdings of museums and galleries identifies the former as the kind of objects exalted in the wake of the sacralization of the consumer ethic. Here Galdós offers rather damning testimony of a society predicated upon artifice and upon the total schism of nature and culture. It is interesting to note that no one in Galdós's *Novelas contemporáneas* collects seashells, stones, plants, or whale teeth, only cheap trinkets of mass manufacture that serve no individual economy of needs. As Jean Baudrillard explains, these objects "no longer 'designate' the world, but rather the being and social rank of their possessor."[27] This same system of industrial capitalism and mass production which so radically affects the tastes of nineteenth-century consumer society can also be seen to affect interpersonal relationships. Individuals, too, become objects, to be collected by those with more money and power than their hapless victims: witness the life stories of Fortunata and Tristana, or the prostitution of Isidora Rufete, Rosalía Bringas, and Refugio Sánchez Emperador. The pale, paper-doll Tristana symbolizes the ultimate collectible that Galdós sees destined for the pathetic storehouse that the museum has become in his society; she is physically beautiful but utterly useless, especially so after the amputation of her leg. Don Lope does not mince words in categorizing her as his most valuable and only remaining museum piece:

> At every stage, at every step I was losing some of the good and comfortable things that used to surround me. Now I deprived myself of my wine cellar, replete with exquisite wines, now of my Flemish and Spanish tapestries; after that, my paintings, then my very precious weapons; and finally all I have left are a few indecent pieces of junk . . . But I shouldn't complain about God's rigor, since I still have you, who is worth more than all the jewels I've lost. (5: 1561)

No less vivid examples of this fusion of art and commerce that typify the nineteenth century can be found in *Fortunata y Jacinta* (1886–1887). The house of Bonifacio Arnaiz, crammed with the products of the Manila and the China trade, is simultaneously a museum and a monument to mercantilism triumphant. In fact, the narrator speculates that perhaps Arnaiz became too attached to his wares and "was more of an artist than a merchant." By contrast, the indolent Juanito Santa Cruz is a different sort of museum-keeper. He neither works nor creates; he merely accumulates passively his dynastic family's capital. What distinguishes Juanito is his serial collection of lovers, and Fortunata, a rare phenomenon of nature within her conventionalized society, is a perfect specimen for him to acquire.

Indeed, ironically, she is the only one worthwhile, although Juanito can never fully comprehend her value. In part three, tired of his mistress and longing only to return to the domestic tranquillity of his life with Jacinta, Juanito lodges the following complaint: "The poor girl doesn't learn, she makes no progress at all in the art of pleasing; she has no instinct for seduction and doesn't know the feline ruses that give men pleasure. . . . In all the arts you need assimilative faculties, and this dumb woman who has come my way is always herself" (5: 320–21). Despite Fortunata's obsessive idea to imitate her rival Jacinta, she is, as the Delfín says, always and only identical to herself: not a replica, not a reproduction or imitation, but a unique and original presence. If the test for admittance to the museum is the criterion of authenticity, then Fortunata, whose curators include Juanito, Maxi Rubín, and Evaristo Feijoo, passes that test with unsuspecting ease. Of course it is no mere coincidence that it is Galdós's women characters who are specifically singled out as museum artifacts. Given the familial relationships that obtain psychologically among the miser, the collector, and the fetishist, what better object to enlist for one's own than woman, viewed by nineteenth-century society as source of property value, cipher of artistic beauty, and stimulus of erotic arousal?

In all fairness, it should be pointed out that not all of Galdós's characters consider themselves victims or objects of the museum's reign. Some, on the contrary, triumphantly trumpet their status as a kind of human museum, a living repository of knowledge and events. One such walking archive in *Fortunata y Jacinta* is Estupiñá, the former shopkeeper turned itinerant fabric seller, who prides himself on being an eye witness to all of Spanish history since his birth in 1803. Still another is the astonishing General Morla, "a veritable historical-anecdotal encyclopedia of Madrid from 1834 to our own day," who regularly attends Eloísa's Thursday luncheons and is a source of some amusement for the narrator of *Lo prohibido*:

> He didn't need to exert himself to satisfy all doubts, since the admirably catalogued archives of his memory immediately supplied him with the datum, news item, or affair he was being asked about. When he recounted for us some intrigue, he would mention the street, the house number, the floor. He would name all the members of the family and, if no one cut him short, would relate the imbroglios of the father or mother during the previous generation. (4: 1739)

Morla's is the threat of all museums: the uncontrolled accumulation of objects and data and the corresponding fall into irrelevancy. Ironically, when history becomes consigned to the museum's storerooms, where it is reduced to the concern of a few cranks and eccentrics, it effectively ceases to be historical. The links between past and present are severed, Galdós observes, and what should be a living tradition whose dynamics inform the current situation is instead cast aside by a bourgeoisie intent on abolishing all but the new. As the philosophical narrator of *El amigo Manso* laments: "Every day, History has less applicable value among us and is all in the unfeeling hands of the archaeologist, the curiosity seeker, the collector, and the dry and monomaniacal scholar" (4: 1202).

On another level, the museum metaphor and its dependence upon the structural principle of heterogeneity has far-reaching implications for the realist premises upon which the *Novelas contemporáneas* series is posited. As Eugenio Donato has detailed, the museum represents an ultimately unsatisfactory attempt to portray and interpret human reality; it situates objects in a neutral environment divorced from their original context, and is itself trapped within an "anthropocentrism of meaning."[28] Scarcely less devastating than the assault upon representation that Donato uncovers in Flaubert, the concept of the museum as seen in Galdós's novels helps explain why realism, defined as the attempted correspondence of the art work to the phenomenal world in its totality, is *a priori* a hopeless undertaking. Unlike the *Wunderkammern* of the sixteenth and seventeenth centuries whose varied contents were intended to present in microcosm a coherent and organic model of the universe, the storehouses depicted in the *Novelas contemporáneas* are usually assembled according to solely quantitative criteria and do not admit such a classification of human knowledge. The emphasis on the quantitative aspect, however, reveals a peculiar deficiency, not unlike the Derridean notion of the supplement, whose addition paradoxically functions to highlight what is missing.[29] Rosalía Bringas, no matter how many dresses she already owns, is irresistibly compelled to purchase more. Torquemada will continue to accumulate more gold; the amount of bric-a-brac squeezed into José María Manso's parlor stretches toward infinity. Yet the most highly valued objects of such collections are always those very ones still lacking. As Galdós categorically states, the collector "will never find himself free of the anxiety to own rare objects nor of the torment produced by seeing them in the hands of others."[30] More recently, E. H. Gombrich has reiterated this sentiment that "the didactic collection has a built-in need of expansion. There are always gaps in its displays which ought to be filled so as to illustrate the story more fully and cogently."[31]

This inherent incompleteness of the serial collection poses a basic problem for the museum, and for the novel as well. If, as the disparate elements gathered together in the museum indicate, the borders of reality cannot be encompassed satisfactorily, then how can a realist novel pretend to be an adequate representation of the referential world? Can the frame ever hope to achieve closure? If the novel-frame is itself rather paradoxically framed by part of its contents, does it not become parasitical rather than definitional, a *passe-partout* that dismantles borders and disallows the fixity of the outer limits between reality and fiction?[32]

Poststructuralist critics have charged that in its claim to totality the nineteenth-century novel is little more than a mortuary erected upon the decaying fragments of an ideologically tainted literary system that pretends to naturalize what is in essence pure fabrication, in much the same way that the modern museum draws its authority from fictitious suppositions presented as immutable truths. Even such an ardent defense of Galdós's novelistic production as that of Ramón María Tenreiro, coming at a moment (1920) when realism was squarely under attack by Ortega, unwittingly seems to acknowledge the monumental, funerary quality to realism by describing Galdós's novels as a "vast and admirable museum of scenes of public and private life in Spain during the time of the author."[33] Similarly, Clarín's review of *La incógnita*, although meant as a tribute to the author's skill in sketching characters that ring true to their social milieu, alludes to Galdós's novel as a static accumulation of social vignettes, hung willy-nilly on its pages like so many portraits lined up on a gallery wall: "The collection of portraits with which he begins the series of his letters is a priceless one, and would be the pride and joy of any museum."[34] Readers may well ask themselves if in his novels Galdós has created such a musty museum, or if the task he sets himself—to render faithfully Restoration society, to criticize its defects and better comprehend the process of its *devenir* since Trafalgar—is as massive and ultimately self-defeating as that of the museum to display "history as an eternally present spectacle with transparent origins and anthropocentric ends."[35]

In following what might be called an aesthetic of linguistic and stylistic accumulation, Galdós does initially appear to be caught in this trap of more-is-less. He is the author not just of numerous series of *Episodios* but also the *Novelas contemporáneas*, themselves consisting of lengthy two-, three-, and four-part works. Yet what is the magic number of novels that completes a series? How much print must accrue to Galdós's name before his attempt to provide an "image of life" is accomplished? Even at the level of individual novels it is possible to detect this narrative urge toward accumulation. Most of Galdós's novels contain extensive descriptive inventories, ranging from household goods to complex family genealogies and psychological profiles. Additionally, as his handling of the novelistic form evolves, Galdós employs ever more eclectic narrative strategies. In the *Novelas contemporáneas* series alone, one finds the use of multiple points of view (traditional omniscience, first person narration), the amalgamation of dramatic and narrative techniques (epistolarity, monologues in indirect free style, pure unmediated dialogue), oscillating narrative stances and focalizations even within a single novel—a veritable catalog of variants assimilated to the genre. Similarly, Galdós's oeuvre represents a compendium of forms of language: oral and written, popular and literary, Madrilenian and rural. Surely his novels, in this sense reminiscent of Balzac's *Comédie humaine*, bear all the signs of the nostalgia for the encyclopedia. If the nineteenth-century novelist is par excellence a master of description, then author and narrator are equally as guilty as their characters in indulging in the extravagant behaviors of accumulation and obsessive classification. The pleasure experienced by the narrator-describer and his or her reader is not unlike that felt by Eloísa, Isabelita Bringas, and their counterparts; the former collects words, the latter collect objects. All of them share "the pleasure of amassing, exchanging, constituting series of objects that are at the same time 'equivalent' yet different, managing stocks, extending the series to the saturation point, neutralizing synchrony and diachrony."[36]

And yet, despite this evidence, it would be jumping to conclusions to assume that Galdós is guilty of erecting his novelistic edifice upon the same naïve faith in the representational power of the museum that he so often criticizes in his characters. On the contrary, it is possible to discern three distinct phases in Galdós's search to extricate himself from the traditional realist impasse. These strategies, admittedly provisional and only partially executed, still manage to demonstrate Galdós's awareness of the paradoxes generated in trying to capture the simultaneity and plenitude of human experience using linguistic signs which are by nature sequential, finite, and arbitrary and thereby to reconcile the novel with the inescapable artificiality of art.

The first phase is distinguished by Galdós's express recognition of the overthrow of unity as governing principle of late nineteenth-century Spanish society. As we have seen, the museum aspires to create the impression of homogeneity; the objects in its collections should somehow relate to each other, either by chronology, style, or theme. Nonetheless, it only succeeds in revealing the heterogeneous character of all it assembles under one roof. Galdós, implicitly in the *Novelas contemporáneas* and explicitly in his speech to the Real Academia in 1897, renounces the project of imposing a spurious vision of unity upon his work or his world. In his address Galdós discusses "the relaxation of every principle of unity," which he regards as the hallmark of his era, seen especially in the absence of social cohesion. In this generalized move toward heterogeneity, Galdós perceives a positive force for literary creation: "The lack of principles of unity favors the flourishing of literature."[37] Clearly he finds in this nonunity a method for the emancipation of literature, which can now focus upon the isolated individual. This individual, in turn, is no longer necessarily representative of eternal human archetypes, or even the generic social types found in *costumbrista* literature (the ragpicker, the unemployed bureaucrat, the actor, etc.). More likely, he is a member of one of many distinct, competing segments particular to the society of his own historical moment; although he frequently shares with other novelistic characters an antagonistic relationship to society, he is nonetheless the unique protagonist of his own personal drama.

In a second tactic designed to contest the museum's abortive efforts to achieve completion, Galdós begins to espouse more deliberately the open-ended possibilities of fiction in his *Novelas contemporáneas*. The museum obviously operates upon the principle of containment. Its art and artifacts, neatly displayed on walls and in rows of glass cases, are defined by their placement within a building specifically dedicated to the purpose of their confinement. Galdós's novels, however, are only rarely discrete, self-contained entities whose frames constitute impermeable boundaries. Instead, they spill over from one work to the next. Characters exit and then reappear in subsequent works; plot lines cross back and forth, irrespective of the formal, printed endings arbitrarily intended to divide one novel from the next. The dialogue which concludes *El doctor Centeno* is picked up at the beginning of *Tormento*, while the explanation of Federico Viera's death, described in *La incógnita*, is postponed until *Realidad*.

Moreover, the endings of many of the *Novelas contemporáneas* are left purposely ambiguous, their frames incomplete, as the composition of *Fortunata y Jacinta* and *Tormento* (chapters 2 and 4) duly confirm. From the earlier to the later novels there is a clear progression toward the indeterminate ending that refuses to clarify major interpretive questions for the reader. The dogmatic ending of *Doña Perfecta*, although not without its own ironies, conforms more generally to expectations of novelistic closure: "This is all we can say for now about persons who appear to be good and are not." *La desheredada*, the first of the *Novelas contemporáneas*, leaves off with an ironic epilogue which raises the cynicism of the moral at fable's end to new heights: "If you feel the urge to arrive at a difficult and risky height, don't trust in false wings . . . the best thing, believe me, will be for you to take the stairs." By the decade of the 1890s, the endings of many of Galdós's novels are unabashedly unresolved. *Tristana* concludes with the apparent marriage of convenience of the heroine and her guardian-seducer, as the narrator asks in the final line: "Were the two of them happy? . . . Perhaps." And *Torquemada y San Pedro* concludes without settling whether the "conversion" of which the protagonist speaks from his deathbed refers to his soul or the national debt. Neither possibility can be confirmed, and the narrator's last word to the readers is "¡cuidado!" 'watch out!' Readers discover Galdós's increasingly adamant refusal to permit the traditional principles of closure in nineteenth-century fiction (marriage, death, moral resolution of conflict) to rule his novels. Having intuited that the ending of a novel, like the completion of a museum's collection, is simply illusory, he worries less and less about closing the gaps in the narrative frame and constructing novels based on a belief in their own finality of meaning. The gradual eclipse of the omniscient narrator (by indirect free style and monologue in *Fortunata y Jacinta*; by a relatively uninformed narrator in *La incógnita*; by unmediated speech in the dialogue novels) reinforces this tendency by means of which authoritative interpretation of reality and of the text gives way to the unresolved competition between relativized, opposing viewpoints.

As the third step in distancing himself from the specious logic of the museum, Galdós confronts and dismisses the notion that novels can masquerade as history, or philosophy, or sociology—as anything other than the fictions that they are. Rather than attempt to mask or actively combat this fictionality of the text, Galdós turns it to his advantage by explicitly exposing the artifices and conventions upon which the realist novel is predicated. In fact, the *Novelas contemporáneas* are notable precisely for their acute properties of self-reflexivity. Not just in such overtly metafictional works as *El amigo Manso, Tormento,* and *Misericordia,* but also in more traditionally structured works, the reader detects Galdós's growing awareness that realist literature is sustained principally by the fiction, as much metaphysical as epistemological, that the world is meaningfully ordered and that its experience can be captured and its signification can be satisfactorily reproduced for an audience, in the same way that the museum "testifies to an archaeological memory that cannot be recovered except through fabulation."[38] More and more, Galdós engages with the only realities available to him—those of language and the imaginative faculty—in the recognition that "intensified truth and created truth . . . enter with just as much right into the truth of the text."[39] In this context, it is more accurate to say that in the textual truths that Galdós offers his reading public, reality is achieved or invented, rather than reflected or (re)collected. The operations of a mimesis of the second order oblige Galdós to reframe the presentation of the world in his fiction, even as his characters, so many of them museum-goers and collectors, are frenziedly engaged in the framing of their own reality, collective and individual.

Nonetheless, it is a fact that Galdós can still appeal (albeit cautiously) to reality through language, and it is this continuing, implicit faith in language's power of representation and signification that separates Galdós's work as a realist from the later texts of modernism. It would, in fact, be historically inappropriate to disregard the epistemological and aesthetic foundations of Galdós's narratives, so firmly rooted in nineteenth-century notions of positivism, scientism, and progress. Tony Tanner, by way of illustration of the impact that such a conceptual framework exercised on the realist novel, has concluded that in *Moby-Dick* Melville "gathers together every possible definition and description of a whale that's ever been, and what he shows is that you can never catch a live whale. You can only have a dead whale."[40] For Galdós, Spain's Isabeline and Restoration societies effectively take the place—metaphorically speaking, of course—of Melville's dead whale. There is no question as to the imperative need he sees to dissect them from all angles in the *Novelas contemporáneas*, using massive accretions of detail and description and multiple narrative strategies. Only at this point can he lay the cadaver to rest in his novelistic tomb. Galdós clearly argues that such a literary project is necessary for Spaniards with an eye to the future, since what he chronicles is both a matter of historical record and a means of understanding the national psyche as it engenders patterns of conduct which will undoubtedly repeat themselves even as new historical circumstances arise. To this end, the traditional value of the museum-novel in retaining the past, particularly in light of the often vertiginous dynamics of the historical process, serves Galdós well. But the realist endeavor of capturing the live whale, that is, rendering in novelistic terms the lived reality of pre- and postrevolutionary Spain as refracted through the shimmering but inconsistent fabric of human experience: this necessarily remains an elusive task, though as Ricardo Gullón has indicated, Galdós may begin to suspect that it lies not so much in archaeological documentation as in dreams and the unconscious, madness, or the flight toward the symbolic.[41]

To the extent that Galdós dwells within the ranks of nineteenth-century realist writers he remains a literary curator and taxidermist, although perhaps one who is optimistic enough to emphasize the value of the subject over that of the object. That is, he creates his novel-museums not so much for what they contain as for the effects (artistic, moral, social, and political) these contents can exert upon the readers who interact with them, not unlike that utopian vision in which "the visit to the museum no longer entails . . . a cold monologue of objects removed in time and space from the public but instead the gradual approximation of an open dialogue between the work and the beholder, both of them influenced by the intermediary role of the museum and its directors."[42] At the same time, it might be noted that for all their awareness of the reversals and displacements of discursive systems such as realism entail, contemporary readers and critics are scarcely less likely to escape the thrall of the museum's delusions. The fact that sooner or later so many Galdós scholars convene on the island of Gran Canaria, conducting research at the Casa-Museo de Galdós, is a gently ironic postscript on our own readiness to search for origins, historical referents, and interpretive certainty in the shadow of that same imaginary museum that subtends the creation of the *Novelas contemporáneas* and frames our reading of them.

THREE

Critical

Frames

It is a general error, which long has passed for a law of art, to consider that every literary work should fit a sort of architecture that has peculiar rules which do not resemble at all those of the world in their movement and relations of symmetry. Just as there are canons governing the harmony of the parts of a building, there also exist precepts governing the parts and their relationship among themselves and to the whole in the literary work, and it has even been said—what barbarous formalism!—that this is what is essential, that beauty rests principally on this.—Leopoldo Alas, "Del naturalismo"

Those who have written on the problem of frame analysis agree that frame construction and interpretation are crucial activities in the realm of cognitive response. As organizational devices, frames control the intelligibility of our encounters with the world, with human social behavior, and with symbolic constructs such as art and literature. In Goffman's words, "the individual's framing of activity establishes its meaningfulness for him" (*Frame Analysis* 345). Nowhere is this more true than in the reading process. When readers confront texts, they attempt to make sense of them by integrating their elements into larger systems of signification.

This they learn to do by relying upon preexisting models which act in the manner of a template, guiding their ordering of the textual elements. These models have been variously labeled by critics as codes, conventions, or frames.[1] Since more than a single model may be available, readers must actively discriminate between competing models and then apply one of them to the text at hand. Quite evidently, then, the handling of models or frames is conceived as a highly dynamic process. The reader's participation in this process, moreover, is not limited to the initial application of the frame but also extends to subsequent modification and revision of it. Neither reading nor the frame that directs reading can remain static: "To use a frame . . . is to ground a hypothesis in a *déjà-vu* model of coherence . . . The dynamics of reading can thus be seen not only as a formation, development, modification, and replacement of hypotheses, but also—simultaneously—as the construction of frames, their transformation, and dismantling."[2]

Frames prompt readers to fill in what gaps they may find. As Menakhem Perry notes, "*Most of the information* a reader derives from a text is not explicitly written in it; rather it is the reader himself who supplies it by the mere fact of choosing frames."[3] But which frame to choose? Faced with this conundrum, the reader at the outset will opt for what are called default assignments or default assumptions: expectations and presumptions of a predictive nature, based on past experience and knowledge, but whose continued supposition is not specifically warranted by the current situation. Default assumptions deal in the typical, and although they may or may not prove correct in the long run, they are surely indispensable to any sort of generalized thinking: "unless we make assumptions, the world would simply make no sense."[4]

When actual experience contradicts default assignments, the reader must somehow reconcile the disparity. Normally when this occurs, the reader will salvage what can be salvaged and then reconstruct a more adequate frame that is compatible with what is in reality found in the text—normally, but not always. Perry, for instance, describes a rather arduous scenario in which stubborn readers try to avoid frame substitutions wherever possible and only grudgingly engage in the acts of comparing and repatterning frames. By refusing to cancel out or replace default assignments that have proved inadequate to the interpretive task, readers risk relying upon misinformation or forcing facts to fit the theory. Additionally, it must be remembered that frames, codes, and theories are scarcely naturally occurring systems. Like contexts, they are made, not given, and incorporate social and cultural biases to which readers and critics may be blinded by their very conventionalized nature.

Many are the default assignments that have commonly been applied to realist writing. Several of them are outlined in the introduction and, uncontested, inform the basic premises of this study. At the same time, the chapters of this book have tried to suggest that on occasion we may find it useful to reposition our reading frames as a way of enlarging our understanding of literary realism and the ways that Galdós pushed up against the limitations of realist representation. One such default assumption that has already been dealt with in connection with *Fortunata y Jacinta* is that of closure and the culturally motivated preference for endings that, if not happy, are at least coherent and unambiguous.

Still another assumption that has shaped the reading of the nineteenth-century novel has been the idea that realist narrative invariably assumes the form of a linear, organic, unified composition. Because Galdós's *El doctor Centeno* does not outwardly conform to this prototype, it has effectively been "framed," that is, accused of structural defects and marginated to a position of near invisibility in the corpus of Galdós's texts. As Jonathan Culler describes the effects of default assignments upon reading, "Framing can be regarded as a frame-up, an interpretive imposition that restricts an object by establishing boundaries."[5] In a situation where the frame does not match the experience of the text, the presumption is not that the frame (or who holds it) is in error, but that the text itself is incompetent to measure up to the frame's specifications. A closer inspection of *El doctor Centeno*, one that is open to the possibility of a readjustment or transformation of the reading model, may yield insights into the author's framing strategies on the one hand, and, on the other, a clearer vision of the deeply ingrained patterns of critical analysis and interpretation that are commonly applied to the class of texts of which *Centeno* is a charter member.

More than any other novel in the Galdosian canon, *El doctor Centeno* (1883) has stood since its publication at a critical impasse, occupying the position of poor relation or stepchild to the rest of Galdós's literary output. Despite the recent proliferation of Galdós studies, it is perhaps the least discussed of all the *Novelas contemporáneas*, and has received far less scrutiny—though, possibly, more criticism—than even the most glaringly tendentious novels of the first epoch. We know that even at the time of its publication *El doctor Centeno* did not make the same kind of splash as did, say, *Doña Perfecta* or the early *Episodios*. In a piece addressed to the critic Luis Alfonso, Pardo Bazán observed that the audience for *Centeno* was rather small, not, she maintained, because it was a piece of naturalist fiction that some Spaniards might find offensive, but because it was a novel that demanded too much of its readers: "I don't wish to omit that if *El doctor Centeno* was Galdós's least read novel, it is not because it is lacking in precious filigree work; it is because . . . it is a two-volume work! To buy, or borrow, or read two volumes is an effort that exceeds the heroism of almost all Spaniards. One bulky volume, all right, but two!"[6]

Pardo Bazán was, of course, referring to the almost legendary recalcitrance of the Spanish reading public to invest its time and powers of intellection in lengthy and more technically challenging works of literature, a complaint aired by Larra, Galdós, and Clarín as well. However, the extension of this particular novel to two volumes and the manner of its division has in fact been the source of much antagonistic press. The accusations of major novelistic defects levied against *El doctor Centeno* in the late nineteenth century and ofttimes reiterated by twentieth-century readers are legion. According to prevailing judgments, *El doctor Centeno* is a novel plagued by its disperse thematic content and highly problematical form. Most often, it is described disparagingly as a work without a plot. More than one critic has affirmed that the eponymous protagonist, Felipe Centeno, is not really the dominant figure but is instead overshadowed by such characters as Pedro Polo and Alejandro Miquis. Parts one and two of the novel, it is claimed, are separated by virtue of the independence of their respective story lines, leading William Shoemaker to declare that "the structure of *El doctor Centeno* is loose, disjointed, and poorly articulated."[7] The entire first book is said to be merely a lengthy exposition which prepares the way for the 'real' novel, that is, the tragic consequences of Alejandro Miquis's romantic delusions, in the second volume. Both parts are found to be cluttered with a number of digressions, purely picturesque in nature. Their presence in the novel is grudgingly tolerated on the evidence that they are charming but rather transparently autobiographical vignettes drawn from the author's own experiences of student life in Madrid during the 1860s, contributing to the sensation that narrator and reader are in intimate contact with social reality.

Notwithstanding the neo-picaresque series of adventures that befall the itinerant Felipe and his two masters, it is somehow sensed that the novel paradoxically suffers from a dearth of novelty or a lack of plot. For Ortega Munilla this represented one of the novel's virtues. As he elaborated in a letter to Galdós: "The best part of this book [referring to part one] is that *nothing happens*. Let whoever is looking for [illegible] and riotous action at the service of logic commit himself to the lunatic asylum for dramatists or the fools' asylum for serial novelists. The good novel consists of analysis and nothing more than analysis."[8] Other readers, however, were at the very least nonplussed by the lack of significant developments in the plot. As if this paucity of action at odds with the novel's unwieldy, episodic framework were not disconcerting enough, *El doctor Centeno* also apparently refuses to make good its contractual obligations as narrative by regularly defrauding the readers' expectations. Various plot lines and symbolic motifs are introduced in the initial volume only to be abandoned in the succeeding one. To give only two frequently cited examples, the prominence of the pedagogical theme (Polo's school, Felipe's schooling), the focus of part one, is then deemphasized in part two. In another obvious instance, the protagonist is heralded as both a doctor and a hero in the novel's title and its opening sentence respectively, yet despite what the use of these epithets may lead the reader to believe, Felipe never achieves such stature, at least not as these terms are conventionally defined.[9]

The real novel of Centeno's exploits and those of his acquaintances, we are told, is not to be found within the text of the first part of *El doctor Centeno* but rather somewhere outside of it or beyond it, either in part two, or in the subsequent *Novelas contemporáneas*, or perhaps even in the germ of another work that ultimately was never written. This rather remarkable case of displacement is summed up by Montesinos, one of the most candid of all critics in his incomprehension of the novel's form, when he remarks that "the novel remains outside, beyond that horrid school [Polo's]" and again that "the novel, of course, is in what is insinuated more than in what is said."[10] Of course if the novel does not lie in what the novel says, then we have a right to ask where exactly it is to be found. There are events that this novel does not or cannot recount, such as the details of Polo's involvement with Amparo, or Miquis's dalliance with the unidentified la Tal (the nonnarratable or unmentionable). There are events that the novel elides either for reasons of choice or ignorance, seen in such narratorial asides as "The hero's story presents here a great gap" or "It is better that this very principal part of Centeno's story remain unpublished" (the unnarrated or unmentioned). And, just as there are things this novel means but does not say (ellipses, cryptical allusions, textual repressions), there are conversely things this novel says but does not mean (the many examples of irony).[11]

The charges laid at *Centeno*'s doorstep, however, relate to a larger absence: that neither individually nor together do the two books deliver the promised novel of young Felipe. Has it been lost somewhere in the gaps mediating between authorial intention and reader's reception? Not unlike Miquis, who confesses that "My self is an alien self" (4: 1424), or Jesús Delgado, who writes letters to himself-as-other signed in his own name which he then answers in kind, or even Centeno, whose identity undergoes endless transmutations (Felipe, Celipín, El Iscuelero, el doctor Centeno, el gran Quevedo, Flip, Aristóteles), the novel and its parts would appear to be marked by the signs of autoincompatibility, of nonidentity of meaning with itself.[12]

Thus defined by most critics as a novel, so to speak, "beside itself," *El doctor Centeno* has given rise to a series of studies whose very language alludes to the otherly status of its contents. "Enough, too much pedagogy. But all of it marginal to the novel," Montesinos states, adding: "Everything we are told about [Felipe's] excursions and his games is undoubtedly very good, but it is not compatible with the actions of Polo or Miquis" (70, 72). Shoemaker is no more forgiving of what he considers to be the peripheral nature of so much of the novel's material. He comments that the majority of the literary references and comparisons in *El doctor Centeno* are "merely cultural and ornamental enrichments of the text," just as its social and national criticism (the topic of education excepted) is "opportune, tangential and occasional" (200, 202). These critics' choice of adjectives is especially revealing. What is marginal, ornamental, or tangential by definition stands alongside of something else, at the margins of another discourse which is really the central one, although in this case distinguished precisely by its absence. In this context, it is not surprising to find that most critics have judged *El doctor Centeno* to be a "prelude," "novelistic pretext," "preamble," or "first act" to a novelistic cycle or series whose continuation is to be found in *Tormento* and *La de Bringas*.[13] Again, the play of meaning in the novel is, to all practical purposes, infinitely deferred outside itself to these other novelistic texts.

Obviously, for those readers who insisted upon what Montesinos identifies as "a unified and tidily concluded novel (119), *El doctor Centeno*'s structural discontinuities and its refusal of closure must have seemed at worst a failure, at the very least a puzzlement. Of those few critics who have written on the novel, many have felt compelled to defend what they perceive to be a weak or deviant novelistic design. Joaquín Casalduero, for one, excuses both the lack of focus on the protagonist and the simplicity of the plot on the grounds that these are typically procedures governing the naturalist novel, which "has no beginning or conclusion; it is a slice of life."[14] Arguing from a not unrelated angle, Montesinos attributes the slack qualities of the novel and its dissociative organization to Galdós's overly intimate dependence upon real-life models (pepole and incidents drawn from his memories of his early years in Madrid), with adverse effect upon his fictional creation: "Galdós, who could judge all of that, could feel satisfied with the fidelity of the copy. Not the reader. The extremely faithful copy of an uninteresting model is no more interesting, because of its accuracy, than the model" (90).

Both these explanations ultimately rest upon the notion that the realist work of art may present itself as shapeless, the better to reflect the aimless or unpredictable sequence of events that besets the individual as part of the uncensored flow of everyday experience it chronicles. Yet it is abundantly clear that realist novels are neither artless nor formless. They are in fact highly codified entities that rely upon certain basic conventions of form (omniscience; fidelity to physiognomic, environmental, and psychological detail; documentation; reproduction of linguistic patterns characteristic of popular, local, or colloquial speech) and subject (the history of the recent past as it is bound up with the destiny of the individual; fixation on the sphere of activity of the middle and/or lower classes). Underlying these conventions is the acceptance of a posited correspondence between verbal constructs and a predicated external reality. The pretense that such novels offer a transparent and unmediated transcription of human social circumstances is, however, mounted upon an "alternative order which the artificiality of art provides," by means of a symbolic structure invented by the writer and imposed upon his material.[15] The problem with the statement that *El doctor Centeno* is as amorphous as life is that while it may describe some actual readers' perception of empirical reality, it leaves the fictional order unexplored. Novelistic discourse, as defined by its literariness, is never simply (or just) a window onto Taine's famous "race, moment, and milieu." It is inevitably a textual assemblage built upon a series of narrative choices and refusals, selections and omissions, roads taken and not taken, and must be examined as such.

This is not to imply that *El doctor Centeno* has not had its revisionist defenders. Some recent readers have disputed its being labeled as a meandering or disjointed work and have tried to recoup its value by demonstrating the existence of novelistic unity based upon recurring patterns of thematic features and structural traits. Geraldine Scanlon for one finds that despite its raising of such diverse and seemingly unrelated concerns as Spanish pedagogy, Miquis's philanthropic dementia, the clash of reality and imagination, and the psychological growth and adjustment of the individual, *El doctor Centeno*'s coherence as a novel is sustained by the reiterated opposition of obsolescent, sentimental values to modern, utilitarian ones, adding: "The key to the problem of the novel's unity lies, I believe, in its extraordinary thematic richness."[16]

Rodolfo Cardona and, later, Germán Gullón, locate the key to the novel's

unitary structure in the use of the *Bildungsroman* pattern which documents
the apprenticeship to life and subsequent psychological maturation of the
young Felipín. In one of the more persuasive arguments to date, Gullón
comments that "Felipe is a line of force, a constant; he transmits everything the novel contains, leaving in chiaroscuro what is outside his reach."
He admits that "at certain moments, the lines of force slacken a bit," but
in general, the care Galdós takes in describing the novelistic development
of Centeno allows the reader to perceive this novel as "a harmonious and
complete whole." [17] In a stimulating semiotic reading, Akiko Tsuchiya regards *El doctor Centeno* as the expression of a conflict regarding the nature
of the linguistic sign. Felipe places his faith in the concept of natural language, even though he is surrounded by evidence of the arbitrariness of
the sign. Therefore, Felipe's "interpretive journey," his attempts to locate
an immutable truth behind the deceptive appearances of the social world,
may be seen as "the unifying force of the novel." [18]

Clearly, in attempting to evaluate a novel such as *El doctor Centeno* we
must engage not only those questions already posed by the novel's detrac-
tors, but also the critical prejudices, philosophical and historical, inherent
in the approach of the questioners themselves. What can be deduced from
this brief survey of successive readings that have been performed upon
El doctor Centeno, corresponding to the *mittlere Ebene* or middle level of
institutionalized reading (including the press, critics, and other educated
readers) as defined by Hans Robert Jauss in his theory of literary historical reception? [19] Above all, one detects as the common refrain in all
these essays the repeated recourse to the criterion of novelistic unity, described exclusively in linear terms, as the touchstone for measuring the
merits of this or any other of Galdós's works or for highlighting its flaws
and inadequacies when such unity is lacking. Awarded a special place
of prominence in the aesthetics of romanticism, this concept of organic
unity—the integration of disparate elements into the equilibrium of a continuous and totalizing structure, dictated by a single external organizing
principle—formerly occupied a role as "the unquestioned telos of critical
interpretation." [20]

It may be, however, that the preference for a closed and unidirectional
literary structure is precisely that: an unexamined preference or culturally conditioned bias on the part of the reader, rather than an absolute
value inhering in the text itself. Necessary to sustain an entire armature
of belief, the linear model of both history and fiction can be read as "an
unearned form of metaphysical self-assurance." [21] Questioning the validity

of such claims, recent critical inquiries have focused on heterogeneous texts that defy reduction to a single totalizing logic or structure. In fact, one of the most sharply drawn lessons of modernist and postmodernist fiction has been that of the legitimization of fragmentary, polyphonic, and discontinuous narratives.

But what of the realist novel, where such discontinuity or disarticulation is not expected to surface? When it does, the prevailing strategy has been to dismiss it as an anomaly, a case of technical incompetence on the part of an author unable to make his novel conform to the normative paradigms of realist fiction. An alternative and more profitable strategy might be to acknowledge that nineteenth-century fiction is especially rich in narrative textures and unconventional strategies, so much so that, even before the break signaled by modernism, writers such as Galdós in Spain were broadening the formal repertoire of the novel to include techniques not usually associated with the realist canon, continually pushing back the limits of realism to the point where it dissolved amid the pressures of its own theoretical contradictions.

Objections to "unruly" realist texts are not solely the province of twentieth-century readers; they are frequently voiced by nineteenth-century readers as well. In his essay on *Tormento*, Clarín sees the oft-maligned construction of *El doctor Centeno* as symptomatic of just such an unruly text, and rejects the straitjacketed definition of literary realism that would condemn it and like novels to the proverbial critical doghouse: "Owing to Pérez Galdós's respect for the forms of social life, some readers have considered his *Doctor Centeno* inferior to other books that seem to them 'more complete' . . . A novel that doesn't begin with Leda's egg and doesn't conclude with the burial of the protagonist: why shouldn't it be a work of art, and harmonious, and everything else you say?" Alas challenges the idea that artistic satisfaction can only be derived from novels that follow a unified, linear plan culminating in an airtight closural gesture: "Show even once that there cannot exist art, harmony, Greek lines, and everything you demand in works which copy a piece of reality without pretending to construct a *microcosm*, nor to represent, in an action that is *complete in itself, an entire order* of ideas."[22] Yet even he tends to view *El doctor Centeno* as a novel that must be read in conjunction with *Tormento* to achieve a sense of completion, explaining that Galdós has embarked upon "a new series that begins in *El doctor Centeno* and will stop who knows where." Here Clarín echoes what he had already written about the novel in his generally positive review for the Madrilenian periodical press:

> It is necessary to consider *El doctor Centeno* . . . as a portion of the
> episodes in the life of the character who is the protagonist, or at least
> the constant witness, to a series of narrations whose chief concern
> will be the contemporary life of our people.
>
> Therefore, *El doctor Centeno* will be able to be judged properly as
> a composition when the whole of which it is a part can be seen all at
> one time.[23]

Such persistent critical unease occasioned by *El doctor Centeno*'s apparently digressive structure and irreducibly plural themes logically invites a rereading of the novel that squarely confronts the compositional problem. Might it not be possible to speak of a basic coherence of signification which guarantees the novel's intelligibility, without necessarily resorting to linear metaphors or the notion of a single structural armature? In fact, a rereading of the novel unencumbered by rigid frame-structures discloses that *Centeno*'s unique emplotment is governed not by a sole framework but instead by two contrastive internal structures. There are in fact two discrete paradigms, one superimposed upon the other, governing the novel's proairetic code. Although there are occasional points of contact between them, the novel's signification—and especially its irony, its deflation of the ideals of progress and personal heroism—by and large is generated in the spaces of nonintersection of the two axes. That such a structure should form the basis for a novel that has so clearly been labeled "realist" means that it may be necessary to rethink the definition of literary realism: "The 'simple' linear terminology and linear form of realist fiction subverts itself by becoming 'complex'—knotted, repetitive, doubled, broken, phantasmal."[24]

On a superficial level, the fabula of *El doctor Centeno* is characterized by a purely linear structure, what Sherman Eoff has referred to as a "simple chronology of events in the life of a boy."[25] Felipe is introduced in February of 1863 as a youngster of thirteen or fourteen, newly arrived in Madrid from the fictional province of Socartes, and the novel proceeds to recount in episodic manner the events that befall him until the death of his second master during the summer of 1864. The model in this case is one of direct linearity, psychological and physical growth, and orderly passage from beginning to end. In part one Felipe plunges headlong into the bewildering and harsh urban world of Polo, Ido, Ruiz, and Morales y Temprado. In part two he observes the inexorable decline of his new master Alejandro, set in counterpoint to his own increasingly independent capacity for action and judgment. In many ways this pattern parallels the experience of Galdós's readers, who go through their own sort of decompression process upon finishing the book, emerging from the deceptive waters of fiction once again into the clear light of the real, nonliterary universe to which they belong. The linear path taken by both characters and readers is strongly suggested by the second volume's final three chapter titles: "Beginning of the End," "End," "End of the End."

At the same time, it has frequently been noted that Felipe Centeno represents that rare instance in Galdós's fiction of a recurring character who both enters and also departs the novelistic universe still a child, without having experienced any radical alteration or reversal of his social circumstances. *El doctor Centeno* is not a rags-to-riches fable, nor is Felipe a self-made man as exemplified by Agustín Caballero. On the contrary, Centeno begins his working life in this novel in the service of Pedro Polo and later of Alejandro Miquis, briefly earns his keep as an itinerant petrol-seller, clerks in the Cipérez general store, and finally exits from *Tormento* a servant still, in the employ of Agustín. Granted, he has finally met up with a master whose honesty and industriousness are values worthy of emulation, and like the contented Lazarillo when he acquired his first pair of shoes, he can now boast of owning a watch. Nonetheless, he has failed to achieve economic independence or any real social or artistic distinction. These facts do not constitute in and of themselves a negation of the *Bildungs* pattern convincingly argued by Gullón and Cardona; social stagnation on the one hand does not of necessity invalidate personal maturation on the other. Nonetheless, Felipe's perennial adolescence and his visible lack of advancement in material terms indicate the workings of a second, underlying structure at the level of the novel's discourse, one which is profoundly circular in nature and has gone undetected in the rush to set *El doctor Centeno* on the path of the straight and narrow.

The opening sequence of part one, by its very construction and also by the explicit manner in which it heralds the concluding scenes of part two, offers ample evidence of the circularity of novelistic design which overwhelms the linear impulse. In discussing this initial chapter it may be useful to draw upon the well-known ending of Balzac's *Le Père Goriot* for a frame of reference. *El doctor Centeno* is a novel bursting with literary allusions, ostentatious in its reworkings of earlier models and genres, and most candid in the homage paid by its characters to Balzac.[26] The student Arias Ortiz owns an almost complete set of the *Comédie humaine* and refers to Rastignac and the baron de Nucingen, among other characters. Even more tellingly, Felipe discovers a copy of *Le Père Goriot* in Miquis's room (4: 1399, 1390). These are not unlikely clues that *El doctor Centeno* propounds a dialogic meditation on Balzac's famed ending in which his protagonist Rastignac ascends the high ground of the Père Lachaise ceme-tery and from this elevated position surveys the mighty world of Paris's *beau monde* at twilight.

With his defiant cry of "It's between the two of us now!" and the decision to dine at Madame Nucingen's house, Rastignac epitomizes the ambitious hero of nineteenth-century fiction. Having successfully completed his edu-cation in the inner workings of his society and abandoned his youthful illusions, he comes into possession—first with his gaze, then later by his actions—of all he desires. Rastignac's totalizing vision of the city liter-ally and figuratively at his feet "testifies to a career whose direction and final felicitous destiny are so assured that it can go without telling."[27] For this reason, the novel may effectively come to a stop with the premonitory sentence: "And as the first act of defiance he threw in Society's face, Ras-tignac went to dine at Madame de Nucingen's home."[28] Standing upon the hill looking down, Rastignac sets himself at a critical remove from society even as he declares his intention to assimilate himself to it.

At the opening of Galdós's *El doctor Centeno*, Felipe Centeno likewise climbs to a high point overlooking Madrid: "With a resolute stride, our hero rushes up the steep slope of the Observatory" (4: 1312). From his vantage point what he espies are not the symbols of elegant society (the Place Vendôme, les Invalides, the banks of the Seine) but instead the astronomical observatory, itself surveyed and transformed into an object of scrutiny, and the outposts of early industrial Madrid: "Then he is capti-vated and transported by the suburban landscape that stretches before his view, which includes the hospital, the train station, remote factories and workshops, and, finally, the arid hills of the limits of Getafe and Leganés" (4: 1314). As opposed to the luxury anticipated by Rastignac's virtually erotic fascination with Paris, the inauguration of Galdós's novel suggests poverty and the multiple miseries of the organism: cold, hunger, dizzy spells, and nausea. Twice Felipe looks down and spits, a prelude to such graphic naturalistic motifs in the novel as the sexual drives that ravage Polo and Miquis, Alberique's outbursts of brutality in Doña Virginia's pensión, and Miquis's protracted bout with tuberculosis.[29]

It must be remembered that although *Le Père Goriot* concludes with Rastignac's graveyard scene, the final paragraphs of that novel actually comprise a paean to life, vitality, and social and sexual conquest. When Rastignac descends the hill, it is to go make his fortune. Galdós accom-

plishes the ironic inversion of this whole sequence by placing it in his
initial chapter within a thoroughly burlesque context. Felipe, like Rastignac, descends the hill, but not under his own power. Rather, he passes
out from the cigar he has been attempting to smoke and "falls down, stu-
pefied; he loses his color and then consciousness, and finally rolls down
the steep slope like a dead body until he ends up in a pit. Silence . . .
nothing happens . . . Seconds pass, minutes pass . . ." (4: 1315). The
sad, redundant trajectory that will be traveled by the characters is noticeably anticipated from the first page. *El doctor Centeno* already opens with
a simulacrum of death in Felipe's faint, and after several hundred pages
comes full circle to its concretization in the physical death of the twenty-
two-year-old Alejandro Miquis, who, in the company of his servant, has
moved from one overlook (the observatory on the hill) to another (the in-
salubrious garret apartment of doña Cirila). With the untimely death of the
quixotic Miquis, even the normal linear, biological movement from youth
to old age is aborted. When the novel finally ends, with the funeral cor-
tege pulling up to the cemetery gates, what the reader encounters is not a
Balzacian hymn to life but a monument to waste and death.

As indicated by the prominence of the verb "rodar" 'to roll,' the circular
movement of the novel, far from providing just a simple linkage between
the first and last chapters, can be traced over the course of the entire narrative, which contains a series of plot lines and leitmotifs that appear to
advance toward the denouement yet keep looping back upon themselves.
Felipe's mock-titanic effort to smoke the cigar, his feint of death, and resurrection by a hearty meal is soon followed by Miquis's financial resurrection,
the result of the windfall of his aunt Isabel's money. During the long coach
ride through the streets of Madrid which concludes the first volume of the
novel—an echo of Calvo Asensio's winding funeral procession (4: 1364–
65) and emblem of the novel's serpentine structure—Miquis stops to buy
boots for his servant and cigars for himself. Then the two, dubbed "heroes"
and "boys" by the narrator, go off to eat (not at Madame Nucingen's, of
course, but at a local inn).

Volume two opens with another shared meal, this one at doña Virginia's
rooming house. Here what turns is not the carriage wheels of the previous scene but time itself: "Consider how the turning of the wheels of time
over twenty years has changed things and persons" (4: 1383). The second
half of the novel sees Alejandro's circumstances worsen as he is forced
to move to cheaper rooms and sell off his clothes and even his books,
which "were exiting in mournful procession." In the concluding pages of

part two, Felipe takes the money given him by the dying Alejandro to help
Cienfuegos pay his debts and instead buys himself another pair of boots.
Then comes the final reprise: Miquis's demise and the grim procession of
coaches that snakes its way, "slowly, through streets and roads" on the way
to the cemetery (4: 1464).

The narrative continuum pointing toward decline and death is set against
the alternate internal narrative mechanism of cyclical repetition and its
minute variations. Many have challenged the validity of *El doctor Centeno*'s
seemingly unmotivated juxtaposition of the first book (the story of Centeno
and Polo) against the second book (the story of Centeno and Miquis). They
note that the priest and the student never intersect, quite an oddity considering that the dense and inescapable nets of human relationships of the
kind exemplified in *Fortunata y Jacinta* are what specifically characterize
so many of Galdós's works.[30] Yet one might counter that the crucial factor
here is not the interconnectedness of the characters but rather the similarity of circumstances that beset the young Centeno. Felipe first serves
a priest without true vocational calling, a man who doggedly labors as a
teacher despite his lack of training or commitment to pedagogy. Then he
serves a university student who never attends class, foolishly dedicating
himself to the dramatic arts in spite of his lack of originality or aptitude.
The faces have changed, but the situation is identical: earnest servant,
ineffectual master. Within this compositional play of repetition and difference, Galdós sketches the fundamentally nonprogressive character of
Centeno's own career, a twice-told tale. Such repetition, of course, functions as a troubling or confounding of the narrative line.[31]

The illusion of progress undone, of linearity overruled by an inevitable
circularity, is even built into the verbal structures of the novel's opening.
Both syntactically and semantically, the beginning of chapter 1 is constituted by a peculiarly ironic yes-no movement. No sooner is one proposition
stated than the very next clause modifies it so as to invalidate it, in a
constant dialectical ploy pitting the linearity and sequentiality of language
and writing against the transformations and turns that occur in meaning
as each word, read in seriatim fashion, modifies the semantic horizons of
those preceding it. And so the text tells us that "With a resolute stride the
hero rushes up the steep slope of the Oberservatory," but readers' comfortable assurance that they know where the story is headed evaporates
when this information is reversed by the following sentence: "He is, to say
it, a pallid little hero, poorly endowed with flesh and even more skimpily
dressed to cover that flesh, so insignificant that no passerby, of those who

are called persons, can believe upon seeing him that he comes from a line of heroes and a race of immortals" (4: 1312). Felipe is the hero, but only if the concept of hero is redefined, for his name and deeds will never be immortalized: "although he may not be destined to hurl one more name into the enormous and already suffocating inventory of human feats." The narrator-chronicler promises to tell us where Centeno acquired his cigar, but since there are two possible historical versions, he decides to suppress the polemic and not tell us after all.

When the narrator slips into free indirect style and Felipe marvels at the size and novelty of all he surveys from the hilltop, the effect is quite opposite: "He contemplates the large mass of the hospital. Boy, is it huge! . . . this seems like heavenly glory. Good God, Madrid!" (4: 1315). This is a child's-eye view of a panorama which, though it appears vast in size and great in achievement to an uneducated youth from the countryside, in reality may very well be drab and circumscribed. After all, this is the same character for whom smoking a cigar is equivalent to taking up Vulcan's bellows to do battle with a carbonized monster or a volcano, or for whom the Manzanares resembles "pieces of a little mirror that has just broken in the hands of some river nymph." These precious conceits, with their baroque and literary-mythological overtones, obviously belong to the narrator's voice, not Felipe's. And so this precious image is then flatly contradicted by the next line in the text: "It is the river, which owes its fame to its smallness" (4: 1314).

The figure of the line turned back upon itself in a circle finds its maximum expression in the linguistic fusion of prefix and root characteristic of Felipe's speech in this first chapter. Regardless of what he actually intends to say, Felipe's erroneous addition of the *des-* prefix neatly serves to undo the meaning of his words. As Centeno unwittingly affirms, positivistic analysis actually discourages active intellectual inquiry. Astronomers do not examine the sun; they "desaniman el sol" 'unexamine/discourage the sun.' People do not so much learn as unlearn; asked if he can write, Felipe replies: "Desaprendí las letras" 'I unlearned my letters' (4: 1318). He explains that he is searching for a gentleman who will employ him and perhaps leave him time "para destruirme" 'to uninstruct/destroy myself' (4: 1317). Not instruction, but rather self-destruction. It would be difficult to imagine a clearer indicator of the novel's dual structural paradigm than this unique conjunction of lexical meaning and unmeaning, culture and *incultura*, weaving and then unraveling itself in Felipe's peculiar mode of self-expression. It further reminds readers of the pathetic self-consumption of his master Alejandro, identified with the phoenix (4: 1398, 1414), and of the writing, editing, and final dismemberment of his *Osuna* manuscript that occurs at the novel's conclusion. When doña Angela uses the pages of act one to make curlpapers for the ringlets in her daughters' hair, the poetic lines that Miquis had written are then literally folded back upon themselves in circles.

Even more than Galdós's opening gambit, it is the novel's games with chronology that provide incontrovertible proof of the circular shape lurking beneath the novel's outer linear skeleton. Though *El doctor Centeno* picks up the story of the protagonist in 1863 and carries it over into the following year, its temporal dimension is anything but simple. In the first chapter, the narrator warns readers to "note carefully the date, which was sometime in February of 1863" (4: 1315). Using this date as a point of reckoning, the novel pretends to establish a twenty-year gap between the actions of the principal characters and the moment of their written recording by the narrator. This is the motivation behind the invocation that prefaces part two, clearly intended to underline the preterit value of the story, with its rhetoric of *ubi sunt:*

> Remember, dear reader, when you and I and other important persons used to live in doña Virginia's house, and consider how the turning of the wheels of time over twenty years has changed things and persons. The house no longer exists: doña Virginia and her husband, or whatever he was, are now God knows where . . . Those handsome boys, those other gentlemen of diverse condition whom we saw enter, stay, and leave there during a two-year period: what became of them? What happened to so many a boisterous student, what became of such varied people? (4: 1383)

Just as Virginia's boarding house has been demolished, so in the first volume of the novel the leveling hand of progress and urban renewal has obliterated the oddly antiquated domicile of Miquis's aunt Isabel Godoy de la Hinojosa. But here the narrator offers the clarification that twenty years ago, when Centeno visited it, Isabel's house and the street on which it was situated represented a small piece of seventeenth-century Spain coexisting simultaneously alongside the Madrid of 1863: "It seemed a trap set for the careless passerby; and anyone who walked into it—not like Felipe, who, because he was a child, didn't see the meaning of things—would believe himself more in Toledo than in Madrid, or under the rule of the Austrian kings, menaced by Rinconete's light fingers. Today, Almendro

Street is secluded and silent; judge how it must have been twenty years ago" (4: 1365).

If historical past and present seem to inhabit proximate spaces uneasily on the calle de Almendro, in the novel's second part they are drawn even closer together, temporally as well as spatially, with the episode of the prank played on the *eautoepistológrafos* don Jesús Delgado. When the student boarders discover that Delgado's mysteriously time-consuming epistolary tasks consist of composing, sending, and answering numerous letters to himself decrying the national educational system, they conceive of the idea of also writing him a letter. They use his same paper and ink, imitate his handwriting, address it to "señor don Jesús Delgado," and affix a forgery of his own signature at the bottom. Then, in a flourish intended to further unsettle the mild-mannered "peaceful madman," they postdate the letter by twenty years to November 8, 1883 and inform him that his eminently sensible dreams for the reform of *Complete Education* have by now become reality: "You, my wise friend, immersed in the tumultuous ocean of letters sent to you from distant regions, shores, and continents, have not appreciated the swift passage of time. *Twenty years have gone by without your realizing it!* (4: 1405).

Of course the contemporary reader could not have failed to note the mordant irony of reading this novel in the year of its publication—the very same 1883—and observing that despite the efforts of Sanz del Río, Giner, and the Instituto Libre de Enseñanza, pedagogy in Spain had not advanced much beyond the counterproductive methods of Polo, Ido, or such Dickensian counterparts of theirs as Gradgrind (*Hard Times*) or Podsnap (*Our Mutual Friend*). More significantly, the forged letter to Delgado completes the temporal circuit of the novel. The narrator situates the events he is recounting twenty years in the past, yet one of those events is a trick letter dated forward twenty years, to the time of the narrator's writing. In this manner, Galdós produces a work that rushes forward, only to circle ceaselessly back upon itself, an example of narrative become tautology.

Though narrative is retrospective by definition, and the process of its telling can never be exactly simultaneous with that which it retells, *El doctor Centeno*'s initial sequence has already begun to attempt to narrow that gap by its consistent use of verbs in the historical present tense: "With a determined stride the hero rushes up the steep slope of the Observatory." By the time we reach volume two of the novel, however, that already minimal gap has been rendered functionally invisible. The narrator's use of the present indicative is continually deferred to the past, while the characters' present lives are projected toward the future in an interlocking then-is-now movement that would seem to overthrow the notion of diachrony. *El doctor Centeno* turns in the same repeated, circular pattern as the solitary Jesús Delgado's self-directed epistolary correspondence, the latter standing as a *mise en abyme* in which we see reproduced the novel's overall structure.[32]

Galdós's incorporation of two complementary organizing principles in *El doctor Centeno* is, one suspects, intimately related to the novel's meditations on Spanish history. Though usually subordinated to the story of Felipe's transformation into the observant and experientially wise *Aristóteles*, a ubiquitous preoccupation with history is also displayed in the novel. Galdós's attention to such problems as the definition of history and the methods of historical investigation, writing, and transmission as they may resemble or differ from fiction is already visible in the first chapter, with its apostrophe to Clio and its mock-epic prose. The technique in this particular *Novela contemporánea* has, in fact, been likened to that of an *Episodio*. Moreover, the criticisms aimed at *El doctor Centeno* are remarkably similar to the ones directed at the fourth series of *Episodios*, which, not coincidentally, also deals with the final years of the Isabeline monarchy (1847–1868). Among these criticisms are the fact that no one protagonist predominates for the entire work or series and that the heroes as portrayed are mostly unheroic characters.[33]

Nor is *El doctor Centeno*'s vision of this period of Spanish history any more optimistic than that of the fourth series of *Episodios*. In comparison with a novel such as the *Le Père Goriot*, *El doctor Centeno* presents the model of dynamism thwarted, both in Felipe's personal development and the historical trajectory of the Spanish nation. In contrast to the ambitious or Napoleonic figure at the center of so many nineteenth-century novels, Galdós portrays in this work a frustrated hero-conquistador (Pedro Polo Cortés), another who is the obverse of the heroic paradigm (the passive dreamer Miquis, taking refuge in the literature of Spain's glorious imperial past), and a third, the novel's subject, who at best represents an "unknown and obscure hero," a "colorless little insect." All three are observers rather than participants in the dramas of life and history; they stand to one side of the movement of history, gazing inward, unable to influence its outcome.

Similarly, if plot as it functions in nineteenth-century narrative is a "dynamic activity that moves the narrative—and the reader—forward, toward the 'promise of progress toward meaning,'" if plotting, to quote Peter Brooks, offers "some simulacrum of understanding of how meaning can be construed over and through time," then the plot of recent Spanish history as portrayed in *El doctor Centeno* culminates in a deceptive anticlimax, the line detoured before reaching its anticipated end.[34] It gives the outward illusion of progress in railroad trains, factories, Federico Ruiz's careful astronomical and meteorological observations, and the razing of old buildings, but it is actually cyclical and nonprogressive. In the circular patterns remitting characters, narrator, and readers from 1863 to 1883 and back again, real forward movement is arrested. By portraying these years as interchangeable, the novel in a sense equates late Isabeline society with Restoration society; it thereby denies that the revolutionary and republican interlude of 1868–1874, still an anticipated event for the characters in the novel but a reality for the narrator and the novel's extrinsic readers, had exercised any lasting historical impact. Galdós's depiction of the repetitive and unproductive course of Spain's development even manages to anticipate with prescience Canovas's and Sagasta's signing of the Pacto del Pardo in 1885 formalizing the *turno pacífico*, that is, the regular and monotonous alternation of the liberal-conservative and liberal-fusionist parties: the figure of the circle institutionalized as political reality.

Shiny and periodically renewed on the outside, but unchanged within: this is the historical premise of the novel, best symbolized by Felipe's friend Juanito del Socorro. In yet another symbolic representation of Spain's shift from republic to restored monarchy, Juanito in book two finds the perfect trade for his era when he abandons his job in the office of a liberal newspaper and becomes apprenticed to a gilder. Henceforth it will be Juanito's job to apply multiple layers of gold leaf, skillfully disguising the wizened core of the wood beneath. This is the very reverse of Felipe, who at novel's conclusion appears transformed on the inside (compassionate, better educated, realistic) but unchanged without (young, unsituated, and disempowered). The gilder's illusionistic quick fix finds its political equivalent in the September Revolution. Abandoned all too soon by the middle classes, it effected cosmetic changes while leaving intact much of the old power structure and value system, thus dashing any real hopes for progressive reform in Spain. Such is the object lesson that Galdós, in a circular repetition compulsion of his own, will return to obsessively in virtually all the subsequent *Novelas contemporáneas* as well as the fourth and fifth series of *Episodios*. At the novel's end Felipe has grown in stature as a positive force, but can accomplish little in the face of Alejandro's escapism, Morales y Temprado's vacuous oratory, Ruiz's positivism, Polo's antipedagogy, and the university students' dissipation. For what ails Spain of the 1860s (and 1880s), Galdós can find no doctor proper, save perhaps in the house of fiction.

At this point, readers may very well ask whether the existence of two competing structural and temporal paradigms in *El doctor Centeno* truly results in a realist novel that is fragmentary or discontinuous, unfettered by the myth of linearity and organic unity; whether *Centeno* is, in effect, a modernist or quasi-modernist narrative. Quite clearly, this is not the case. Closure has not been abolished, nor does the presence of both linear and circular plotting result in the internal combustion of the text. One may argue, in fact, that the reading presented in this chapter has still not disengaged from the telos of organicism but has, instead, simply found a way to conjoin the two patterns so that the premise of thematic and structural unity is once again confirmed. There is a good deal of truth to this argument; certain default assignments, certain reading practices die very hard indeed. In the face of the impossibility of reading without some sort of model, it proves difficult not to exchange one historical and ideologically motivated frame for another that is equally motivated, or at the very least to search for new ways to guarantee that critics will end up with the same frame as was applied at the outset. Nonetheless, stepping back from these received frames and entertaining the possibility of other structural prototypes for nineteenth-century fiction may allow readers to discover aspects of a text that have gone undetected or been undervalued. *El doctor Centeno* may still strike us as less accomplished than other of Galdós's novels, but by reframing their approach to it, by not prejudging its structural attributes and compositional peculiarities as defective, critics may come to appreciate the insights into the representational conventions of realist writing that Galdós offers the truly receptive reader.

> # 7
>
> **Criticism, the Framing of the Canon, and the Nineteenth-Century Spanish Novel**

The great affliction of modern literature is that the awful book is read as much as the good one. All are equally favored; all are called to the great arena, to an immense literary competition in which reputations of all sizes, aspiring to immortality, fluctuate for many years. But in the end few are chosen, few are the ones that posterity selects from the multitude destined to an eternity of oblivion.—Galdós, Crónicas de Madrid

By now it has become a commonplace to repeat the etymology of the word *canon*, which in Latin signified "measuring line, rule, or model" and, in the earlier Greek, "rod, rule." As the preceding chapters have made clear, the line is in fact the figure of the border or boundary, that which separates: the picture from the wall behind it, the cultivated garden from the untilled field encircling it, one citizen's country from the many nations that would encroach upon its frontiers. When readers today speak about the canon, they refer to a similar demarcation between object and field, in this instance between works that are vaguely and sometimes reductively classed as truly outstanding examples of literature and those that dare claim for themselves only a lesser province of importance.

Of course to describe literature as good is implicitly to ask: good for what? The answer to this question has varied over time and across cultures, perhaps indicating how very sensitive frames are to displacement and reconstruction. At various moments in Western history the idea of the canon has been based upon literature's condition of normativeness, its reproduction of models of communicative behavior: one reads literary texts in order to imitate and perpetuate competence in writing. At other moments the canon has been erected upon the criterion of morality: people read literature so as to improve their characters and collectively ameliorate society's wrongs. Finally, there have also been periods when the distinguishing feature of the canon was good taste: reading literature showed one's recognition of cultural superiority and aesthetic refinement.[1] Simply put, then, the canon is a frame, variable in nature, that encloses a series of texts privileged at a particular moment in time for their moral, artistic, or historical value.

The canon is without doubt one of the surest examples of a frame whose construction is inconceivable without taking into account the pressures and value judgments brought to bear by social and institutional forces. In this respect silence counts; the canon is every bit as significant for what it omits or consigns to the periphery as for what it encompasses. Moreover, by raising the distinction between classic and ephemeral, superior and inferior, included and excluded texts, the concept of canon represents an exercise of authority. It necessarily draws another Maginot line dividing literary from critical discourse, categorizing the former as separable yet dependent, a subset of the latter. For canons to exist, criticism (or theory, if you will) must function as a metalanguage that frames definitively the universe of imaginative literature. Since such a metalanguage is employed by schools, universities, journals, scholarly presses, the media, and other influential institutions, it becomes evident that the definition and transmission of canons is neither simple nor disinterested.

In literary studies today one of the most frequently addressed topics concerns the whys and wherefores of the canon: where it has already been (the story of the establishment of the original, authoritative Christian canon, followed by the emergence of an alternative, secular canon beginning in the eighteenth century) and where it is going now (the debate over its legitimacy and its continued ability to classify knowledge or monitor human values). The case of the nineteenth-century novel in Spain offers in this respect a fruitful field of inquiry, in that it is particularly compelling as an example of a genre that has swung widely between extremes of great favor and utter disrepute over a relatively brief period of time. It has variously been charged as having everything, or nothing, to say to its readers, depending upon who was doing the evaluating of it and when.

A schematic survey of the historical reception of the realist novel dating from the 1870s, followed by a synchronic look at the closely intertwined fates of contemporary literary theory, realism, and the novel form, together suggest a picture of how and for what purposes value has come to be assigned to this particular class of literary texts. Implicated in the earliest construction of a realist canon in Spain were notions of social reformism, literary taste making, and ideological control. The lines of this canon in its current incarnation are not quite so clearly drawn. The novels and authors now accorded privileged status seem to have been granted that distinction on the basis of a formula that, purged of transcendentalism, instead weighs the archaeological value and formal characteristics of a given work, asking whether it can stand as a source of information about nineteenth-century society or as a worthy model in a typology of realist narrative. But other factors, including lightly veiled ideological concerns, also have their say; and in some instances about equal parts of received wisdom, serendipity, and critical inertia seem to have determined which nineteenth-century novels most deserve to be kept or added to the list of works we study and teach, and which others displaced from center to margin.

Because they are so tightly bound up not just with literary but also with cultural, social, and even political values, the issues of how and why the canon is constituted in its present fashion demand much closer scrutiny. The nineteenth-century novel is repeatedly referred to in manuals of literature as the beginning of the modern novel in Spain. Today's readers and critics are likewise citizens of that extended historical moment or condition known as modernity and its aftermath. Hence a deeper understanding of the forces that shape the canon of these crucial nineteenth-century texts necessarily tells us much about these novels, and equally as much about our own intellectual prejudices and preoccupations that are put into play as we set about reading them.

In the preceding chapter an attempt was made to trace the critical fate of *El doctor Centeno*, a Galdós text largely ignored by the reading public of the nineteenth and also the twentieth century. If nothing else, the narrative of *Centeno*'s dereliction demonstrates the power of canon-makers to determine what readers actually read. Little has been written on this novel, and it is unlikely that at present many university departments, either in this country or in Spain, see fit to include it in a course syllabus or list of required books upon which students will be examined. At the same time, it is entirely plausible to assert that certain attitudes, ideologies, and modes of reading are also partly responsible for the way *El doctor Centeno* has been dismissed with scarcely a second look. What this suggests is the need to situate Galdós's novels, both the uncontested masterpieces and the lesser known works, within the context of realist fiction in general, and then to examine the whole of this from within the frame of the modern critical enterprise.

Certainly, at the moment of its first flowering the realist novel occupied a place all its own in contemporary culture. Reviewing *Doña Perfecta* for *El Imparcial* in 1876, the well-respected Krausist critic González Serrano affirmed without equivocation that "the Novel, because of its very special conditions, can constitute itself as a work of social, political, and even religious transcendence, and form the Canon for all of life."[2] With the exception of the occasional author like Valera, ever the elegant stylist, who chose to emphasize the ends of the novel as strictly aesthetic, most Spanish novelists and critics of the final third of the nineteenth century specified in their writings that the novel merited consideration not just as a literary object but also as a sociological document, ideological manifesto, and highly individualized expression of national culture. No less so than the editorial columns of newspapers, the pages of the novel—what this same critic called a "fictitious syncretism of this absorbing incoherence that surrounds us everywhere"—provided a forum where those representing opposing factions in the contest between the two Spains could take account of contemporary reality, newly perceived in its problematic historical dimensions. By the last decades of the century the novel came to symbolize a literary genre that was, historically speaking, not only possible but also necessary. If, after all, it was the political stability of the Restoration that made cultivation of the novel artistically and economically feasible, it was in fact the preceding turmoil stirred up by the Revolution of 1868 that had made its cultivation ideologically imperative. As the genre continued to evolve on its somewhat belated timetable in Spain, this ideological burden that the novel was made to bear was somewhat lessened. Nonetheless, even an author and critic as pledged to defend the autonomy of art as Leopoldo Alas was able to claim that the novel, conceived of in a spirit of free inquiry and without ceasing to be a "beautiful and entertaining work," could actually serve physiologists, philosophers, and psychologists (he mentions Taine and Spencer) as a source of data and insights into the so-called social question.[3]

Two specific constellations of metaphors, frequently repeated in prologues, essays, and articles appearing in the periodical press, indicate the weighty role accorded the novel as preeminent literary genre of the Spanish revolutionary and Restoration eras. The novel was alternately compared either to a representational device (photograph, mirror, painting, or still life), reflecting a closely observed class, region, or society, or else to a diagnostic tool (scalpel, microscope, dissection laboratory), serving to probe the etiology and record the pathology of social maladies, even if an actual remedy lay beyond the novel's reach. The novel's function, hence, was perceived as being actively critical; the means for implementing this objective was the system of literary mimesis broadly labeled as realism. Working in concert, these two aspects (one ethical, one aesthetic) enthroned the novel as the most powerful of all literary forms, marking the first of four broad moments in the history of the realist novel in Spain, and the only one to allow it a transcendental role in both the arbitration of standards of literary taste and the determination of a potential model for human action. More than just a convenient label for a class of works within a literary taxonomy, the novel genre was extolled in typically hyperbolic fashion by Alas as nothing less than "the all-comprehensive style of literary art."[4] Like many of the writers and critics of his day, Alas owed his intellectual formation to Krausism, which valued disciplines such as literature and pedagogy because of the decisive contribution they made to the process of the perfectibility of society and its individual members. At perhaps no other moment in Spanish history did so many feel that the novel mattered, and not just to the progress of the literary arts but to that of humankind itself.[5]

This imperious domination of life and letters by nineteenth-century narrative was broken with the appearance of a new brand of novel cultivated by Spain's so-called Generation of 1898: deliberately subjective (Unamuno), antirhetorical (Baroja), plotless and tending to dissolve chronology and characters into a fractured mosaic of disparate sensorial impressions (Azorín). During this second moment in its history the nineteenth-century novel, anchored as it was in a specifically bourgeois value system, held little currency among the intellectuals of the new era, who were intent on divorcing themselves from bankrupt Restoration politics and its cultural manifestations, and even less currency in the face of Ortega y Gasset's aesthetics of "dehumanization" and the various artistic agendas of the vanguard. From the turn of the century until the outbreak of the civil war, one can point to a proliferation of novels in which the ventilating of abstract intellectual concerns from a limited and highly personalized authorial perspective supplanted previous efforts by novelists to re-create in a concrete, detailed, and ostensibly objective fashion a microcosm of the totality of society in that segment of it being depicted. What such diverse novels as Unamuno's *Niebla*, Miró's *El humo dormido*, Pérez de Ayala's *Belarmino y Apolonio*, and Jarnés's *Locura y muerte de nadie* have in common is their

studied cultivation of literariness and their no less studied disregard for
the external referent in pursuit of what Ortega called "the new art." They
are self-conscious literary exercises that reject such stock-in-trade notions
of the realist novel as verisimilitude, psychological development of character, causality, historical consciousness, documentation, and organic structural unity, judging such techniques to be anachronistic and artistically
limiting, no longer descriptive of an existence perceived as a chaotic succession of fleeting and discontinuous moments of consciousness. Intoning
that "Lucas or Sorolla, Dickens or Galdós, have character but not style,"
Ortega had few qualms in relegating the novel, along with other art forms
of the preceding century, to the cluttered attic of cultural history.[6] As the
surrealist poet Vicente Aleixandre, by his own admission a fervid reader
of Galdós in his adolescence, was nonetheless forced to recognize, the
realist aesthetic had become a casualty of the ludic new art proposed by
Ortega: "I imagine I've lived through the lowest point on the curve marking
Galdós's 'purgatory.' From 1920 (from his death) to 1935, the new literary
generations as a rule had nothing to do with this novelist. His realism and
the very material upon which he operated were quite removed from the
preoccupations of the epoch."[7]

The ground lost by the nineteenth-century novel was recovered only in
piecemeal fashion during the post–civil war period, the next significant
moment in its life as a genre. Because the study of literature was instru-
mentalized and pragmatized during the Franco dictatorship as part of the
ideological apparatus wielded by the Movimiento, literature and other art
forms were valued in postwar Spain insofar as they could furnish an unequivocal display of Catholic orthodoxy and patriotism, or be utilized as
tools in the inculcation of such values in the masses. Thus co-opted for official propagandistic purposes, those nineteenth-century novelists' works
remaining when the canon was adjusted to legitimate the regime were seriously mangled at the hands of the Francoist machine of censorship and
educational control. Writers including Fernán Caballero, Pereda, Alarcón, Coloma (and, with certain reservations, Palacio Valdés and Valera),
officially sanctioned by the *Cuestionario de lengua y literatura* appearing
in the Orden del 14-IV-1939 of the Ministry of Education and endorsed
in such journals as *Atenas* and *Razón y Fe*, were indeed recommended
study toward completion of the *bachillerato*, but for reasons extraneous to
their relative merits as novelists. Rather, these authors were praised for
their doctrinaire conservatism in political, theological, and moral matters.
When the contemporary novelist Juan Goytisolo writes of matriculating at

the University of Barcelona in 1948 "after a high school course of study in which the only literary work we were given to read was Father Coloma's *Pequeñeces*,"[8] he is describing an instructional experience not atypical of that of many Spaniards channeled through the largely Church-controlled educational system during the 1940s and 1950s, when lesser works that conformed to prevailing notions of *lo castizo* found their way onto approved reading lists. In this instance the work in contention was a late nineteenth-century serial novel written by a Jesuit in which the story of a decadent aristocracy's desertion of its social mission is played out as a drama of sin, loss, and redemption. That such a work was more vigorously promoted over other realist fictions that were perhaps less programmatic (or less ideologically congenial to the political right) in their representation of Spanish society's values is indication enough of the norms being invoked by Francoist literary hagiolaters.

The fortunes of other significant nineteenth-century writers aligned on the wrong side of the ideological fence were considerably less felicitous during the Franco years. Valera was sometimes considered a skeptic who failed to understand true Christian mysticism. Pardo Bazán's novels were damned as crudely naturalistic, and many of Blasco Ibáñez's works of the tenor of *La araña negra* were prohibited from being reedited on grounds of their irreligiosity. While the *Episodios Nacionales* passed muster as suitably patriotic texts and *Marianela* was dismissed as a harmless sentimental interlude, virtually all of Galdós's social novels were condemned for the sins of anticlericalism and liberalism—"those toxins," as Luis Araujo Costa identified them in his 1957 edition of *Trafalgar*—which imperiled Galdós's standing as a nineteenth-century paladin of Spanish national consciousness.

As one manual of Spanish literature explained, Galdós presented the unfortunate case of an "author of great literary merit but reprehensible moral character or erroneous ideological or religious tendencies."[9] The centenary celebration of Galdós's birth in 1943, which, fueled by the impetus of Spanish critics in exile, achieved considerable momentum in Latin America, was with few exceptions suppressed on the Iberian peninsula.[10] By contrast, Clarín was not so much refuted as ignored. In particular, his *La Regenta*, centered on the adulterous passion of Ana Ozores for Alvaro Mesía and the mutual attraction between her and the vicar general Fermín de Pas, himself embroiled in a series of ethically questionable maneuvers to increase his personal and ecclesiastical power over the citizens of Vetusta, was perceived as the jewel of anticlerical sentiment in the crown of an author already suspect for his liberal, Krausist values. Descriptions in manuals of literary history of his contributions to the novel were either edited drastically or else expunged altogether. The apparent conspiracy of silence greeting the publication of *La Regenta*'s two volumes in 1884–1885 was outdone by the postwar policy that, in banishing the Oviedan novelist from the roster of the literary establishment or emphasizing only such potentially negative features as his novel's great length and abundance of description, deflected the attention of Spanish readers away from one of the most important practitioners of nineteenth-century fiction.[11] Writing about the difficulties Alas faced in gaining critical acceptance for the body of his critical and literary work—a struggle that began even in his own lifetime and continued unabated until at least the 1950s, when the centennial of his birth saw the publication of the first studies that undertook to recuperate Clarín for the canon of the Spanish novel—Gonzalo Sobejano offers the following corroborative testimony: "Those of us who began our intermediate studies at the end of the civil war were allowed to read, of the epoch and genres to which I refer, as many of Pereda's novels as we wished, some by Valera and Palacio Valdés, those by Father Coloma, and even specific books by Azorín, Baroja, or Unamuno, but very little, almost nothing by Galdós or Leopoldo Alas."[12]

It should be stressed that the deep fissures that make of Spanish culture and its evaluation such a contentious affair were already visible during the latter portion of the Enlightenment and firmly in place by the time of the Cortes de Cádiz of 1812. In other words, attempts to recruit the nineteenth-century novel in support of one or another ideology, irrespective of formal and literary concerns, are scarcely unique to the post-1939 era. Overtly biased readings were already a feature of the criticism that prevailed when the novel dominated the literary scene during the previous century. At their best, such readings attempted to place Spanish literature within a unified, and unifying, cultural context, as exemplified by Menéndez y Pelayo's situation of Spanish masterpieces within an uninterrupted continuum of Catholicism and Latinate and national tradition. At their worst, they turned criticism into an outlet for self-righteous moral pronouncements of the tenor of Father Blanco García's vituperative *La literatura española en el siglo XIX*.[13] Ironically, the very same *Pequeñeces* to which Goytisolo had been subjected in the 1940s, presumably for its edifying moral tableaus, was itself at the time of its publication in 1891 at the center of the *algarada*, an obstreperous critical free-for-all played out in the press and the pulpit between progressives and reactionaries along strictly partisan lines, in blatant disregard for the successes or failures of the book as narrative per se. As Pardo Bazán lamented in her discussion of the outstanding features of the book (the apologetics of Catholicism and the critique of the venality of the nobility under the Restoration), "the question has been degenerating from a literary issue into a social and political one."[14]

Coloma's tract, or the religious thesis novels of Galdós and Pereda, are among the many works submitted to a criticism that so often substituted moralization for stylistics or poetics. Only half in jest did doña Emilia write in *La cuestión palpitante* that in the minds of many Spaniards the blame for the decline in national standards of morality, previously reserved for the lottery and the bullfight, now deserved to be ascribed to the ascendancy of a low-minded, pornographic naturalism in literature.[15] Set in this context, the application of an ideological litmus test in lieu of axiological criteria based on notions of taste or aesthetic form to determine a novel's eligibility for canonical status can be seen to belong to a well-bearded tradition that antedates the Franco project by almost a century.[16]

As a case of attempted blanket institutional control of interpretation, however, the postwar shaping of the novelistic canon under the direction of the Ministry of Information and Tourism is particularly instructive as to how glaringly blind the institution could often be to challenges to its hegemony. The *Episodios*, for example, were never proscribed as unfit reading for Spaniards, despite the fact that from one series to the next Galdós becomes increasingly pessimistic regarding the nonprogressive course of Spain's history, more vocal in his condemnation of factionalism, quixotic idealism, political abstraction, religious intolerance, and the empty pursuit of military glory as holdovers from a feudal past. It has been amply demonstrated that the Franco regime never managed to create a coherent ideology of its own, much less a Francoist intellectual culture, and that its policies governing editorial censorship were more often than not perceived as arbitrary and contradictory.[17] On the basis of the anomalous configuration of a novelistic canon which simultaneously interrogated and found wanting the nonpolitical Valera yet included Galdós's unflinchingly critical examination of national conscience and motives in the *Episodios*, one is forced to conclude that the architects and servants of Spanish postwar editorial and educational policy were not only muzzy ideologues but bad readers as well. At the very least, they must have been lazy ones who never read beyond the more heroically conceived novels of the first series, since of the later series, each grows progressively more disillusioned with the course of Spanish politics. Instead, they were content to parrot Menéndez y Pelayo's judgment that the *Episodios* "have educated youth in the cult of their native land."[18] Through all of this, the notion of mimesis itself was rarely attacked. In fact, rehabilitated from the disrepute into which it had fallen during the heyday of the vanguard, realism was lauded as a perennial and transgeneric impulse of Spanish literature, virtually an expression of national character, recurring in the epic of the Cid, Rojas's *Celestina*, the picaresque novel, Cervantes, and many other texts leading up to its full flowering in the nineteenth-century novel. It was instead the chosen object of a realist novel's gaze or the expression of a negative judgment on traditional Spanish society compared to European norms that earned certain realist writers the displeasure of the regime's censors.

Since the 1960s, simultaneous with the transformation of Spain's economic and social infrastructure, realist fiction has once again become the object of increasing critical attention. The resurgence of interest in nineteenth-century Spanish fiction occurred providentially at a time when the rise of studies in the fields of narratology and semiotics championed by Genette, Barthes, Todorov, Bal, Bremond, Greimas, Prince, and others had shifted attention primarily to the genre of prose narratives. The chronology is probably coincidental, given the relative slowness with which Hispanism has responded to particular strains of Continental criticism. Nonetheless, it is evident that it is the application of contemporary literary theory that has wielded greatest impact, affecting somewhat Hispanists' current constitution of the canon and to an even greater degree the manner in which these privileged texts are being read and exploited in conformity with postrealist expectations of the novel.

As renewed interest in Galdós, Pardo Bazán, and Alas has grown, so has also a general awareness of most recent theoretical approaches to literature as either text-centered (structuralism, poststructuralism, and deconstruction) or text-and-reader interactive (reader-response criticism and reception theory). What this means is that without altogether abandoning the notion of the nineteenth-century novel as Stendhalian mirror held up to the road, readers are now beginning to admit that the much-touted relationship between literature and social reality exhibited in realist fiction is a nonexclusive one; that, on the contrary, inter- and intratextual relationships are of paramount importance and are certainly no less intense for their being non-representational. Jonathan Culler observes:

> When critics study nineteenth-century novels as elaborate self-referential, self-deconstructive structures, there is often a claim im-

plied that any reader who experiences them as referring to a particular society is hopelessly deluded, but it ought to be possible to maintain both that reading and interpretation necessarily involve the positing of a referent, and that investigation of literary structure requires the displacement of any particular proposition or reference. Literary study has gained in range and subtlety from theories of language and literature that urge us to postpone as long as possible the moment of reference, the rush from words to world, and to concentrate on patterns of relations within texts and between them . . . There seems to be no coherent and convincing alternative to anti-referential or propositional theories of literature—accompanied, of course, by an account of the referential movement in interpretation.[19]

Culler posits that the reading of realist fiction ought to consist of two separate moments: the first, in which the referent is held in abeyance, the better to focus on the structures and systems circulating within the text itself, and the second, in which the referent is brought back in, in recognition of the role played by context and culture. Hispanists who are sympathetic to the above view often find themselves dissatisfied with simple glosses of the plot or the numbingly mechanical recounting of sources, historical particulars, and biographical tidbits fostered by a fossilized tradition of positivist scholarship. They no longer see as their principal task the manipulation of the novel as just one more document pertaining to the archaeology of nineteenth-century society.

Expositions of an author's political and philosophical agenda and reconstructions of social and historical circumstances have, of course, their very pertinent uses and applications. The explanation of Pereda's antirevolutionary politics in *Pedro Sánchez* or of Galdós's affinity for Krausist philosophy in *León Roch* makes for a more informed and therefore richer reading of these novels. Similarly, analyses of Galician social oligarchies as portrayed in Pardo Bazán's Marineda or the phenomenon of urbanization in Galdós's Madrid reveal the specificity of the novel and the conditions of the society in which it was produced. Yet while these discussions shed light on significant preconditions of the text's creation and thereby offer needed clarification to the present-day reader, they scarcely qualify as interpretive analyses or evaluations of literary discourse per se. Instead, or at least initially, purveyors of the new critical idiom are directing their attention to the works themselves, to their structural properties and the ways that their relational arrangement into patterns can create meaning(s). They pose the question not so much of what the text means (for this may be variable and plural) as how it means, a question which can only be answered by considering the novel as dynamic process rather than static product—"literature as system," as Claudio Guillén would have it.[20] John Rutherford's programmatic statement in the introduction to his summary guide to *La Regenta* is illustrative:

> I shall concentrate on the text itself, leaving aside questions of its external relationships (with the society of its time, with the national literary traditions to which it belongs, with its literary, philosophical and ideological sources, with the life, intentions and other works of its author) . . . My approach will, therefore, be analytical and non-historical; I shall try to indicate how *La Regenta*, as an organized system, communicates its meanings to its readers, who, to read and understand it, do not need to be aware of the particular causes or circumstances of its writing.[21]

This is certainly not to imply that contextual readings of Spanish realist fiction have been banished by purely textual readings, or by hollowly formalist ones into which they may degenerate. Actually, the former continue to abound, especially in the feminist perspectives brought to bear in the work of Charnon-Deutsch, Blanco, Jagoe, and Aldaraca and the Marxist-oriented inquiries of Goldman, Sinnigen, Blanco Aguinaga, Rodríguez Puértolas, and Fuentes. Yet even those who approach the production of the Spanish realists from a more traditional historicist (or, now, "new historicist") perspective, attuned to issues of gender and/or class, are alert to the fact that the nineteenth-century novel is almost never an internally consistent ideological vehicle. Often, they point to dislocations, slippages, and contradictions at precisely the level of structure and language as proof of the ways in which the ruling ideologies of texts, their authors, and society at large may be involved in a high-stakes game of concealment and self-betrayal.

The tendency to contextualize, to pledge one's allegiance to a historically specific narrative in recounting the genesis and development of realist fiction, also seems rather more acute in Spanish critics as opposed to so many Hispanists (Spaniards included) trained and/or working currently in the Anglo-American university system. Lacking an autochthonous reservoir of narrative poetics upon which to draw, and, until recently, not always receptive to imported theory that proved incompatible with the canonized exegetical methods of the critical elite in early postwar Spain (Menéndez Pidal, Dámaso Alonso, Carlos Bousoño, Amado Alonso, Joaquín Casalduero, et al.), one segment of literary scholarship in Spain continues to approach the study of the nineteenth-century novel relying upon "a renewed historicism which combines circumstances of the period and the biographical aspect with stylistic observations."[22] One can sympathize with the discomfort provoked by the specter of relativism as raised by contemporary criticism and which the reliance upon traditional historicism is designed to assuage. Nonetheless, the insistence upon viewing a realist novel as a closed, self-contained "work" in contradistinction to Barthes's open and plural "text" has the potential to impoverish substantially the critical dialogue rather than expand its parameters.

Consider, for instance, the following assertion made by Francisco Caudet in the introduction to his edition of *Fortunata y Jacinta*: "The dialectical relationship of the writer to the sociohistorical referent, which the realist artist has deliberately turned into the raw material for his work, makes defending the realist text as something gratuitous and fully autonomous a distorted dispute."[23] While such a statement appears at first glance to expound a perfectly commonsensical vision of the realist novel generated as an imaginative response to experiences and circumstances in the writer's milieu, it invokes some very serious corollaries. Caudet's and other like declarations in effect posit three tasks incumbent upon the critic. First, to accept that there exists a single master trope or interpretation that holds the key to the novel's meaning: in this case, an unvarying, one-to-one relationship between the novel and the real world. Next, to assume that, given a sufficient quantity of historical information, this meaning can be laid bare. And, finally, to agree to eventual professional retraining, since the achievement of the arch-exegesis must logically arrest both the need for future commentary and one's further services as critic.

Nonetheless, the awareness that the movement of reading and interpretation must be centrifugal rather than centripetal, departing from the foregrounded text in itself and only later annexing the broader range of critical preoccupations (historical, social, or ethical) that characterize the sphere of the extratextual, informs some of the best criticism being written today on the nineteenth century. As one possible example among many, most previous studies of Galdós's *Miau*, to quote Eamonn Rodgers, have relied on perspectives "much more appropriate to moral choices in real life than to the elucidation of literary texts."[24] The story of an unemployed bureaucrat's unrelenting solitude, both in the workplace and at home with his family, has elicited abundant commentary over the years on the possible meaning of his eventual suicide. As a result of the sociothematic nature of this emphasis, however, replete with discussions of the phenomena of *empleomanía* and *cesantía* as provoked by Spain's turbulent politics, the examination of the novel as an operative system of literary discourse is relegated to the critical periphery. By redefining the "moral pressure" that inhabits this novel as really "the need for meaning" in the face of verbal dialectics that can assure no certainty regarding reality, Noël Valis attempts a reversal of this priority of content over form and context over text. In putting aside such nonliterary debates as whether or not Ramón Villaamil is meted out justice by his society, Valis can instead refocus the discussion on the protagonist's frustrated search for absolute and determinate meaning and the novel's own manner of straddling the line between sense and nonsense, "the border between meaning and non-meaning, in the uncertain and fragile zone of *miau*" (427), never losing sight of the fact that the text's existence as a specifically literary artifact must command primacy over our attention.

These, then, could be considered the current program: the return to the text, the discovery of textuality. But which precisely are the texts being read? Curiously, if we discount Francoist readings of nineteenth-century fiction as a lamentable literary-historical parenthesis that has now been closed off, the current canon—understood as encompassing those books which consistently turn up as the subject of college course syllabi, symposia, articles and reviews in scholarly journals—looks in some ways remarkably similar to the canon proposed at the turn of the century.

Presumably, canons may be modified in one of two basic ways, either through the wholesale inclusion or exclusion of particular writers, or through adjustment and fine-tuning of the list of canonized titles (some previously sanctioned works demoted, others newly valued or revalued and duly added) by writers whose place in the literary establishment remains secure. Isolated examples of both have indeed modified the shape of the Spanish novel canon. The one truly meteoric revision that has occurred in the last few decades is the unqualified admission of Clarín, on the basis of his two novels and several volumes of short fiction, to the pantheon of great Spanish realists. This development stands in direct contrast to earlier evaluations, including Menéndez y Pelayo's, that accorded singular weight only to Alas's critical and philosophical thought. It is also true that certain previously staple works are generating proportionately less interest while others have become objects of more intense inquiry. Studies of naturalism in *Los pazos de Ulloa*, for example, have given way to explorations of decadentism, aesthetic consciousness, and the voice of the feminine, especially in Pardo Bazán's later novels *La quimera* and *La sirena negra*. The *Episodios Nacionales* are no longer dismissed as simply hack writing in the tradition of the serials novel. Similarly, some of Galdós's *Novelas contemporáneas* traditionally held in lesser esteem (*El doctor Centeno, La incógnita, Realidad, Tristana*) are now being more judiciously scrutinized. Are they indeed lesser works, as has sometimes been maintained, or are they instead texts that violate the principles of unity or closure that have typically framed discussion of the realist novel and so disappointed the expectations of earlier generations of critics? It has already been seen in the preceding chapter that *El doctor Centeno* has been singled out for commentary on relatively few occasions, and only then to pick away at its supposed shortcomings. Another example is provided by *Tristana*, often considered to be brief, unnecessarily ambiguous, and inconclusive.[25] Both these novels are only now beginning to be considered in a different light. Until recently, *Tormento* similarly attracted little attention; if interest has revived in this novel, it is undoubtedly a result of criticism's fascination with metafiction, parody, and the novel's interrelationships with popular literature.

On the whole, though, more or less the same evaluative hierarchy continues to obtain. We still read *Fortunata y Jacinta* (or now, alternately, *La Regenta*) as the maximum representative of nineteenth-century narrative. We still prefer *La de Bringas* or *La desheredada* to *Doña Perfecta* or *Gloria*, the *Novelas contemporáneas* to the *Episodios*, Galdós and Clarín over Pereda, Pardo Bazán, and Valera, and all of these over Alarcón, Palacio Valdés, Coloma, Picón, Ortega Munilla, and so forth. In fact, the relative (in)frequency with which the present study refers to certain authors and titles reflects my own tacit recognition of a prevailing pecking order.

In the face of this relative stability of the canon, what indeed has changed dramatically is the position of realist fiction vis-à-vis later developments in the novel. If these works no longer provide the canon or model for life, neither do they provide the canon for the novel, although they continue to be taught and studied for their historical importance as Ur-forms of the genre, now superseded. Put another way, "the nineteenth [century] is not the fashionable favorite among younger Hispanists these days. Only Galdós and Clarín are the exceptions, and they have attracted veritable cults. For the rest, when there is a choice between Gil y Zárate and Borges, the choice is clear."[26] The reason for that choice seems equally clear, and appears to rest on the inevitability of our reading through the screen of literary modernity, with its attendant rejection of the claims staked out by the realist novel as both naïve and deceptive, unrealizable and undesirable.

Whether or not one accepts as conclusive (or even convincing) recent reports regarding the death of realism, no discussion of the current position of the nineteenth-century novel is complete without taking into account the degraded status of realism in contemporary theoretical debates. Earlier definitions were based upon formalist criteria (realism as encompassing a specific series of techniques: omniscience and impartiality; identifiable formal patterning; fidelity to social, historical, psychological, and linguistic detail) or ontological ones (realism as a means of conveying knowledge regarding human experience of a predominantly social and historical nature through its intricate depiction of man- and woman-in-the-world). Grounding both these definitions was the assumption of an imperturbable correspondence between the lived world and its linguistic simulacrum in the novel, a correspondence which has been shrugged off in the post-Saussurean universe of signifiers irremediably sundered from signifieds and meanings generated by difference (that is to say, deferral or absence) rather than presence. More recent forays into the subject have accordingly redefined realism as a kind of rhetorical ploy whose intended function is notably pragmatic; and this function, seen as authoritarian and paternalistic, has engendered objections on aesthetic, ideological, and philosophical grounds. In what amounts to a major turnaround, realism is no longer recognized as a baring of previously hidden or ignored social realities but instead as a stratagem that prolongs their occultation and hence must be demystified and unmasked. Where once the realist author was a reliable cicerone, leading the reader into previously uncharted regions of social experience, now he is himself a tourist, a voyeur.

Barthes pinpointed that element of the realist endeavor most vulnerable to attack when he charged that realism as a literary mode attempts to naturalize and make transparent something which is in fact arbitrary and conventional. Realism is imposed upon texts by their authors; it does not stem from nature itself:

> The realist mode of writing, is a combination of the formal signs of Literature (preterite, indirect speech, the rhythm of written language) and of the no less formal signs of realism (incongruous snippets of popular speech, strong language or dialect words, etc.), so that no mode of writing was more artificial than that which set out to give

the most accurate description of Nature . . . The writing of Realism is far from being neutral, it is on the contrary loaded with the most spectacular signs of fabrication.[27]

Others have, like Kermode, chided the nostalgia for a "secretarial realism" that propounds "an anachronistic myth of common understanding and shared universes of meaning."[28] Even assuming that such a correspondence theory of realism based on consensually established values were acceptable, the very notion of a secretarial aesthetic would limit an artist's creativity by implying that the best a writer can aspire to is the office of copyist, like Flaubert's inane pair Bouvard and Pécuchet or Alas's pathetic Bonifacio Reyes.[29] As an aesthetic that endeavors to transcribe objective reality with a minimum of stylistic interference, realism "exalts Life and diminishes Art, exalts things and diminishes words"[30]—in effect, an art of the anti-artful that would become indistinguishable from documentary (as indeed was naturalism's supposed goal) and ultimately would write itself out of existence as literature. Respect for the laws of realistic probability shrinks the scope available to the artist's imagination. Concomitantly, studies of realist fiction generally pay greatest attention to the aspects of *dispositio* and *elocutio* while routinely ignoring that of *inventio*.[31] But as a corollary to linguists' and philosophers' rejection of the correspondence theory, the project of realist art holding a mirror up to nature also becomes illusory, a fiction in itself. Such a project is yet another manifestation of the ocular/specular metaphor that has been foundational to Western culture ever since the advent of the mind-body problem in philosophy.[32] The praxis of realism, in which the implied author engages with an objective, preexisting reality that is separate and independent from the observer, in fact presupposes a metaphysics of dualism. This sharply defined subject/object dichotomy, however, is invalidated by the fact that reality can never be known or communicated independently of language, a system which inheres in the individual as observing self. It is at this point that the dualist proposition breaks down, since logically speaking, "one cannot use a part of one's present theory to underwrite the rest of it," as Richard Rorty notes (294). The post-Kantian writing or speaking subject is therefore inevitably confined to an aesthetic of subjectivity.

The unmasking of the conventions and rhetoric of realism is equally central to Marxist considerations of the problem. As dictated by the logic of the Marxist position, the framing of realist discourse is no mere benign drudgery, no formulaic schoolboy exercise in transcription carried out by an uninspired lot of writers. Rather, it indulges a willful exercise of power that comes to be obscured as such by the very familiarity of the techniques that are employed and the day-to-day reality that is thematized. Terry Eagleton admonishes those critics (Lukács included) who, like the nineteenth-century realists they exalt, are responsible for "having made a fetish of one historically relative literary form,"[33] and this gravamen is reiterated no less forcefully by Fredric Jameson:

> This is the situation in which the great realistic novelists, "shepherds of Being" of a very special ideological type, are forced, by their own narrative and aesthetic vested interests, into a repudiation of revolutionary change and an ultimate stake in the status quo. Their evocation of the solidity of their object of representation—the social world grasped as an organic, natural, Burkean permanence—is necessarily threatened by any suggestion that that world is not natural, but historical, and subject to radical change.[34]

Barthes's dismay over the masquerading of contrived signs as natural ones finds its parallel in Marxist discourse on ideology, a "complex structure of social perception which ensures that the situation in which one social class has power over the others is either seen by most members of the society as 'natural', or not seen at all."[35] In brief, realist writers dupe themselves and their readers. On balance, the conclusion seems to be that since literary realism represents an aesthetic and ideological cul-de-sac, the faster novelists freed themselves from its strictures the better.

The upshot has been that, as regards the exegetical activities of Hispanists working in the field of nineteenth-century studies, the academy has seen the balance of pressure shift from canonical to hermeneutical restrictions, as Kermode distinguishes between them.[36] That is to say, since the actual canon has not been substantially altered even as realism's aims have been disallowed as ingenuous, erroneous, or repressive, these same works must now be read according to sharply differing criteria if critics are to preserve the text's viability as something that continues to speak to the late twentieth-century reader. Accordingly, under the influence of structuralist and deconstructive strategies, these novels are being probed to expose disturbing marginal excrescences, unwitting inversions in the declared logic of the text, self-reflexive properties of the narrative and its language, and metafictional devices that undermine the epistemological certainty that realism sought to project. In short, much of nineteenth-century fiction is being considered, proleptically, in the context of early twentieth-century texts and the latter's rupture with previously sanctified forms and themes of the novel, with highest praise (and the greatest number of articles, papers, and dissertations) going to those novels which seem to exceed or diverge from traditional norms and forms of the novel and presage the advent of literary modernity. This is scarcely a phenomenon unique to the critical community of Hispanism. Looking within the ranks of French authors, Walter Benjamin and Jonathan Culler respectively single out Baudelaire and Flaubert as writers who incarnate the contradiction between traditional modes of art and the radical break that modernism represented.[37] In Spanish literature, Clarín and Galdós are the authors who, while writing well within the parameters of nineteenth-century bourgeois fiction, are most frequently cited—and with good reason—as harbingers of the course of the novel in the following century.

The change of critical venue is most readily apparent in recent readings of *La Regenta* and Galdós's *Episodios*. The former work, previously valued as a faithful re-creation of fin-de-siècle provincial society descended from *costumbrismo* and naturalism, is now described as a novel turned in upon itself in meditation upon its own creation as narrative: what Alarcos Llorach, looking at the circularity of its structure, called a "work that chases its own tail."[38] Recent studies have focused on such features of the text as entropy, spatiality, indeterminacy, the presence of *écriture*, and the degradation of language and culture as seen in the proliferation of self-doubting "signs, and lettered and bookish forms" in Clarín's massive work.[39] In one suggestive reading of Alas's tale of adultery, hypocrisy, and disillusionment, the slow and sometimes halting progress of the novel is explained by the narrator's obsessive need to go back over nearly every episode of the plot he narrates, with less concern for the story itself than for the manner of its verbal presentation as text. Sentences, paragraphs, and entire sequences are in effect placed *sous rature* and subsequently reedited or rewritten. In this hypertrophic reflexivity of the novel's discourse, Clarín is seen as a "traveling companion of the modernists."[40]

A similar critical telos may also be discerned, albeit as a minority voice, in the ongoing dialogue surrounding Galdós's *Episodios Nacionales*. The latter, usually considered a vast explanatory frieze of national history, is in the work of certain recent critics taken as proof of just the opposite: the impossibility of all historiography's claims to truth, knowledge, and absolute origins, its indistinguishability from fiction.[41] Those same seismic tremors that have been detected in Clarín's work—"The ground is trembling beneath the realistic foundations of *La Regenta*"[42]—can in fact be felt rumbling through many a Spanish novel after 1881.

On the one hand, these new readings have had the salutary effect of forcing a reevaluation of the concept of literary realism. Realism can no longer be seen as a transparent and uncomplicated reproduction of the referent and instead must be redefined as a considerably more opaque strategy that harbors the seeds of its own impending negation. Examples of this can be found in numerous nineteenth-century texts that purportedly signify the external world yet only end up signifying themselves as literary entities. This, after all, is the irony that reverberates in Máximo Manso's opening words to the novel he narrates: "I do not exist . . . I swear and forswear that I do not exist." Moreover, the questioning of realism reflects a more general dissatisfaction with the inadequacies of nomenclature and periodization as they apply to certain exceptional or transitional novels, *La Regenta* among them, that overflow the boundaries and categories allotted to them. What exactly does the term *realism* stretch to include? Can classically "readerly" texts be lumped together with more experimental ones without destroying the descriptive value of the word?

On the other hand, by virtue of reading "back to the future," the inadvertent winner—the deliberately designated winner, as Gerald Graff glumly maintains in his analysis of the politics of antirealism—is still not nineteenth-century narrative, but rather the narrative of modernity and even postmodernism extending from Azorín, Valle-Inclán, Gómez de la Serna, and Miró to Goytisolo, Benet, and Torrente Ballester.[43] In *El misterio de la cripta embrujada*, Eduardo Mendoza's spoof of detective fiction that doubles as a squint-eyed critique of Spain during the transition to democracy, the narrator defines the raison d'être of the entire period 1939–1975 with the epithet "the pre-postFranco era."[44] It is tempting to relabel analogously the nineteenth-century novel as the era of "pre-(post)modernism." Is this an example of the Derridean claim that texts are neither original nor originary but instead always already snared in a chain of continually proliferating signifiers, part of an intertextual weave that nullifies historicization? Or, to the contrary, is it an example of a radical disfigurement of history that, in fostering a rapprochement between realist texts and modernist ones, ignores the distance that the writers themselves of the period 1898–1936 consciously sought to establish and reductively locates realism's value in its precocious rehearsal of modernism? As must be readily apparent, along with so many other aspects of contemporary theory that have become part of their working vocabulary, Hispanists have also absorbed some of the unresolved contradictions generated by the individual critical positions they hold or by their combined usage under the umbrella of a new critical pluralism.

Two such inconsistencies surface repeatedly in recent treatments of nineteenth-century Spanish fiction. For one, despite the repudiation of a criticism as practiced either during the Bourbon Restoration or subsequently by the Franco regime, according to which a literary work was judged on the basis of its promotion of political allegiances or exemplary Christian conduct, it is difficult to see how such an approach differs substantially from the moral spin that has been put on the current binary opposition of realism versus modernism. In the hierarchical relationship integrated by these two concepts, modernism has become the privileged term, realism the derelict one, characterized in a language of strong moral connotation as deceptive, imitative, or oppressive. Criticism of the novel in late eighteenth- and early nineteenth-century Spain was effectively born under the sign of a moral imperative; reading of secular literature, including the ever-suspect novel, was permissible insofar as it instilled love of virtue and country and obedience to God and church. Almost two centuries later, and proceeding from the opposite end of the political spectrum, criticism still finds itself enmeshed in ideologico-moral judgments. This is not to imply that such judgments have no place in the study of literature. Once the critic has moved beyond the level of descriptive empiricism ("*Pepita Jiménez* was originally published in four installments" or "Pereda's novels feature rural environments more frequently than urban ones"), these may in fact be the most frequent kinds of judgments he or she may make. If there is no denying the existence of a politics of nineteenth-century representation, neither is it possible to ignore that there also exists a politics of discussing and representing representation.

It is very much a part of the modern critical enterprise to strip the polite veneer off entire systems of thought, to point out the socially significant differences they exploit, to show how they attempt to pass themselves off as natural and normative discourses when in fact they are constructions of a most unnatural order. This is, in fact, the thrust of the redefinition of realism as a mode of writing that employs signs to speak of other signs, rather than of some transparent and easily accessible world of essences. It is, however, important to recognize that these critiques may also inadvertently set themselves up as equally exclusive and univocal—rather a case of the pot calling the kettle black (or the contemporary critic calling the realist writer a covert ideologue), since current readers are no less caught in a web of local interests and ideologies than their predecessors. If there is no *hors-texte*, neither can there be any position outside of ideology, or history. Subjects are always situated within the range of social practices and systems of representation governing the societies in which they live, and necessarily speak from a view of self and society generated within those parameters. The following observation might profitably be applied by analysts of the phenomenon of nineteenth-century Spanish realism: "The problem with specific ideological discourses and practices is not *that* they are ideological, but exactly *how*, and to exactly *which* 'social conditions of existence,' they 'form, transform and equip' men and women to respond."[45]

In another troublesome vein, the attempt to jettison historical ballast from the exegetical process has met with only partial success. Those critics who read back to the future, claiming to be unfettered by a potentially distorting vision of the diachronic organization of literature, are themselves trafficking in a notion circumscribed by a clearly historical premise: that of progressivism and evolution, the old nineteenth-century notion that institutions are evolving toward an ultimate perfectibility of form. Here that premise is expressed in the idea that realism ultimately culminates in the more excellent novel that represents the triumph of modernism.

Equally complex is the problem of how to explain the relative constancy of Hispanism's nineteenth-century great books list, when, given the current critical climate, there has been perhaps every encouragement to question the validity of canons in general. Despite noteworthy critical and philosophical efforts, it has proved virtually impossible to establish a more resolute definition of literature than the following: particular writings that are highly valued by certain members of a society. Logically, the exclusivity postulated by a canon suffers when it is admitted that there are no intrinsically distinctive features that mark literature, or that Valera's limpid novelistic discourse may be subjected to the same kinds of analysis as a billboard ad for Tío Pepe sherry. As Eagleton explains: "This, indeed, is the embarrassment of literary criticism, that it defines for itself a special object, literature, while existing as a set of discursive techniques which have no reason to stop short at that object at all."[46] This is not so very different from Stanley Fish's statement that "literature is language . . . but it is language around which we have drawn a frame, a frame that indicates a decision to regard with a particular self-consciousness the resources language has always possessed."[47]

Moreover, by definition any discussion of the concept of canon necessarily entails the delimitation of a certain class of privileged works that
have received the imprimatur of the academy, to the exclusion of entire
sets of competing or complementary texts. Canon versus non-canon implies a breach between mainstream and margin, high and low culture, one
group of aesthetic responses deemed acceptable and even ennobling and
another group deemed impoverished or threatening. Because, however, of
the nature of the presuppositions upon which such distinctions are made,
the notion of a literary canon is often no less suspect than that of realism,
with which it shares many features.

One of the axioms regarding the nature of the realist novel is its undis-
puted representative value of the society and types it depicts. Furthermore,
while it provides a lasting record of the society it chronicles, the very
necessity of the act of such recording testifies to the immense mutability
of social forms, always poised—but especially so in the nineteenth century—on the brink of change. Similarly, a literary canon is assumed to be
representative (in this case, of a range of literary forms and innovations,
and of received human values reflected in them), and it also exemplifies
the dialectic of permanence and (r)evolution. Canons, paradoxically, lead
to the preservation of order by offering models of tradition to emulate,
but at the same time, owing to the evolutionary nature of art, style, and
genre, they function as a record of the production of cultural change. More
pointedly, even staunch defenders who eloquently argue for the humanist
concept of the canon as "the fantasy of a best self to be excavated from the
past" and see the canon as a source of both artistic models and human wisdom must admit that, like realism, "canons are not natural facts" but rather
institutional constructs which can as easily conceal exercises of power and
the "pursuit of self-representations that satisfy narcissistic demands" as
embody norms of taste and conduct.[48] Like the vision of society displayed
by the novels of realism, the values and standards promoted by canons are
presented as immutable yet are often highly contingent.

Finally, the theoretical division between canon and non-canon was
already established and then undermined in practice by nineteenth-
century authors. The latter distinguished between serious novels (which
qualified as great art) and *folletines* and penny dreadfuls (which did not),
yet it is clear that in Spain there was a good deal of crossover from the
universally lambasted serial novel to the so-called "high" novel. Extensive
work done on the structure and sociology of the serial novel and the re-

ception of popular literature by Ferreras, Romero Tobar, Botrel, Marco, Ynduráin, and Andreu has helped clarify the numerous instances in which the forms, themes, and techniques of non-canonical literature were profitably incorporated into the novels of Galdós and his contemporaries as a way to attract a larger readership while also examining and even subtly parodying the conventions that structure the novel.[49] At the same time, a modest increase in the number of modern annotated editions of nineteenth-century works brought out by publishing houses such as Cátedra, Castalia, and many of the regional presses has again made available certain of these minor novels (for instance, Coloma's *Pequeñeces*, Picón's *Dulce y sabrosa* and *La hijastra del amor*, Ortega Munilla's *Cleopatra Pérez*) as well as magnified the visibility of oft-neglected novels by more prominent authors (Valera's *Doña Luz* and *Genio y figura*, Pereda's *La puchera*, Pardo Bazan's *La tribuna*, etc.). Yet these novels are rarely found in classrooms and scholarly journals.

Some critics have advocated enlarging the canon with *folletines* and other similarly marginal texts, although they then face the nagging question of how to reconcile the image of the nineteenth-century novel as popularly influenced with the competing image of this same novel as an anticipation of modernist, that is, elitist or minoritarian art forms. Others have decried the refusal to grant equal and serious consideration to Spanish women novelists, whose toehold on claims to literary excellence and canonicity has traditionally been far more precarious. Most Hispanists, however, pay scant lip service to the writings of Picón, Alarcón, Fernán Caballero, Gertrudis Gómez de Avellaneda, and many others, regardless of their increased accessibility, leaving unchallenged the canon as inherited from previous generations of readers and literary historians.[50] This unchanging reproduction of the canon, we have seen, can scarcely pretend to be based upon a commonality of aesthetic value judgments among critics of the past several decades. Instead, the repeated omission or inclusion in the canon of any particular novel by Galdós, Pardo Bazán, or their contemporaries must be understood as arising from a tangled confluence of discrete circumstances, "the product neither of the objectively (in the Marxist sense) conspiratorial force of establishment institutions nor of the continuous appreciation of the timeless virtues of a fixed object by succeeding generations of isolated readers, but, rather, of a series of continuous interactions among a variably constituted object, emergent conditions, and mechanisms of cultural selection and transmission."[51] In the continuing exploration of the intricate cultural dynamics governing the status of any given work relative to the nineteenth-century canon, we find a prime example of the textual as it comes back full circle to the contextual.

These constitute only a few of the paradoxes surrounding current evaluations of the Spanish nineteenth-century novel. In an ironic twist, readers are now being told by the media in certain quarters that they are tired of postmodernism, experimental prose and film, what is on occasion referred to as the "literature of exhaustion."[52] And so Ricardo Gullón, writing on *Cien años de soledad*, comments that "the difference between him [García Márquez] and certain contemporary novelists is based upon the fact that the latter lose themselves in the labyrinth of techniques, and he does not."[53] In comparing Macondo to the Compsons's Yoknapatawpha, Goriot's Paris, or Fortunata's Madrid, he calls them all "inventions reserved for those who, like García Márquez, succeed in reviving the very ancient and almost forgotten art of storytelling and practice it with the complex simplicity that this art demands," offering a noble defense of the nineteenth-century novel as archetypal example of this class of fiction.

In fact, the nineteenth-century novel is not infrequently identified by the distinctly positive connotations attendant upon the tag of "classical" form of narrative. Classical realist novels embody those features of storytelling that encourage the public to read for the plot, to identify with the characters and situations portrayed, to seek out in the written word the imaginative expression of their own private desires; they provide the guilty pleasures of the good read furtively enjoyed by Aleixandre and Lorca as they discovered their mutual and unabashed enthusiasm for the then-unfashionable Galdós: "We discovered we were both impassioned admirers of Galdós (in that epoch!) and friends by personal experience and without fail, since we were kids, of Jacinta, la Peri, Orozco, and León de Albrit."[54] Nonetheless, in another indication of the postmodern bias within which they move, critics heap their plaudits on twentieth-century authors who manage to rework, transform, or otherwise reinvent the underpinnings of the realist novel, yet simultaneously denigrate the original nineteenth-century model by which these successive adaptations are judged. And so García Márquez is congratulated for his revival of storytelling "in an almost classical mode," while the traditional and originary narratives of Alarcón go unread: "Those who assert that Pedro Antonio de Alarcón is the best narrator of the nineteenth century surpass in number those who assiduously frequent his texts."[55] There is little cause for surprise here. Did not Borges already apprise us that Pierre Menard's achievement in writing the *Quijote* surpassed that of Cervantes?

Yet even as this latest version of the myth of the golden age nourishes the drive to return to an earlier, more communal sort of narrative, others deride those twentieth-century heirs of realism who "continue to write frantically, headless chickens unaware of the decapitating axe."[56] Nostalgia for the great age of classical realist narrative notwithstanding, neither writers, readers, nor critics can go home again and duplicate under identical conditions the nineteenth-century experience of composing and encountering realist novels. Both the acts of writing and reading are irreversible. Fixed in time and place, they can scarcely be performed within a climate of cultural neutrality; so to impugn readers who don the lenses of (post)modernity when interpreting the text placed before them is a largely ineffectual gesture. But further inquiry directed to specific nineteenth-century Hispanic texts, canonical or not, can contribute to refining and revising the master narrative constructed to date on what Andreas Huyssen has dubbed "the great divide" separating the age of realism from the age of modernity and beyond.[57] Critics are inevitably situated on one or the other side of that great divide, that framing borderline. In perusing these recent accounts of theirs of the Spanish nineteenth-century novel Hispanists can, if they choose, read their own critical autobiography as well. Having seen where and how the critical frame has been imposed upon the texts of Spanish realism, they may be better able, or better disposed, to reframe the debate in the future along other lines.

Conclusion

Although it is certainly true, as Henry James observed, that "really, universally, relations stop nowhere," the construction of frames offers a means of imposing order and structure upon a world that is in principle unbounded. The frame isolates and distinguishes a figure from its ground, thereby lending definition to both. Studies written by scholars working in disciplines as diverse as semiotics and narratology, the fine arts, sociology, cognitive psychology, linguistics, and artificial intelligence all converge in their explicitation of the role of the frame; their work tells us that frames organize the world in such a way as to make it meaningful.

There is nothing intrinsically natural about frames, despite the fact that we rely upon them so continuously as to scarcely be aware that we do so at all. Frames, like conventions generally, are made, not found, for even the perceptual Gestalten behind them may be imbued with cultural assumptions and the regulating force of social institutions. When we expect that a painting will be executed on a squared-off picture plane, or anticipate that a nineteenth-century novel will conclude on a strong note of formal closure and thematic resolution, or presume that the arguments in a work of scholarship should be flanked, as by bookends, by a preface and a conclusion, we are in fact applying a knowledge of frames that has its roots deep in the presuppositions and values of our culture. Given this fact, it becomes clear that the way we manipulate frames, modifying or even canceling them when they prove insufficient, is indicative of the modes of problem solving that are authorized by a given society.

One such mode of problem solving can be found in nineteenth-century fiction. Realism endeavors to present an encyclopedic portrait of modern society in all its detailed splendor. This being an impossible task, it must content itself with a partial view, cut at random from the field of observation. In this manner, realism establishes itself as a system that operates upon the principle of synecdoche: the framed part stands for the all-inclusive but unrepresentable totality. Galdós and his fellow Spanish authors, in describing their works as *cuadros de costumbres contemporáneas*, that is, pictures of contemporary social customs, clearly allude to the framed character of the novelistic miniatures in which they reproduce the workings of their society.

Yet the visual and narrative framing operations that are indispensable features of realist writing reflect a selection and reproduction of data that occur only secondhand. Before putting pen to paper, the author must first perform an act of imaginative or symbolic framing, and this is what realism imitates, not reality itself. Two important qualifications regarding realism hinge upon this redefinition of mimesis as second-order framing, the copy of another copy. First, the recognition of this two-tiered frame structure wrests authority from realism's claim to represent the social universe in perfectly transparent fashion. A form of representation that had been considered self-evident and genuine can be seen to be arbitrary and conventional, its conventionality supported and fostered by an ideological position congenial to the middle class that is both the subject and the object of realist fiction. Second, since the frames applied by realist authors actively shape their contents rather than passively support them, realist writing does not simply transcribe reality; it configures it through language. What this means is that in spite of the constraints that govern realist discourse, nineteenth-century novelists exercise a higher degree of creativity than has generally been acknowledged.

Studies of realist fiction often imply that the acts of framing found in its texts are for the most part unremarkable, just as they imply that the frames themselves are unproblematic in their structural integrity and completion. Hence it is revealing to note that the vast novelistic production of Benito Pérez Galdós is distinguished by its attention to frame devices in all their many forms: narrative overtures and endings, intertexts and embedded stories, genres. This heightened attention does not destroy the frame outright—this is the accomplishment, rather, of the modernist text—but instead exposes its artifice while still allowing it to function as frame. By thwarting closure, reproducing themselves in nesting sequences, or circumscribing an empty field, Galdós's frames seriously question many of the received conventions of realist fiction. As the examples of *La de Bringas*, *Fortunata y Jacinta*, *Torquemada en la hoguera*, and *Tormento* illustrate, such frame shifts are part and parcel of Galdós's fiction; they can be found as well in the doubled pseudoclosure of *La desheredada*, the dissolution of barriers between real life and theater in *La corte de Carlos IV*, and the epistolary brackets that surround the text of *La familia de León Roch*. They highlight the contingency of the entire process of frame construction and the easily displaced centrality of the objects that are framed as social or cultural knowledge. Galdós's framing strategies also demand a special agility on the part of his readers. Time and again, as the narrative frame is repositioned, they are forced to reexamine their expectations regarding not just narrative but society and its truths as well.

Recent critical studies of realism, many of them written under the influence of structuralist and poststructuralist theories of textuality, demonstrate another mode of problem solving through framing. In this case, new frames of reference are applied to the key texts of nineteenth-century realism so that neither their canonical status nor their appeal to contemporary exegetical practices are jeopardized. This relocation of the reading frame, the better to align it with the position of postmodern theory, is often a productive tool that accommodates an unanticipated, more nuanced understanding of familiar texts, as the exercise in rereading *El doctor Centeno* confirms. Yet it may suggest other problems, the most extreme ones being the peremptory dismissal of realist narrative overall, or the situating of the frame so as to exclude Galdós altogether from the discourse on European realism. This is an infelicitous critical move at best, for Galdós's fiction is as vital to the evaluation of the compass of the realist aesthetic as the frame is to the discernment of the stature of art, ornamentation, and their relationship to social practice in the nineteenth century.

Appendix:

The Political

Intertext in

Torquemada

en la

hoguera

What follows is a comparison of passages from Galdós's novel that cite Bailón's written and spoken words with corresponding passages from J. Landa's translation of Lamennais, *Palabras de un creyente (La regeneración de la humanidad* (Barcelona: Hijos de Domenech, 1868). The fragments from *Torquemada* are cited by volume and page number from the *Obras completas* of Galdós. The selections from Landa's translation are cited by chapter and page number. Readers may also wish to consult the original French language edition: Hugues-Félicité Robert de Lamennais, *Paroles d'un croyant*, ed. Louis LeGuillou (Paris: Flammarion, 1973).

Pérez Galdos *Torquemada en la hoguera*	Lamennais *Paroles d'un croyant*
Gloria a Dios en las alturas y paz. . . . (5: 911)	Gloria a Dios en las alturas, y paz en la tierra a los hombres de buena voluntad. (I, 29)
Los tiempos se acercan, tiempos de redención, en que el Hijo del Hombre será dueño de la tierra. (5: 911)	El tiempo de vuestra regeneración no está lejos; preparad vuestras almas, porque ya se acerca el día más feliz para la humanidad.
	El Cristo, enclavado en la cruz por vuestras culpas, ha prometido redimiros. (Introducción, "A los hijos del pueblo," 27)
	Estad preparados, porque los tiempos se acercan. (XXIV, 88)

El Verbo depositó hace dieciocho siglos la semilla divina. En noche tenebrosa fructificó. He aquí las flores. (5: 911)

Hace diez y ocho siglos, el Verbo depositó en tierra la semilla divina, que fecundó el Espíritu Santo. Los hombres la han visto florecer, y han comido de sus frutos, frutos del árbol de la vida, plantado nuevamente en esta su pobre morada . . . Pero después la tierra se ha tornado tenebrosa y fría. (I, 29–30)

¿Cómo se llaman? Los derechos del pueblo. (5: 911)

Si hay algo de grandioso en la tierra, es el ver a un pueblo firme y resuelto, que camina bajo la égida de Dios a la conquista de sus derechos . . . (XXXVIII, 130)

He aquí el tirano. ¡Maldito sea! (5: 911)

Por eso han sido maldecidos los tiranos y los magnates de la tierra, porque no han amado a sus hermanos y los trataron siempre como a enemigos. (IV, 35)

Aplicad el oído y decidme de dónde viene ese rumor vago, confuso, extraño. (5: 911)

Aplicad el oído, y decidme de qué procede ese rumor vago, confuso, extraño, que por todas partes se escucha. (II, 30)

Posad la mano en la tierra y decidme por qué se ha estremecido. (5: 911)

Posad la mano en la tierra, y decidme por qué se ha estremecido. (II, 30)

Es el Hijo del Hombre que avanza, decidido a recobrar su primogenitura. (5: 911)

Hijo del hombre, ¿qué ves?
—Veo a Satanás huyendo, y al Cristo, rodeado de sus ángeles, que viene a reinar en la tierra. (II, 33)

¿Por qué palidece la faz del tirano? ¡Ah! El tirano ve que sus horas son contadas . . . (5: 911)

Veo a los pueblos sublevarse, y a los reyes tornarse pálidos como el oro de sus diademas. ¡Guerra se han declarado entre ellos: guerra de exterminio! (II, 31)

Joven soldado, ¿adónde vas?
(5: 911)

—Joven soldado, ¿a dónde vas?
—Voy a pelear por Dios y los
altares de la patria.
—¡Benditas sean tus armas, joven
soldado!
—Joven soldado, ¿a dónde vas?
—Voy a pelear por la justicia, por
la causa santa de los pueblos y por
los sagrados derechos del hombre.
—¡Benditas sean tus armas, joven
soldado! (XXXVI, 123 ff.)

He aquí que el hombre vacila y se
confunde ante el gran problema.
¿Qué es el bien? ¿Qué es el mal?
Hijo mío, abre tus oídos a la
verdad y tus ojos a la luz. El bien
es amar a nuestros semejantes.
Amemos y sabremos lo que es el
bien; aborrezcamos y sabremos lo
que es el mal. Hagamos bien a los
que nos aborrecen, y las espinas se
nos volverán flores. Esto dijo el
Justo, esto digo yo . . . Sabiduría
de sabidurías, y ciencia de
ciencias. (5: 921)

El que tenga oídos, que escuche;
el que tenga ojos, ábralos y mire,
porque los tiempos se acercan.
(I, 29)

El amor reposa en el fondo de las
almas puras, como una gota de
rocío en el cáliz de una flor.
(XV, 68)

¡Decís que amáis a vuestros
hermanos . . . ¿Qué haríais, pues,
si los aborreciérais? Yo os digo que
el que, pudiendo, no socorre a su
hermano enfermo, es enemigo de
su hermano, y quien pudiendo no
da paz a su hermano hambriento,
es su asesino. (XV, 68–69)

—Valor, amigo mío, valor. En
estos casos se conocen las almas
fuertes. Acuérdese usted de aquel
gran Filósofo que expiró en una
cruz dejando consagrados los
principios de la Humanidad.
(5: 932)

Armaos de mucha paciencia y de
constante valor, porque no
lograréis vencer en un solo día.
(XXXVIII, 128)

. . . cuando al pie de la cruz en
que expiró el Justo hayáis jurado
morir unos por otros, entonces
brillará sobre vuestras cabezas el
sol glorioso de la Libertad.
(XX, 80)

Notes

List of Abbreviations

Editions of Galdós's Works

All references to the novels correspond to Benito Pérez Galdós's *Obras completas*, ed. Federico Carlos Sainz de Robles (Madrid: Aguilar, 1963–1968), 6 vols. References will be made parenthetically throughout the text, indicating the appropriate volume and page numbers. All translations are my own.

Periodicals

AGald	Anales Galdosianos
BHS	Bulletin of Hispanic Studies
CHA	Cuadernos Hispanoamericanos
CritI	Critical Inquiry
FMLS	Forum for Modern Language Studies
HR	Hispanic Review
IL	Ideologies and Literature
JMMLA	Journal of the Midwest Modern Language Association
KRQ	Kentucky Romance Quarterly
MLN	Modern Language Notes
MLR	Modern Language Review
NLH	New Literary History
PMLA	Publications of the Modern Language Association of America
PSA	Papeles de Son Armadans
PT	Poetics Today
RCEH	Revista Canadiense de Estudios Hispánicos
REH	Revista de Estudios Hispánicos
RHLF	Revue d'Histoire Littéraire de la France
RQ	Romance Quarterly
RR	Romanic Review
RSH	Revue des Sciences Humaines
YFS	Yale French Studies

Introduction

1 Linda Dittmar, "Fashioning and Re-fashioning: Framing Narratives in the Novel and Film," *Mosaic* 16.1–2 (1983): 195.

2 In fact, many of Galdós's texts disprove Franco Moretti's blanket statement regarding the immobility of both form and intent that supposedly inheres in realist fiction. Moretti claims that only in the nineteenth century does the novel start "behaving like a genre in the strong sense—reproducing itself with abundance, regularity, and without too many variations . . . indeed for multiplicity of forms or narrative experiments the nineteenth century is truly the nadir, the lowest point in the history of the novel. It is a monodic age, surrounded by two polyphonic ones, and it wouldn't be inaccurate, in this respect, to speak of 'the novel' for the nineteenth century only, and of 'novels', plural, in the other cases [the eighteenth and twentieth centuries]." In *Signs Taken for Wonders: Essays in the Sociology of Literary Forms*, trans. Susan Fischer, David Forgacs, and David Miller, rev. ed. (London: Verso, 1988), 263. When applied to so many examples of Galdós's fiction, Robert Alter's remarks on the supposed eclipse of the self-conscious novel in nineteenth-century narrative once again point up how limitedly current discussions of literary realism are framed. See *Partial Magic: The Novel as a Self-Conscious Genre* (Berkeley and Los Angeles: University of California Press, 1975), 84–137.

3 H. Verdaasdonk, "Conceptions of Literature as Frames," *Poetics* 11 (1982): 87.

4 For a rejoinder that advocates a more balanced approach, see Geoffrey Ribbans, "Social Document or Narrative Discourse? Some Comments on Recent Aspects of Galdós Criticism," in *Galdós' House of Fiction* (Oxford: Dolphin, 1991), 55–83.

5 See especially John W. Kronik, "Galdosian Reflections: Feijoo and the Fabrication of Fortunata," *MLN* 97 (1982): 272–310, reprinted in *Conflicting Realities: Four Readings of a Chapter by Pérez Galdós ("Fortunata y Jacinta," Part III, Chapter IV)*, ed. Peter B. Goldman (London: Tamesis, 1984), 39–72 and "*El amigo Manso* and the Game of Fictive Autonomy," *AGald* 12 (1977): 71–94; Germán Gullón, *El narrador en la novela del siglo XIX* (Madrid: Taurus, 1976), chapters 4–6, and studies such as "*Tristana*: literaturización y estructura novelesca," *HR* 45 (1977): 13–27; Diane F. Urey, *Galdós and the Irony of Language* (Cambridge: Cambridge University Press, 1982), and *The Novel Histories of Galdós* (Princeton: Princeton University Press, 1989); Akiko Tsuchiya, *Images of the Sign: Semiotic Consciousness in the Novels of Benito Pérez Galdós* (Columbia: University of Missouri Press, 1990).

6 Jurij Lotman, *The Structure of the Artistic Text*, trans. Ronald Vroon, Michigan Slavic Contributions 7 (Ann Arbor: University of Michigan Press, 1977), 95.

7 See Marvin Minsky, "A Framework for Representing Knowledge," in *The Psychology of Computer Vision*, ed. Patrick H. Winston (New York: McGraw-

Hill, 1975), 211–77. A greatly condensed version of this article is included under the same title in *Frame Conceptions and Text Understanding*, ed. Dieter Metzing (Berlin: Walter de Gruyter, 1980), 1–25. Other basic concepts of frame theory that I refer to in the following pages have been drawn from Terry Winograd, "Frame Representation and the Declarative/Procedural Controversy," in *Representing and Understanding: Studies in Cognitive Science*, ed. Daniel G. Bobrow and Allan Collins (New York: Academic Press, 1975), 185–210; Benjamin J. Kuipers, "A Frame for Frames: Representing Knowledge for Recognition," in Bobrow and Collins, 151–84; and R. C. Schank and R. P. Abelson, *Scripts, Plans, Goals, and Understandings* (Hillsdale, N.J.: Lawrence Erlbaum Associates, 1977).

8 Wolfgang Iser, *The Act of Reading: A Theory of Aesthetic Response* (Baltimore: Johns Hopkins University Press, 1978), 111. For further discussion of Iser's distinction between theme and horizon (a demarcational relationship between foreground and background) and of reading as the filling in of "structured blanks" (i.e., gaps in the frame), see parts 3 and 4, "Phenomenology of Reading" and "Interaction between Text and Reader," 107–231.

9 Erving Goffman, *Frame Analysis: An Essay on the Organization of Experience* (Cambridge: Harvard University Press, 1974), 8, 10–11.

10 Gregory Bateson, "A Theory of Play and Fantasy," in *Semiotics: An Introductory Anthology*, ed. Robert E. Innis (Bloomington: Indiana University Press, 1985), 139.

11 Susan Stewart, *Nonsense: Aspects of Intertextuality in Folklore and Literature* (Baltimore: Johns Hopkins University Press, 1978), 22, 122.

12 Mary Ann Caws, *Reading Frames in Modern Fiction* (Princeton: Princeton University Press, 1985), 4. See chapters 1–2 for a rapid review of the literature dealing with the subject of frames in the fields of aesthetics, psychology, and letters.

13 Meyer Schapiro, "On Some Problems in the Semiotics of Visual Art: Field and Vehicle in Image-Signs," *Semotica* 1.3 (1969): 223–42.

14 Boris Uspensky, *A Poetics of Composition: The Structure of the Artistic Text and Typology of Compositional Form*, trans. Valentina Zavarin and Susan Wittig (Berkeley and Los Angeles: University of California Press, 1973), 140.

15 Stewart, *Nonsense*, 24.

16 Jonathan Culler, *On Deconstruction* (Ithaca: Cornell University Press, 1982), 198–99. In a subsequent book, appropriately titled *Framing the Sign*, Culler takes up such questions as how literature comes to be bracketed by criticism and how certain critical discourses themselves have become institutionalized during the twentieth century.

17 The bibliography regarding these various debates is too immense to be reproduced here. For examples pertaining strictly to the question of genre delimitations, which will be discussed in chapter 4 on *Tormento*, see the overview in Paul Hernadi, "Order without Borders: Recent Genre Theory in the English-Speaking Countries," in *Theories of Literary Genre*, ed. Joseph P. Strelka (University Park: Pennsylvania State University Press, 1978), 192–

208, as well as his *Beyond Genre* (Ithaca: Cornell University Press, 1972). On the breakdown of genre frames, readers may consult Clifford Geertz, "Blurred Genres: The Refiguration of Social Thought," *The American Scholar* 49 (1980): 165–79, and Jacques Derrida, "The Law of Genre," trans. Avital Ronell, *Glyph 7* (Baltimore: Johns Hopkins University Press, 1980), 201–29. The seemingly inescapable reliance upon generic boundaries and definitions is discussed in Ralph Cohen, "Do Postmodern Genres Exist?", *Genre* 20 (1987): 241–57. In a more general vein, Alistair Fowler's *Kinds of Literature* (Cambridge: Harvard University Press, 1982) is a historical consideration of the concept of genre in literature and a defense of its validity as communicational system rather than taxonomic map.

18   For a definitive treatment of the metafictive frame structure in *El amigo Manso*, see John Kronik's "*El amigo Manso* and the Game of Fictive Autonomy." The shattering of boundaries that normally separate the narrative frame from its contents is also the subject of his "*Misericordia* as Metafiction," in *Homenaje a Antonio Sánchez Barbudo*, ed. Benito Brancaforte, Edward R. Mulvihill, and Roberto G. Sánchez (Madison: University of Wisconsin Press, 1981), 37–50.

19   In addition to Lotman's *The Structure of the Artistic Text* and Uspensky's *A Poetics of Composition*, some of the recent books on narrative that offer excellent discussions and examples of the internal and external narrative framing techniques here enumerated are: Tzvetan Todorov, *Introduction to Poetics*, trans. Richard Howard (Minneapolis: University of Minnesota Press, 1981); Gérard Genette, *Narrative Discourse: An Essay in Method*, trans. Jane E. Lewin (Ithaca: Cornell University Press, 1980), and *Narrative Discourse Revisited*, trans. Jane E. Lewin (Ithaca: Cornell University Press, 1988); Seymour Chatman, *Story and Discourse: Narrative Structure in Fiction and Film* (Ithaca: Cornell University Press, 1979); Shlomith Rimmon-Kenan, *Narrative Fiction: Contemporary Poetics* (London: Methuen, 1983); and Gerald Prince, *Narratology: The Form and Functioning of Narrative* (Berlin: Mouton, 1982).

20   Michel Foucault, *The Order of Things: An Archaeology of the Human Sciences* (New York: Random House, 1970; rpt. Vintage Books, 1973), 251.

21   The inventorying of phenomena, objects, and individuals that fills the pages of the nineteenth-century novel has frequently been described as tedious, conscientious, laborious, and so forth. Ironically, even when the value of such labor is ridiculed, as occurs with the massings of nonsignifying details in *Madame Bovary* or *Bouvard et Pécuchet*, it simply emerges elsewhere, in Flaubert's idealizing fetishization of writing as work. See chapter 1 for a related discussion of the painstaking but ultimately meaningless labors of Francisco Bringas, the failed artist of realism.

22   José Ortega y Gasset, *Investigaciones filosóficas*, *Obras completas* (Madrid: Alianza-Revista de Occidente, 1983), 12: 450.

23   Damian Grant, *Realism* (London: Methuen, 1970), 14.

24   Harry Levin, *The Gates of Horn* (New York: Oxford University Press, 1963), 16, 56.

25   D. A. Williams, "The Practice of Realism," in *The Monster in the Mirror*, ed. D. A. Williams (Oxford: University of Hull/Oxford University Press, 1978), 257.

26   Farris Anderson discusses the framing action implicit in the pictorial modality of *costumbrismo*, in which reality is perceived as a series of unconnected "hermetic vignettes," and compares it to realism's adoption of an "integrative" or "structural vision" in which these scenes are linked through an evolutive, historical continuum. See his "Madrid, los balcones y la historia: Mesonero Romanos y Pérez Galdós," *CHA* 464 (1989): 63–75.

27   Stephen Gilman, *Galdós and the Art of the European Novel: 1867–1887* (Princeton: Princeton University Press, 1981), 78.

28   More information on Galdós's cartooning can be found in Peter Bly, *Vision and the Visual Arts in Galdós* (Liverpool: Francis Cairns, 1986), 7–8, 73.

29   Fredric Jameson, *The Political Unconscious: Narrative as a Socially Symbolic Act* (Ithaca: Cornell University Press, 1981), 111.

30   Roland Barthes, *S/Z*, trans. Richard Miller (New York: Hill and Wang, 1974), 55.

31   Germán Gullón, "Un paradigma para la novela española moderna: *Amor y pedagogía*, de Miguel de Unamuno," *MLN* 105 (1990): 227, 231.

32   Mary Ann Caws, *Reading Frames in Modern Fiction* (Princeton: Princeton University Press, 1985), 11. The emphasis that she places on the frame (as opposed to the contained semantic field) can also be found, however, in very unmodern examples of literature. The overriding importance of the frame to contain the dispersion of meaning and control interpretation in didactic medieval works such as the *Conde Lucanor* has been persuasively argued by, among others, James F. Burke, "Frame and Structure in the *Conde Lucanor*," *RCEH* 8.2 (1984): 263–74, and Aníbal A. Biglieri, *Hacia una poética del relato didáctico: ocho estudios sobre "El Conde Lucanor"* (Chapel Hill: North Carolina Studies in the Romance Languages and Literatures, 1989), especially 88–112.

33   Thomas G. Pavel, *Fictional Worlds* (Cambridge: Harvard University Press, 1986), 146.

34   E. H. Gombrich, *Art and Illusion: A Study in the Psychology of Pictorial Representation*, 2d ed. (Princeton: Princeton University Press, 1969), 5, 236.

35   Jacques Derrida, *The Truth in Painting*, trans. Geoff Bennington and Ian McLeod (Chicago: University of Chicago Press, 1987), 61. Here Derrida is discussing the role played by the figure of the *parergon* (frame) in Kant's *Critique of Aesthetic Judgment*. Derrida has also pursued relentlessly the implications of the undecidable status and deconstructive action of margins in other threshold figures: the signature, the prologue or preface, the lineaments of the genre-clause, and the hymen and invagination of textual boundaries. See particularly *Signéponge-Signsponge*, trans. Richard Rand (New York: Columbia University Press, 1984); *Glas*, trans. John P. Leavey, Jr. and Richard Rand (Lincoln: University of Nebraska Press, 1986); "Signature Event Context," in *Glyph 1* (Baltimore: Johns Hopkins University Press, 1977), 172–97; *Dissemination*, trans. Barbara Johnson (Chicago: University

of Chicago Press, 1982); "Living On: Border Lines," in *Deconstruction and Criticism*, ed. Harold Bloom et al. (New York: Seabury, 1979), 75–175; *Margins of Philosophy*, trans. Alan Bass (Chicago: University of Chicago, 1982), and the previously mentioned "The Law of Genre."

36 Wallace Martin, *Recent Theories of Narrative* (Ithaca: Cornell University Press, 1986), 7.

1 Narrative Beginnings in *La de Bringas*

1 Lotman, *The Structure of the Artistic Text*, 212.

2 Uspensky, *A Poetics of Composition*, 137.

3 Edward W. Said, *Beginnings: Intentions and Method* (Baltimore: Johns Hopkins University Press, 1975), xi.

4 Ricardo Gullón, *Galdós, novelista moderno* (Madrid: Gredos, 1973), 159–70. Gullón suggests that in his treatment of commonplace objects Galdós anticipates the aesthetics of Azorín and the latter's emphasis on "los primores de lo vulgar" 'the beauty of the ordinary.'

5 William R. Risley, "Setting in the Galdós Novel, 1881–1885," *HR* 46 (1978): 23–40.

6 Michael Nimetz, *Humor in Galdós: A Study of the "Novelas contemporáneas"* (New Haven: Yale University Press, 1968), 62–63.

7 Victor Brombert, "Opening Signals in Narrative," *NLH* 11 (1980): 490.

8 In a favorable review of Ortega Munilla's *El tren directo*, Alas rehearses the argument against the immoderate use of detail in literature. Although he ultimately accepts the validity of including even the most humble objects in the novel, he warns that an excess of description often prejudices the balanced composition of a work. As he explains the debate: "Plato, who saw ideas in everything, would ask himself . . . if he ought to attribute ideas corresponding to those miserable artifacts that are the creation of multiple human needs. A bed, a table, an hourglass, a door, a cart: in the world of ideas, do they have their corresponding idea? Juan Pablo Richter answered this by painstakingly saving nails, corks, buttons, and so forth in a chest, because he used to say that nothing that surrounds man, or is the work of his hands and his skill, deserves to be disdained or forgotten." Leopoldo Alas, *"El tren directo* (Munilla)," in *Solos de Clarín* (Madrid: Alianza, 1971), 287. In the same collection of essays, in a far less favorable review of Pereda's *El buey suelto*, Clarín vindicates Zola's density of "extreme details," while criticizing the Spanish novelist as one of the "false realists who copy what is unique and all its details, even at the level of the atomic, but without the *quid divinum* of inspiration, without hitting upon the type, and copying, for the sake of copying, whatever passes before them." *"El buey suelto* . . . (Pereda)," in *Solos*, 230.

9 Leopoldo Alas, "Sobre motivos de una novela de Galdós," in *Mezclilla* (Madrid: Fernando Fe, 1889), 270–71. For Clarín, the inclusion of such repetitious detail is less a function of Galdós's technical inexperience than of his own unique temperament; he finds significance in every object, scene, and

discussion that he encounters in Madrid. He therefore turns a deaf ear when critics suggest that he ought to "reduce reality when he transfers it to his novels" (271).

10   Orlando, "Novelas españolas del año literario," *Revista de España* 100 (1884): 444, cited in Peter A. Bly, *Pérez Galdós: "La de Bringas"* (London: Grant and Cutler, 1981), 13. As Ricardo Gullón concurs, "In Galdós's novels, the atmosphere is saturated with truth thanks to the selection of details . . . In his day, Galdós was reproached more than anything for his prolixity" (*Galdós, novelista moderno* 169).

11   V. S. Pritchett, "Galdós," *Books in General* (London: Chatto and Windus, 1953), 31–36.

12   More detailed descriptions of nineteenth-century mourning jewelry and hair work can be found in Nancy Armstrong, *Victorian Jewelry* (New York: Macmillan, 1976), 72–79, and Charlotte Gere, *Victorian Jewellery Design* (London: Kimber, 1972), 244–47. One of the showstopping exhibits at the 1855 Paris Exposition was a lifesize portrait of Queen Victoria executed exclusively in human hair. Interest in this craft revived after the death of Victoria's consort Albert in 1861, as evidenced by the proliferation of pattern books of copper plate engravings with directions for copying the designs in hair. Readers curious about the execution of this craft can consult Mark Campbell, *The Art of Hair Work: Hair Braiding and Jewelry of Sentiment with a Catalog of Hair Jewelry,* ed. Jules and Kaethe Kliot (Berkeley: Lacis Publications, 1989). A modern reprint of Campbell's *Self-Instructor in the Art of Hair Work* (1875), it offers information on tools and materials and includes large numbers of detailed patterns for the hobbyist undeterred by the truly labor-intensive nature of this pastime.

13   The link that Galdós establishes between the "elementary lack of taste which is so marked a feature of everything connected with our funeral customs" (see Bertram S. Puckle, *Funeral Customs: Their Origin and Development* [1926; rpt. Detroit: Singing Tree Press, 1968], 271) and the pseudoartistic aspirations of the Spanish middle class continues to provide satirical fodder for contemporary authors. Compare the description of the cenotaph with the following passage in Goytisolo's *Señas de identidad:*

> Inaugurated during the period of Barcelona's development and expansion, when the area of the old cemetery revealed itself to be clearly insufficient, the diverse architectural currents and decorative styles of the epoch coexisted in it with profuse and motley aggressiveness: gravestones with crosses, wreaths, garlands, sorrowing virgins and archangels; marble mausoleums inspired by medieval funeral monuments; neo-Gothic chapels with stained glass panes, apse, nave, and transept which were scrupulously reproduced in miniature; small Greek temples copied from the Parthenon in Athens; extravagant Egyptian structures with sphinxes, colossuses, carriages, and mummies as though designed on purpose for a performance of *Aida.* They passed successively before the visitor's eyes like the synthesis and continuation of the economic adventure of their owners.

Juan Goytisolo, *Señas de identidad*, 2d ed. (Mexico: Joaquín Mortiz, 1969), 67.

14   Ricardo Gullón, *Técnicas de Galdós* (Madrid: Taurus, 1980), 113–15, 125.

15   Chad C. Wright, "Secret Space in Pérez Galdós' *La de Bringas*," *HR* 50 (1982): 75–86.

16   Nicholas G. Round, "Rosalía Bringas' Children," *AGald* 6 (1971): 47, 49.

17   See, however, Urey, *Galdós and the Irony of Language*, who analyzes how the presentation of the hair picture undermines the credibility not just of the narrator but of language itself (48–52).

18   Most previous monographs dedicated to *La de Bringas* in fact focus upon the problem of disruptions of visual fields and perspectives. See Peter A. Bly, "The Use of Distance in Galdós's *La de Bringas*," *MLR* 69 (1974): 88–97, and Chad C. Wright, "Imagery of Light and Darkness in *La de Bringas*," *AGald* 13 (1978): 5–12. By far the most complete treatment of what Risley has called the "rigging of physical space" (38) and of the various painterly qualities applied to the cenotaph and to the novel itself is to be found in Bly's *Pérez Galdós: "La de Bringas"*, particularly chapter 2, "Perspective and Vision" (18–29), where the composition of the hair picture, the overall structure of the novel, and the use of a rhetoric of vision by the characters are all related to the notion of *La de Bringas* as a "novel about the correct perception of reality, both physical and spiritual, seeing all of life in the right perspective" (29).

19   Said, *Beginnings*, 41.

20   Might there not exist in this description a lexical echo of the writings of Galdós's friend and historical informant Ramón de Mesonero Romanos? In his essay "El romanticismo y los románticos" (1837), Mesonero had satirized the affected attire of a nephew who claimed that "the figure of a romantic should be Gothic, ogival, pyramidal, and emblematic." Ramón de Mesonero Romanos, *Escenas matritenses* (Madrid: Austral, 1964), 58.

21   Tony Tanner, *Adultery in the Novel: Contract and Transgression* (Baltimore: Johns Hopkins University Press, 1979), 287.

22   Benito Pérez Galdós, "La sociedad presente como materia novelable," *Discursos leídos ante la Real Academia Española en las recepciones públicas del 7 y del 21 de febrero de 1897* (Madrid: Est. Tip., de la Viuda e Hijos de Tello, 1897), 18–19. For Galdós, this leveling tendency is responsible for muddying distinctions of class, language, and regional identity. "The so-called middle class," he writes, "is only a shapeless agglomeration of individuals who come from superior or inferior social ranks, the product, let us say so, of the decomposition of both families" which has created "an enormous mass without any character of its own." Regarding language, "we observe the same direction, contrary to what is characteristic, tending toward uniformity of diction." As for the rapidly disappearing sense of place, "urbanization is slowly destroying the peculiar physiognomy of each city" while at the same time "the distinctive profile [of the countryside] is being eroded by the continual passage of the leveling roller."

23   See especially Victor Shklovsky, "Art as Technique," in *Russian Formalist Criticism*, ed. Lee T. Lemon and Marion J. Reis (Lincoln: University of Nebraska Press, 1965), 3–24. With its focus upon innovative textual elements and forms that distinguish themselves from a horizon or background of customary narrative practice, defamiliarization is very clearly a framing operation.

24   The expression is borrowed from Mary Ann Caws, *The Eye in the Text: Essays on Perception, Mannerist to Modern* (Princeton: Princeton University Press, 1981). "Texturality" refers to knots and bulges in the text that capture the reader's attention and force a rereading.

25   Given the nature of the project in which he is engaged, Bringas is actually fortunate to lose only his sight. The total absence of hierarchization or subordination of detail ultimately leads to a terrifying hyperlucidity bordering on madness itself. The ultimate example is the protagonist of Borges's "Funes el memorioso," unable ever to forget any of the infinite number of images of the universe he has perceived during his lifetime: "In effect, Funes not only remembered every leaf of every tree in every wood, but also every one of the instances he had ever perceived or imagined it." The narrator reiterates: "In Funes's overly replete world, there were only details, almost contiguous ones." Although his death at age twenty-one is attributed to pulmonary disease, one might as easily conclude that Funes aged prematurely under "the pressure of such an indefatigable reality," "a multiform, instantaneous, and almost intolerably precise world." Jorge Luis Borges, *Ficciones* (Buenos Aires: Emecé, 1956), 125, 126.

26   Uspensky, *A Poetics of Composition*, 147.

27   Bly, in *Perez Galdós: "La de Bringas"*, speaks of the narrator's easy surrender of political principles to personal convenience, adding: "His readiness to compromise moral principles is the plot's final surprise" (91). Bly's conclusion is that "our narrator is indeed Booth's unreliable narrator" (92).

28   Steven G. Kellman, "Grand Openings and Plain: The Poetics of First Lines," *Sub-Stance* 17 (1977): 139.

29   Philippe Hamon, *Introduction à l'analyse du descriptif* (Paris: Hachette, 1981), 78.

30   Philippe Hamon, "Qu'est-ce qu'une description?," *Poétique* 12 (1972): 475.

31   The control of Galdós's reader, previously accomplished by means of narrative authority (derived from transmitting information), is thus transferred to the exercise of narratorial authority (derived from arousing interest). For more on this distinction, see Ross Chambers, *Story and Situation: Narrative Seduction and the Power of Fiction* (Minneapolis: University of Minnesota Press, 1984).

32   See Murray Krieger, *Arts on the Level: The Fall of the Elite Object* (Knoxville: University of Tennessee Press, 1981). Krieger explains that "the stimulus in aesthetics for museum and anthology was, I repeat, the Kantian notion of disinterestedness, leading to the need to maintain 'aesthetic distance' (distance between object and subject of aesthetic experience and distance between

object and its sources in man and culture), and from there to autonomy and self-sufficiency of the object (through the internally exploited principle of a purposiveness free of any external interest)" (13).

33 Maurice Rheims, *La vie étrange des objets* (Paris: Plon, 1959), 47.

34 See Galdós's own comments on the "pernicious mania" of collecting as it affects the middle class in his essay "El coleccionista," in *Fisonomías sociales, Obras inéditas*, ed. Alberto Ghiraldo (Madrid: Renacimiento, 1923), 1: 197–208.

35 Susan Stewart, *On Longing: Narratives of the Miniature, the Gigantic, the Souvenir, the Collection* (Baltimore: Johns Hopkins University Press, 1984), 65. One is reminded, of course, that the miniature and its refusal of time may be endowed with a legitimate artistic dimension, as occurs in the shadow boxes of Joseph Cornell. The souvenirs of the artist's past are turned into what Cornell called poetic theaters of nostalgic reverie, "like boxes or caskets stored within each other": "They frame and set aside, into the margin of time as it flows, the idea of preservation itself." See Mary Ann Caws, *The Art of Interference: Stressed Readings in Verbal and Visual Texts* (Princeton: Princeton University Press, 1989), 204–5.

36 Surprisingly, the erotically charged nature of the hair picture has been consistently overlooked by critics of this novel. To my knowledge, only Bly has pointed out the fetishistic qualities of objects found in *La de Bringas*, and only then in connection with Rosalía, observing: "Rosalía really sublimates her sexual needs in her obsession for clothes" (*Pérez Galdós: "La de Bringas"* 59). He categorizes Rosalía's physiological response to the cape she purchases as an "experience comparable to sexual orgasm." There is, however, a marked similarity between Rosalía's experience and the description of how Francisco conceived of the idea for his picture. The building excitement and the wildly spasmodic quality of Bringas's sudden burst of creativity suggests, too, an orgasmic kind of experience.

37 Peter Conrad, *The Victorian Treasure-House* (London: Collins, 1973), 133.

38 Compare Galdós's position with that of Goethe, writing in 1799 on dilettantes and collectors: "They often take up etching because the technique of reproduction fascinates them. They seek out cunning devices, mannerisms, various techniques and arcane means because they usually cannot free themselves from the notion of technical skill and think that if they just knew the trick, they would have no more difficulties." For Goethe, all dilettantes are plagiarists: "They undermine and destroy all natural beauty in language and thought by mimicking and aping it in order to cover up their own vacuity"— that same vacuity, one might add, that is at the center of Bringas's hair picture. Johann Wolfgang von Goethe, "On Dilettantism," *Essays on Art and Literature*, in *Goethe's Collected Works*, ed. John Gearey, trans. Ellen and Ernest H. von Nardroff (New York: Suhrkamp, 1986), 3: 213, 216.

39 Leopoldo Alas, "*Gloria* (Pérez Galdós), Primera parte," in *Solos*, 338.

40 Jerome Buckley, *The Victorian Temper* (1951; rpt. New York: Random House, 1964), 133. The advent of a modern aesthetic based on the nonidentity of representational exactitude and artistic truth is lucidly discussed in Herbert

Read, *A Concise History of Modern Painting* (New York: Praeger, 1968), 44.

In a brief but fascinating article, Nancy Hill indicates that the Victorian church, perhaps in a desire to respond to nineteenth-century science and secularism in kind by stressing materiality and factuality, apparently placed greater doctrinal importance on the Atonement than the Incarnation. Hill maintains that this emphasis on the doctrine of the Atonement, "with its insistence that Christ actually rose from the dead, that the tomb really was empty, and that such promise was held out to believers" characterized a so-called "hard-edged" style of Christianity both in theology and the art placed at the service of theology (she cites the example of the naïve visual literalism of the Pre-Raphaelite painters). Although this childlike literalism was meant to attract churchgoers, in practice it proved an insufficient vehicle of faith for the inhabitants of an increasingly complex, industrialized world. See Nancy K. Hill, "Insisting on the Empty Tomb: The Retreat to Realism in Victorian Art and Religion," *Studies in the Humanities* 8 (1989): 28–32. Hill's article becomes particularly suggestive when read in conjunction with Galdós's treatment of the literalism of detail characterizing Bringas's cenotaph, an artistic rendition of the empty tomb.

41 Roland Barthes, "The Reality Effect," in *French Literary Theory Today*, ed. Tzvetan Todorov, trans. R. Carter (Cambridge and Paris: Cambridge University Press and Editions de la Maison des Sciences de l'Homme, 1982), 11–17.

42 Peter G. Earle, "La interdependencia de los personajes galdosianos," *CHA* 250–52 (1970–1971): 121.

2 Frame and Closure in *Fortunata y Jacinta*

1 Lotman, *The Structure of the Artistic Text*, 53, and Barbara Herrnstein Smith, *Poetic Closure* (Chicago: University of Chicago Press, 1968), 2.

2 In accordance with the customary method of citing from *Fortunata y Jacinta*, I have modified my references to the novel to allow readers to locate each quotation by part, chapter, and subchapter, in addition to the volume and page number of the *Obras completas*.

3 Contrast Anthony Zahareas, "The Tragic Sense in *Fortunata y Jacinta*," *AGald* 3 (1968): 25–34; Michael Nimetz, *Humor in Galdós*, 186–96; and Geoffrey Ribbans, *Pérez Galdós: "Fortunata y Jacinta"* (London: Grant and Cutler, 1977), especially the chapter titled "Confrontations and Reconciliations," 97–113.

4 One notable exception is S. Bacarisse, "The Realism of Galdós: Some Reflections on Language and the Perception of Reality," *BHS* 42 (1965): 239–50. Bacarisse insists that "realism can be defined in terms of the medium [i.e., language as material substance] used to create the illusion, rather than in terms of the impression of *verosimilitud* it produces on readers" (241). On the basis of a careful syntactic, verbal, and metaphorical analysis of a passage from Fortunata's death scene, he concludes that "reality retains its oracular character because Galdós found the means of offsetting the conceptualization

and logic of language." Although I do not fully share Bacarisse's conclusion, his insistence upon defining realism in terms of the representation rather than the represented is not unrelated to the aims and approach I take in this present study.

5 Both *La Fontana* and *Doña Perfecta* show Galdós's vacillation at this early stage in his career between melodramatic and more subdued endings; in the case of the former novel, the ending oscillates between tragic and happy. Regarding the problems of textual reconstruction of this novel see Joaquín Casalduero, "Una novela de dos desenlaces: *La Fontana de Oro*," *Ateneo* 88 (1955): 6–8; Florian Smieja, "An Alternative Ending of *La Fontana de Oro*," *MLR* 61 (1966): 426–33; and Walter T. Pattison, "*La Fontana de Oro*: Its Early History," *AGald* 15 (1980): 5–9. On the successive revisions of *Doña Perfecta*, see C. A. Jones, "Galdós's Second Thoughts on *Doña Perfecta*," *MLR* 54 (1959): 570–73, and, most recently, Geoffrey Ribbans, "*Doña Perfecta*: Yet Another Ending," *MLN* 105 (1990): 203–25. It is important to note that Galdós was constantly revising his novels, as a comparison of the very different Alpha manuscript of *Fortunata y Jacinta* with the actual published version will attest.

6 Gilman, *Galdós and the Art of the European Novel*, 209.

7 D. A. Miller, *Narrative and Its Discontents: Problems of Closure in the Traditional Novel* (Princeton: Princeton University Press, 1981), 279.

8 Frank Kermode, *The Sense of an Ending* (New York: Oxford University Press, 1968), 133.

9 Miller, *Narrative and Its Discontents*, ix, 5.

10 It is instructive to compare the observations of Herrnstein Smith, Miller, and Kermode on the techniques and rationale of closure in literary works with the closural features that characterize such real-life social situations as the conversation and speakers' attempts to disengage from it. On the latter, see Emanuel A. Schegloff and Harvey Sacks, "Opening up Closings," *Semiotica* 8.4 (1973): 289–327.

11 Jan Mukarovsky, "The Concept of the Whole in the Theory of Art," in *Structure, Sign, and Function*, trans. John Burbank and Peter Steiner (Yale University Press, 1978), 80.

12 Williams, "The Practice of Realism," 257.

13 Thomas E. Lewis, "*Fortunata y Jacinta*: Galdós and the Production of the Literary Referent," *MLN* 96 (1981): 329. Lewis interprets the existence of such a contradiction between the novel's structure and its representational practices, seen especially in the chapter titled "Costumbres turcas," in a positive light. As he argues, "by undertaking to articulate elements of a progressive middle-class ideology in the mode of the Imaginary, this text constructs the referent in a manner that replenishes in consciousness the absence of such a practice from the ideological problematic of the Restoration" (339).

14 Henry James, "The Art of Fiction," in *Criticism: The Major Statements*, ed. Charles Kaplan (New York: St. Martin's Press, 1975), 435.

15 Gilman, *Galdós and the Art of the European Novel*, 229–30.

16 Gonzalo Sobejano, "Muerte del solitario (Benito Pérez Galdós: *Fortunata y*

Jacinta, 4a, II, 6)," in *El comentario de textos 3* (Madrid: Castalia, 1979), 214–15.

17   Prince, *Narratology*, 158.

18   Lotman, *The Structure of the Artistic Text*, 211, 214.

19   D. A. Miller, "Balzac's Illusions Lost and Found," *YFS* 67 (1984): 165.

20   Marianna Torgovnick, *Closure in the Novel* (Princeton: Princeton University Press, 1981), 13–14.

21   Geoffrey W. Ribbans, *Reality Plain or Fancy? Some Reflections on Galdós' Concept of Realism*, E. Allison Peers Lectures 1 (Liverpool: Liverpool University Press, 1986), 7. See also Jo Labanyi, "The Raw, the Cooked, and the Indigestible in Galdós's *Fortunata y Jacinta*," *Romance Studies* 13 (1988): 55–68, and Sarah E. King, "Food Imagery in *Fortunata y Jacinta*," *AGald* 18 (1983): 79–88.

22   Peter B. Goldman, "El trabajo digestivo del espíritu: sobre la estructura de *Fortunata y Jacinta* y la función de Segismundo Ballester," *KRQ* 31 (1984): 177–87. In the subsequent "Juanito's *chuletas*: Realism and Worldly Philosophy in Galdós's *Fortunata y Jacinta*," *JMMLA* 18.1 (1985): 82–101, Goldman continues his examination of alimentary metaphors in the context of the novel's theme of moral and artistic authenticity.

23   See also the discussion of these tropes in Maggie Kilgour, *From Communion to Cannibalism: An Anatomy of Metaphors of Incorporation* (Princeton: Princeton University Press, 1990).

24   In *Galdós and the Art of the European Novel*, Gilman attributes Galdós's emphasis upon the rituals of "alimentary time" (the diurnal repetition of marketing, cooking, and dining activities in *Fortunata y Jacinta*) in part to the lingering heritage of naturalism, in part to the author's desire to communicate temporally the human experience at the heart of his novel (372). For a general introduction to this topic as it relates to nineteenth-century fiction, see James W. Brown, "On the Semiogenesis of Fictional Meals," *RR* 69 (1978): 322–35, and Jean-Paul Aron, *Le mangeur au XIXe siècle* (Paris: R. Laffont, 1973).

25   A similar question is posed by Agnes Moncy Gullón, "The Bird Motif and the Introductory Motif: Structure in *Fortunata y Jacinta*," *AGald* 9 (1974): 51–75, that is, whether *Fortunata y Jacinta* can best be viewed by critics as raw fruit (the novel as social document) or as a compote (the novel as "masterpiece of esthetic inventiveness"), concluding that it may feasibly be studied either way (53). Ribbans, *Reality Plain or Fancy?*, points out that neither the guileless Ballester nor the often pompous newspaper critic Ponce are entirely reliable theorists of the creative process in literature (20), therefore concluding that "the reader is left to decide for himself which criterion, if either, the novel he has just read exemplifies" (7). He contends that "Galdós, typically, does not opt inequivocally for either procedure" (*Pérez Galdós: "Fortunata y Jacinta,"* 16). Yet the words granting equal weight to raw fruit and compote belong to the narrator rather than the implied author. At this latter level I hope to demonstrate that there is indeed an implicit preference for the novel-compote.

26 This pun is exercised by Derrida in his deconstruction of the role of the preface, another paradoxical figure of margins like the frame. See Jacques Derrida, "Outwork, Prefacing," in *Dissemination*, especially 3–16.

27 John W. Kronik, "Narraciones interiores en *Fortunata y Jacinta*," in *Homenaje a Juan López-Morillas*, ed. José Amor y Vázquez and A. David Kossoff (Madrid: Castalia, 1982), 290.

28 Embedded narrations are sometimes also referred to as intradiegetic, subordinated, or interior narrations. I use these terms interchangeably to describe a narrative told by some character other than the novel's primary narrator who exercises ultimate control over the communication of the text to the reader.

29 Rimmon-Kenan, *Narrative Fiction*, 91–94. See also Tzvetan Todorov, "Narrative-Men," in *The Poetics of Prose*, trans. Richard Howard (Ithaca: Cornell University Press, 1977), for the section on "Digression and Embedding," 70–73.

30 Angel Tarrío, *Lectura semiológica de "Fortunata y Jacinta"* (Las Palmas: Cabildo Insular de Gran Canaria, 1982), 192. Tarrío has borrowed this expression from Barthes, and uses it to describe the hypersaturation of realist discourse by signs that point to the known social world, which constitutes the referent for Galdós's readers. For a detailed analysis of the shifting markers and functions of this narrator, especially as related to the notion of reality as multifacetic and conflictive, see Kay Engler, "Notes on the Narrative Structure of *Fortunata y Jacinta*," *Symposium* 24 (1970): 111–27.

31 It is ironic that the only time that Nicolás is willing to hear Fortunata out, she is an unwilling narrator. When the priest tells the Rubín family about the scandals Mauricia has caused in Las Micaelas, he invokes Fortunata's corroborating testimony: "The latter, very much against her will, had no choice but to relate the novelistic incidents of the mouse, the visions, and the bottle of cognac, but she gave only a very sketchy account, to get it over with sooner" (5: 3/V, iii, 364).

32 The only exceptions to this are the brief letter that Juanito sends Fortunata when he leaves her in part three and the letter that Fortunata dictates to Estupiñá at the end of part four, entrusting her son to Jacinta. Of course, Ido does write, but his dreadful popular novels are never actually cited in *Fortunata y Jacinta*.

33 Kronik, "Galdosian Reflections: Feijoo and the Fabrication of Fortunata," 299–300.

34 Marvin Minsky, *The Society of Mind* (New York: Simon and Schuster, 1985), 257.

35 See Sherman H. Eoff, "The Treatment of Individual Personality in *Fortunata y Jacinta*," *HR* 17 (1949): 269–89.

36 Kay Engler indicates that in *Fortunata y Jacinta* "characters gradually usurp the function of the narrator: their words take on representational function as well. In other words, with the virtual disappearance of the narrator, modes of presentation become more direct and experimental" ("Notes on the Narrative Structure of *Fortunata y Jacinta*" 120; see also 116 and 119–21). Ricardo Gullón, in *Técnicas de Galdós*, similarly alludes to the way in which "little

by little the narrator becomes contaminated, if he didn't share them from the beginning, by the characters' ideas, attitudes, and points of view" (207). For an overall perspective on the subject, see Roy Pascal, *The Dual Voice: Free Indirect Speech and Its Functioning in the Nineteenth-Century Novel* (Manchester: Manchester University Press, 1977).

37   Jean Rousset, *Narcisse romancier: Essai sur la première personne dans le roman* (Paris: José Corti, 1973), 69–70.

38   José F. Montesinos, *Galdós*, 2d ed. (Madrid: Castalia, 1980), 2: 261.

39   Gilman uses Galdós's recollection of "breakfasting on Balzac" to show that when attempting to describe the creative process, Galdós often employed physiological images of fever and appetite. He concludes that "as against inspiration, which classically descends from above, Galdós clearly suggests that his conscious intentions are implemented by the welling upwards or outwards of the literate unconscious" (224–25).

40   Uspensky, *A Poetics of Composition*, 151–55.

3   The Political Intertext in *Torquemada en la hoguera*

1   Urey, *Galdós and the Irony of Language*, 100. Urey's detailed close reading of the opening paragraphs of the novel uncovers many other instances of irony, which should serve as a warning to readers that they are being manipulated by the narrator. See also Peter A. Bly, "La fosilización de la autoridad narrativa a través de los capítulos iniciales de la serie *Torquemada* de Galdós," *Actas del IX Congreso de la Asociación Internacional de Hispanistas* (Frankfurt: Vervuert Verlag, 1989), 2: 25–29.

2   Pierre L. Ullman, "The Exordium of *Torquemada en la hoguera*," *MLN* 80 (1965): 258–60.

3   Said, *Beginnings*, 22.

4   On the classification of parody as trope, see Gerard Genette, *Palimpsestes: La littérature au second degré* (Paris: Seuil, 1982), 23–26.

5   Laurent Jenny, "The Strategy of Form," in *French Literary Theory Today*, ed. Tzvetan Todorov, trans. R. Carter (Cambridge and Paris: Cambridge University Press and Editions de la Maison des Sciences de l'Homme, 1982), 45.

6   Robert Weber, "Galdós' Preliminary Sketches for *Torquemada y San Pedro*," *BHS* 44 (1967): 16–27, indicates that Galdós had originally planned to reintroduce Bailón in the fourth volume of the series, but then later eliminated all references to him in the final draft of the book. Bailón does return very briefly to the action in *Angel Guerra*.

7   See, for instance, Peter G. Earle, "Torquemada, hombre-masa," *AGald* 2 (1967): 29–43, especially 34–35.

8   This point is made by H. L. Boudreau, "The Salvation of Torquemada: Determinism and Determinacy in the Later Novels of Galdós," *AGald* 15 (1980): 113–28. Boudreau defines the binary structure of this narrative patterning in the following manner: "Each volume of the novel presents the established nature of the protagonist struggling with a need to change in conflict with a basic inability to do so. In each case he is simple and passive but responsive

to an agent of the press for change (Bailón, Donoso, Cruz, Gamborena), a change aspired to by his ego but denied him by the primitive, materialistic core of his being" (114–15).

9 F. García Sarriá, "El plano alegórico de *Torquemada en la hoguera,*" *AGald* 15 (1980): 103–11; also, B. J. Zeidner Bäuml, "The Mundane Demon: The Bourgeois Grotesque in Galdós' *Torquemada en la hoguera,*" *Symposium* 24 (1970): 158–65.

10 Zeidner Bäuml, "The Bourgeois Grotesque," 165n.

11 For a more complete treatment of the inversion of moral values as conveyed by the religious motif in the novel, see Geraldine M. Scanlon, "Torquemada: 'Becerro de oro,'" *MLN* 91 (1976): 264–76.

12 Urey, *Galdós and the Irony of Language,* 104.

13 Jonathan Culler, *Structuralist Poetics* (Ithaca: Cornell University Press, 1975), 154.

14 Roland Barthes, "From Work to Text," trans. Josué V. Harari, in *Textual Strategies: Perspectives in Post-Structuralist Criticism,* ed. Josué V. Harari (Ithaca: Cornell University Press, 1979), 77. Any discussion of the intertextual phenomenon in modern critical parlance must begin with Julia Kristeva, *Sémiotikè: Recherches pour un sémanalyse* (Paris: Seuil, 1969) and *La Révolution du langage poétique* (Paris: Seuil, 1974). Also valuable is Michael Riffaterre's *La Production du texte* (Paris: Seuil, 1979) and "La Trace de l'intertexte," *La Pensée* 215 (1980): 4–18.

15 Jonathan Culler, "Presupposition and Intertextuality," in *The Pursuit of Signs* (Ithaca: Cornell University Press, 1981), 100–118, describes the double bind of theorists of intertextuality as follows: "A criticism based on the contention that meaning is made possible by a general, anonymous intertextuality tries to justify the claim by showing how in particular cases 'a text works by absorbing and destroying at the same time the other texts of the intertextual space' and is happiest or most triumphant when it can identify particular pretexts with which the work is indubitably wrestling" (107).

16 H. Chonon Berkowitz, *La biblioteca de Benito Pérez Galdós* (Las Palmas: Cabildo Insular de Gran Canaria, 1951), 68.

17 Frank Bowman, "Les Pastiches des *Paroles d'un croyant,*" *Cahiers Mennaisiens* 16–17 (1984): 144–54, offers a catalog of both rebuttals and parodies of Lamennais's book, including: J. Augustin Chaho, *Paroles d'un voyant* (1834); Milon de Villiers, *Paroles d'un mécréant* (1834); Elzéar Ortolan, *Contreparoles d'un croyant* (1834); Auguste Martel, *Paroles d'un autre croyant* (1834); F. Ponchon, *Le croyant et ses paroles* (1834); the anonymous *Paroles d'un pensant* (attributed to A. P. fils [de la Creuse], 1834); José Vicente Álvarez Perera, *Paroles d'un chrétien* (trans. from the Spanish by M. Oeuf La Loubière, 1839), and so on. In studying the transformations that Lamennais's *Paroles* undergoes in these and other such works, Bowman notes that "this range of techniques—the polemical refutation of the content, the reprise of the form in order to contradict the meaning, the reprise of the form now emptied of its contents in order to apply it to something else—is found *mutatis mutandi* elsewhere, but there as well as here the characteristic fea-

ture of these reprises is not the sarcasm of parody but rather violence and exaggeration, which certify—as does their polemical objective—that it is a question of a pastiche rather than of an imitation" (150).

18   Felicité (*sic*) de Lamennais, *Palabras de un creyente*, trans. Juan Bauzá (Marsella: Impr. de Julio Barile y Boulouch, 1834); *idem* (Burdeos: n.p., 1834). Bauzá's translation was again published in Cáceres (Librería de Pujol, 1835) and Seville (Librería de Sorís, 1835).

19   See "Cuatro palabras del traductor," prologue to Mariano José de Larra, trans., *El dogma de los hombres libres: Palabras de un creyente por M. F. La Mennais* (Madrid: Impr. de J. M. Repullés, 1836), v–xviii. Larra's translation was reprinted in 1838 in Seville. His translator's prologue is anthologized in Mariano José de Larra, *Artículos políticos y sociales*, ed. José R. Lomba y Pedraja (Madrid: Espasa-Calpe, 1966), 258–68. For the significance of this involvement with the *Paroles* to the development of Larra's political thought, see José Luis Varela, "Lamennais en la evolución ideológica de Larra," *HR* 48 (1980): 287–306.

20   A comparison of Landa's translation of Lamennais and Galdós's retrieval of this text in *Torquemada*, in the original Spanish, has been included in the appendix.

21   Benito Pérez Galdós, "Observaciones sobre la novela contemporánea en España" [1870], reprinted in Iris M. Zavala, *Ideología y política en la novela española del siglo XIX* (Salamanca: Anaya, 1971), 324.

22   John H. Sinnigen, "Literary and Ideological Projects in Galdós: The *Torquemada* Series," *IL* 3 (1979): 6.

23   [Charles Augustin] Sainte-Beuve, "*Paroles d'un Croyant*, par l'abbé Lamennais," *Revue des Deux Mondes*, 3d series, 2: 349 (April 1, 1834).

24   Paul Vulliaud, "*Les Paroles d'un Croyant*" de Lamennais, 3d ed. (Amiens: Edgar Malfère, 1928), 164.

25   V. M. y Flórez, "Estudios literarios. Mr. de La-Menais," *Liceo Valenciano*, 3d series, vol. 2, no. 9 (September 1842): 391.

26   Alec R. Vidler, *Prophecy and Papacy: A Study of Lamennais, the Church, and the Revolution* (New York: Scribner, 1954), 264.

27   Marcelino Menéndez y Pelayo, *Historia de las ideas estéticas en España*, *Obras completas* (Madrid: Consejo Superior de Investigaciones Cientificas, 1940), 5: 41.

28   The smug attitude of the narrator notwithstanding, the fact is that this so-called "sentimental democracy," which drew upon populist religious sentiment in defense of political ends and had developed a numerous following only half a century previously, enjoyed a certain popularity in Spain. In Spain the most widely known works of utopian socialist thought were those of Fourier and the Christian socialists. For a study of how populist conceptions of Catholicism were exploited in France by republican propagandists using religious language and symbols to win the allegiance of the lower classes, see Edward Berenson, *Populist Religion and Left-Wing Politics in France, 1830–52* (Princeton: Princeton University Press, 1984). Also useful is D. O. Evans, *Social Romanticism in France, 1840–1848* (Oxford: Clarendon

Press, 1951). On Spain, see Antonio Elorza, ed., *Socialismo utópico español* (Madrid: Alianza, 1970), and Iris M. Zavala, *Románticos y socialistas: prensa española del siglo XIX* (Madrid: Siglo Veintiuno de España Editores, 1971).

29   Brian J. Dendle, *Galdós: The Mature Thought* (Lexington: University of Kentucky Press, 1980), finds that the "Romantic sickness," which "converts life into literature and, in its pursuit of sterile and illusory goals, denies reality," is a leitmotif of the entire fourth series of *Episodios Nacionales.* In particular, the former theology student García Fajardo "flirts briefly with the theories of Saint-Simon, Fourier, Owen and Lamennais. His vision of socialism is, however, superficial and purely external" (100).

30   Menéndez y Pelayo, *Historia de las ideas estéticas,* 40.

31   Gustavo Pérez Firmat, "Apuntes para un modelo de la intertextualidad en literatura," *RR* 69 (1978): 10.

32   Todorov, *The Poetics of Prose,* 245.

33   Miguel Artola, *La burguesía revolucionaria (1808–1874),* 8th ed. (Madrid: Alianza-Alfaguara, 1981), 344.

34   Rodolfo Cardona, "Galdós y los Santos Padres: hacia una teología de la liberación," *Actas del Tercer Congreso Internacional de Estudios Galdosianos* (Las Palmas: Cabildo Insular de Gran Canaria, 1989 [1990]), 1: 139–47. Since the particular patristic texts that Galdós incorporates into *El caballero encantado* were often suppressed by the Church, which in Spain was especially anxious to protect its interests in the face of the laws of disentailment that had been gradually whittling away its power, Cardona's hunch appears well-founded: "Having examined don Benito's library on several occasions, I am confused in the face of this mystery, and it only occurs to me to hazard one possible source, Lamennais's work, which Galdós knew in part and which might have guided him in the direction of the Holy Fathers" (146).

35   Critical interest in the ways in which Galdós treats the problems of history and historicity is currently very great. See, for instance, Urey, *The Novel Histories of Galdós,* and *Galdós y la historia,* ed. Peter Bly (Ottawa: Dovehouse Editions, 1988), which brings together several recent essays on the topic and includes a comprehensive bibliography on the subject.

36   Linda Hutcheon, *A Poetics of Postmodernism: History, Theory, Fiction* (London: Routledge, 1988), 35. This concept is first articulated in her development of a functional definition of parody in *A Theory of Parody: The Teachings of Twentieth-Century Art Forms* (London: Methuen, 1985).

37   Paula W. Shirley, "The Narrator/Reader Relationship in *Torquemada,* or How to Read a Galdosian Novel," *AGald* 20.2 (1985): 77–87.

38   Cited by Vulliaud, *"Les Paroles d'un Croyant" de Lamennais,* 26, 150.

39   Gelasio Galán y Junco, trans., *Respuesta de un cristiano a "Palabras de un Creyente"* por el Abate [Louis Eugène Marie] Bautain (Madrid: n.p., 1836), vi–vii.

40   Emilia Pardo Bazán, *La literatura francesa moderna* (Madrid: Administración, n.d. [1910–1911?]), 1: 128.

41   Menéndez y Pelayo, *Historia de las ideas estéticas,* 41.

42   Landa, trans., *Palabras de un creyente,* 108.

43   Wolfgang Iser, *The Implied Reader* (Baltimore: Johns Hopkins University Press, 1974), 257–59. See also the important discussion by Frank Kermode, *The Sense of an Ending*, 3–64.

44   In many respects, this process repeats the strategy employed in *La de Bringas*. In that novel a visual object is twice framed: once by Bringas himself when he mounts it under glass, and then again by the narrator, who devotes the entire opening chapter to it. But the contents of the frame are shown to be irrelevant; what matters is the authority of the narrator who first outlines the object and then judges it wanting. In *Torquemada en la hoguera*, it is a verbal entity that is ostentatiously reframed and then divested of all merit by the imperious narrator.

45   Jenny, "The Strategy of Form," 59.

4   Genre and Theatrical Frames in *Tormento*

1   Prince, *Narratology*, 128.

2   Regarding the concept of fraud in the novel, see the discussion of associated terms such as "labyrinth," "secret," and "entanglement" in Anthony Percival, "Melodramatic Metafiction in *Tormento*," *KRQ* 31 (1984): 154–55.

3   Two critics have specifically addressed the question of framing and representation in *Tormento*. In *El narrador en la novela del siglo XIX*, Germán Gullón sees the frame structure of *Tormento* as a means of presenting mutually exclusive versions of reality and thereby creating an impression of objectivity (107–15). Diane F. Urey, "Repetition, Discontinuity and Silence in Galdós' *Tormento*," *AGald* 20.1 (1985): 47–63, analyzes the use of repeated images to frame passages of the text and underscore the "already pre-framed nature of representation" (49). These studies form a necessary complement to my investigation of the use of genre as frame in *Tormento*.

4   On the (re)framing of genres as translation, see Caws, *Reading Frames in Modern Fiction*, 87–120. Lotman, *The Structure of the Artistic Text*, similarly refers to the reflection of one reality in another, that is, the copy of the infinite universe within a finite model of it, as a process of translation (210).

5   Gustavo Pérez Firmat, "The Novel as Genres," *Genre* 12 (1979): 278, 279. The same point is made by Adena Rosmarin: "For genre is not, as is commonly thought, a class but, rather, a classifying statement. It is therefore itself a text. It is writing about writing, distinguished by its topic and its way of handling that topic, the way it takes a set of literary texts and defines their relationship . . . The text called 'genre' is always different from the text it writes about." In *The Power of Genre* (Minneapolis: University of Minnesota Press, 1985), 46. Jenny also concurs: "Genre archetypes, however abstract, still constitute textual structures, ever present to the mind of the writer . . . If the code loses any of its open-endedness . . . then it becomes structurally equivalent to a text. We can then speak of a relation of intertextuality between a specific work and the architext of a genre" ("The Strategy of Form" 42).

6   Jean-Luc Nancy and Philippe Lacoue-Labarthe, *L'Absolu littéraire* (Paris: Seuil, 1978).

7   Roland Barthes, "From Work to Text," 75. Two helpful surveys of the fate of genre criticism in literary history from classical to modern times can be found in Robert J. Connors, "Genre Theory in Literature," in *Genre and the Study of Political Discourse*, ed. Herbert W. Simons and Aram A. Aghazarian (Columbia: University of South Carolina Press, 1986), 25–44, and Heather Dubrow, *Genre* (London: Methuen, 1982).

8   Paul Hernadi, *Beyond Genre*, viii. René Wellek and Austin Warren confronted this issue when they inquired: "Does a theory of literary kinds involve the supposition that every work belongs to a kind? The question is not raised in any discussion we know. If we were to answer by analogy to the natural world, we should certainly answer 'yes.'" In *Theory of Literature*, 3d ed. (New York: Harcourt Brace Jovanovich, 1977), 226. Jacques Derrida is firmer still: "A text cannot belong to no genre, it cannot be without or less a genre. Every text participates in one or several genres, there is no genreless text" ("The Law of Genre" 65). However, he goes on to point out the paradox that genre labels and classifications do not themselves belong to any genre. This is the age-old problem of the frame that is at once included and excluded from that which it frames.

9   Rosalie L. Colie, *The Resources of Kind: Genre-Theory in the Renaissance*, ed. Barbara K. Lewalski (Berkeley: University of California Press, 1973), vii, 8.

10   Rosmarin, *The Power of Genre*, 25. Much of genre criticism has, in fact, been taken up with the workings of the hermeneutical circle and the chicken-or-the-egg question that it raises, that is, whether the definition of a genre on the basis of the features it includes is accomplished inductively or deductively: would readers ever be able to claim they had located these features in certain works if they had not decided to look for them in the first place?

11   Gérard Genette, "Genres, 'types', modes," *Poétique* 32 (1977): 408.

12   The mechanisms that are responsible for the conflation of drama and novel in *Tormento* are studied in Éliane Lavaud, "Presencia y función del teatro en *Tormento* de Pérez Galdós," in *Homenaje a José Antonio Maravall*, ed. María Carmen Iglesia, Carlos Moya, and Luis Rodríguez Zúñiga (Madrid: Centro de Investigaciones Sociológicas, 1985), 2: 415–25.

13   Frank Durand, "Two Problems in Galdós's *Tormento*," *MLN* 79 (1964): 523.

14   Alicia Andreu, "El folletín como intertexto en *Tormento*," *AGald* 17 (1982): 58. Andreu allows that the popular novel is not the only intertext in this novel, merely the most prominent one. Other discourses she sees encrusted in *Tormento* include social criticism (Larra), satire (Quevedo), *costumbrismo*, and journalism (55).

15   For instance, Alicia Andreu, *Galdós y la literatura popular* (Madrid: Sociedad General Española de Librería, 1982); John H. Sinnigen, "Galdós' *Tormento*: Political Partisanship/Literary Structures," *AGald* 15 (1980): 73–82; and Stephanie Sieburth, "Galdós' *Tormento*: Popular Culture, Politics, and Representation," *Journal of Interdisciplinary Studies* 2 (1990): 43–64.

16   Leo B. Levy, *Versions of Melodrama: A Study of the Fiction and Drama of Henry James, 1865–1897* (Berkeley and Los Angeles: University of Califor-

nia Press, 1957), 1–3, 10, 24; Peter Brooks, *The Melodramatic Imagination: Balzac, Henry James, Melodrama, and the Mode of Excess* (New York: Columbia University Press, 1985), 24–55.

17   Brooks, *The Melodramatic Imagination*, 15–16.

18   Caws, *Reading Frames in Modern Fiction*, 4, 86.

19   Goffman, *Frame Analysis*, 132.

20   For a reconstruction of the impact of *Electra* on the younger generation of intellectuals, consult E. Inman Fox, "Galdós' *Electra*: A Detailed Study of Its Historical Significance and the Polemic between Martínez Ruiz and Maeztu," *AGald* 1 (1966): 131–41. Galdós's theater was not infrequently censured for its political and social content, since it skewered such sacred national myths as the themes of Calderonian honor and military transcendence. For a brief account, see Stanley Finkenthal, "Galdós en el teatro: la reacción crítica," in *Estudios de historia, literatura y arte hispánicos ofrecidos a Rodrigo A. Molina*, ed. Wayne H. Finke (Madrid: Insula, 1976), 155–63.

21   Leopoldo Alas, "El teatro . . . de lejos: las tentativas de Pérez Galdós," *Palique* (Madrid: Victoriano Suárez, 1893), 79. On another occasion Clarín explained: "This is commonplace by now: for the theater, and even for drama in general, what does not work is analysis, careful study, with its series of *petits faits* that give us the life of the human spirit. When the theater, principally modern theater, aspires to enter the domain of the novel, it usually comes out badly; and when it succeeds, it does so by not very legitimate means, such as, for instance, excessive monologues, the repetition of *almost identical* scenes, violent scene changes, precipitous use of time, etc." See his review "*Realidad*, novela en cinco jornadas, por don Benito Pérez Galdós," *Revista Literaria* (March 1890), reprinted in *Obras selectas* (Madrid: Biblioteca Nueva, 1947), 1172. Clarín's objections have been echoed by twentieth-century critics as well: "It is not only that Galdós's dramas are not very theatrical . . . In Galdós, the structure of the stage play is an essentially novelistic one." See Francisco Ruiz Ramón, *Historia del teatro español (Desde sus orígenes hasta 1900)* (Madrid: Alianza, 1967), 1: 478.

22   Jesús Rubio Jiménez, *Ideología y teatro en España, 1890–1900* (Zaragoza: Libros Pórtico-Universidad de Zaragoza, n.d.), 75; Levy, *Versions of Melodrama*, 70.

23   The following novels by Galdós were later reworked for the stage: *Doña Perfecta* (novel, 1876; play, 1896), *Gerona* (1874; 1893), *Zaragoza* (1874; 1907), *Realidad* (1889; 1892), *La loca de la casa* (1892; 1893), *El abuelo* (1897; 1904), *Casandra* (1905; 1910)—in other words, one of the novels from his first epoch, two *Episodios Nacionales*, and four relatively late works from the *Novelas contemporáneas* series.

24   Benito Pérez Galdós, "Decadencia," in *Nuestro teatro, Obras inéditas*, ed. Alberto Ghiraldo (Madrid: Renacimiento, 1923), 5: 149–98.

25   Gonzalo Sobejano, "Razón y suceso de la dramática galdosiana," *AGald* 5 (1970): 39.

26   Manuel Alvar, "Novela y teatro en Galdós," in *Estudios y ensayos de literatura contemporánea* (Madrid: Gredos, 1971), 54.

27 On theatricality and melodrama as applied to the early novels, see Roberto G. Sánchez, "*Doña Perfecta* and the Histrionic Projection of Character," *Revista de Estudios* 3 (1969): 175–90, and also his "El sistema dialogal en algunas novelas de Galdós," *CHA* 235 (1969): 155–67, both included in *El teatro en la novela: Galdós y Clarín* (Madrid: Ínsula, 1974). Also of note is Peter Standish, "Theatricality and Humor: Galdós' Technique in *Doña Perfecta*," *BHS* 54 (1977): 223–31.

    A good deal more has been written on the mechanics of the transformation from novel into drama. For a sample, see Matilde Boo, "*El abuelo* de Galdós (de la novela dialogada al drama)," *Sin Nombre* 8 (1977): 42–56; Willa H. Elton, "Sobre el género de *La loca de la casa*," *CHA* 250–52 (1970–1971): 586–607; Luciano E. García Lorenzo, "Sobre la técnica dramática de Galdós: *Doña Perfecta*. De la novela a la obra teatral," *CHA* 250–52 (1970–1971): 445–71; L. A. Brownstein, "*Gerona*: novela y drama de Benito Pérez Galdós," *Yelmo* 23 (1975): 37–41; J. Domínguez Jiménez, "*Gerona* 'Episodio Nacional' y *Gerona* 'Drama,'" in *Actas del Primer Congreso Internacional de Estudios Galdosianos* (Las Palmas: Cabildo Insular de Gran Canaria, 1977): 152–63; Elsa M. Martínez Umpiérrez, "*Epistolario*: el problema de la transformación de la novela en drama a través de algunas cartas de D. Benito," in *Actas del Primero Congreso Internacional de Estudios Galdosianos* (Las Palmas: Cabildo Insular de Gran Canaria, 1977), 106–17.

28 Alicia Andreu, "El folletín como intertexto en *Tormento*," 55–56.
29 Tarrío, *Lectura semiológica de "Fortunata y Jacinta,"* 57.
30 Elizabeth Burns, *Theatricality: A Study of Convention in the Theatre and in Social Life* (London: Longman, 1972), 3.
31 On the problem of theater (reality) versus theatricality (unreality) and its relationship to the topic of the *gran teatro del mundo* in the context of western philosophy, see Marian Hobston, "Du *Theatrum Mundi* au *Theatrum Mentis*," *RSH* 167 (1977): 379–94. It is also helpful to compare how Balzac handled this topic. Lucienne Frappier-Mazur, "La métaphore théâtrale dans *La Comédie humaine*," *RHLF* 70 (1970): 64–89, sees three different aspects to the elaboration of the *theatrum mundi* metaphor in Balzac's work: the "scene from life," the most traditional manifestation of the topic, in which the ignorant actor, performing before an omniscient spectator, confuses reality and appearance; the "social comedy," in which the omniscient actor, well-versed in reality's rules, deceives the spectator, who is a victim of appearances; and the theater which, by means of the creation of illusions, paradoxically is converted into a "superior reality," a higher aesthetic truth. Frappier-Mazur adds: "In these three cases, Balzac's literary ideas on the dramatic genre only play an auxiliary role . . . His point of view is philosophical, moral, and aesthetic" (67). *Tormento* differs from Balzac's cycle of novels in several obvious ways. In *Tormento*, theater always points to a degraded reality, not to an aesthetic ideal—obviously so, since Galdós's models were not the theater of Molière and Racine but rather the decadent theater of his own era. Furthermore, the author's ideas on the genre of drama are not incidental; they are, in fact, a key to the novel's construction.

32   An even clearer example of the theatricality that obtains in contemporary religious practice can be found in the description of the church that celebrates a novena paid for by Milagros de Tellería in *La de Bringas*. Its shiny interior is lit by candles that function as footlights; its cheap velvet curtains are reminiscent of a "third-rate theater" (4: 1616).

33   Eamonn Rodgers, "The Appearance-Reality Contrast in Galdós' *Tormento*," *FMLS* 4 (1970): 394. For an ideological interpretation of the same structural duality, see Sinnigen, "Galdós' *Tormento*: Political Partisanship/Literary Structures."

34   Galdós, "Decadencia," 154–55.

35   David Cluff, "The Structure and Meaning of Galdós' *Tormento*," *Reflexión* 3–4 (1974–1975): 159–67, indicates that the central three characters are torn by the duality of order-disorder, while the peripheral characters are grouped around one or the other of these two poles; they do not suffer from any internal conflict.

36   Colie, *The Resources of Kind*, 127.

37   Pérez Galdós, "La sociedad presente como materia novelable," 24.

5   The Museum as Metaframe in the *Novelas contemporáneas*

1   Aurora León, *El museo: teoría, praxis, utopía*, 3d ed. (Madrid: Cátedra, 1986), 10.

2   Pérez Galdós, "La sociedad presente como materia novelable," 14.

3   J. J. Alfieri, "El arte pictórico en las novelas de Galdós," *AGald* 3 (1968): 79–86. A similar approach is applied by Geraldine M. Scanlon, "Religion and Art in *Angel Guerra*," *AGald* 8 (1973): 99–105.

4   Peter A. Bly, *Vision and the Visual Arts in Galdós*, 224. Bly's book includes a bibliography of studies that deal specifically with visual values in Galdós's narratives: the use of chiaroscuro, color symbolism, distance and perspective, and plastic descriptive strategies. See also his chapter 2 on "Perspective and Vision" in *Pérez Galdós: "La de Bringas,"* 18–29.

5   Mario Praz, *Mnemosyne: The Parallel between Literature and the Visual Arts* (Princeton: Princeton University Press, 1970); Jean H. Hagstrum, *The Sister Arts: The Tradition of Literary Pictorialism and English Poetry from Dryden to Gray* (Chicago: University of Chicago Press, 1958); Helmut A. Hatzfeld, *Literature through Art: A New Approach to French Literature* (New York: Oxford University Press, 1952).

6   Roland Barthes, "The Photographic Message," in *Image-Music-Text*, trans. Stephen Heath (New York: Hill and Wang, 1977), 28–29.

7   Alistair Fowler, "Periodization and Interart Analogies," *NLH* 3 (1972): 498. See also René Wellek, "The Parallelism between Literature and the Arts," *English Institute Annual* (New York: Columbia University Press, 1942), 29–63. One of the few attempts to establish interart analogies between the nineteenth-century Spanish novel and the sister arts is that of Noël M. Valis, who in "Novel into Painting: Transition in Spanish Realism," *AGald* 20.1 (1985): 9–22, sustains that the "iconization of the feminine" in selected

novels written by Picón, Galdós, and Clarín during the 1890s creates a sort of novelistic self-awareness comparable to the "artistic autonomy" of fin-de-siècle paintings of the Impressionist and Postimpressionist schools.

8 Benito Pérez Galdós, "Las bellas artes en España," *Obras inéditas*, ed. Alberto Ghiraldo (Madrid: Renacimiento, 1923), 2: 9–36.

9 The manner in which the ritual or cult function of works of art has been superseded by a decontextualized exhibition value is discussed by Walter Benjamin, "The Work of Art in the Age of Mechanical Reproduction," in *Illuminations*, ed. Hannah Arendt, trans. Harry Zohn (New York: Schocken, 1968), 217–51, especially 224–25.

10 Hugh Kenner, "Epilogue: The Dead-Letter Office," in *Museums in Crisis*, ed. Brian O'Doherty (New York: George Braziller, 1972), 164.

11 Theodor Adorno, "Valéry Proust Museum," in *Prisms*, trans. Samuel and Sherry Weber (London: Neville Spearman, 1967), 175.

12 Emile Zola, *L'Assommoir*, in *Oeuvres complètes* (Paris: Fasquelle, 1967), 3: 655.

13 Romualdo Nogués y Milagro, *Ropavejeros, anticuarios y coleccionistas, por un soldado viejo natural de Borja* (Madrid: Tip. de Infantería de Marina, 1890), 223. One is reminded of Flaubert's critique of the cliché that the museum had become for his century, as found in his entry on the subject in the *Dictionnaire des idées reçues*: "MUSEUMS:—VERSAILLES. Recalls the great days of the nation's history. A splendid idea of Louis Philippe's.—THE LOUVRE. To be avoided by young ladies.—DUPUYTREN. Very instructive for young men." Gustave Flaubert, *Bouvard and Pécuchet, with The Dictionary of Received Ideas*, trans. A. J. Krailsheimer (Harmondsworth: Penguin, 1976), 317.

14 On the founding of the Prado, see Mariano de Madrazo, *Historia del Museo del Prado, 1818–1868* (Madrid: C. Bermejo, 1945). That the museum had already become an important institutional setting in early nineteenth-century Spain can be verified in Ramón de Mesonero Romanos's *Manual histórico-topográfico, administrativo y artístico de Madrid*, nueva ed. (Madrid: Imprenta de Antonio Yenes, 1844), reproduced in facsimile by Ábaco Editores (Madrid, 1977). Mesonero gives detailed information about the Museo Real de Pintura y Escultura (as the Prado was originally known), the Academia de San Fernando, the Museo Nacional de la Trinidad (1838), the Armería Real, the Museo Militar de Artillería (1803), the Museo de Ingenieros (1823), the Real Gabinete Topográfico (1832), and the Museo Naval (1842), as well as a host of scientific establishments. The most prominent among these was the Museo de Ciencias Naturales, which administered the Gabinete de Historia Natural, the Jardín Botánico, and the Observatorio Astronómico. Many of these institutions had already formed a steady clientele. In the Museo de Máquinas y Modelos, dedicated to advances in agriculture and industry, a "staff curator offers the necessary explanations to the workers and other persons who visit." The Prado already had a souvenir stand, in the form of a "collection of lithographic reproductions of the museum's principal paintings, executed in recent years and sold at the entrance."

15 Leopoldo Alas, *Museum (Mi revista)* [*Folletos literarios* VII] (Madrid: Fernando Fe, 1890), 6.

16 See Michael A. Schnepf, "Galdós's *La desheredada* Manuscript: Isidora in the Prado Museum," *RQ* 37 (1990): 321–29, especially 322. The deleted material, which Schnepf here transcribes, spoke of specific paintings which seem keyed to developing aspects of the protagonist's character.

17 For a social history of this phenomenon in Spain, see J. Miguel Morán and Fernando Checa, *El coleccionismo en España* (Madrid: Cátedra, 1985). In *La sombra* there is a clear antecedent for this motif. Don Anselmo's father is described as "the most enthusiastic collector of art works that ever existed" (4: 202). The exterior of his palace conforms to classical norms, but the habitable interior part of the mansion is a "museum of ornamentation" marked by a chaotic jumble of objects, mercilessly enumerated by the protagonist. It is a sign of Anselmo's own madness that in matters of aesthetics he prefers disorder and heterogeneity to "harmony, symmetry, proportion, and grace."

18 Abraham A. Moles and Eberhard Wahl maintain that the kitsch sensibility "is the product of an epoch that puts everything it can find on public sale: Chinese vases, prostitutes' virtue, stock in the Panama canal, opium from Shanghai, or Persian miniatures." They conclude that what is tragic about kitsch is the principle of mediocrity. See "Kitsch et objet," *Communications* 13 (1969): 105–29, especially 110, 119.

19 Pérez Galdós, "El coleccionista," 202. Adorno, in "Valéry Proust Museum," concurs: "Whether artists produce or rich people die, whatever happens is good for the museum. Like casinos, they cannot lose, and that is their curse" (177).

20 Nogués y Milagro, *Ropavejeros, anticuarios y coleccionistas*, 151.

21 On the predominance of narrative in the formulation of traditional knowledge and the breakdown of Western culture's grand narratives, see Jean-François Lyotard, *The Postmodern Condition: A Report on Knowledge*, trans. Geoff Bennington and Brian Massumi (Minneapolis: University of Minnesota Press, 1984), 15, 19–23.

22 Manso explains that his sister-in-law and her relatives went shopping every afternoon and came home loaded down with "prendas falsas y chucherías de bazar" 'fake jewels and cheap trinkets' (4: 1206). The image of the bazaar, a shop or fair that trades in miscellaneous articles, recurs not just in fiction but also in the periodical press of the time. There was even an illustrated weekly called *El Bazar* published in 1875 (Madrid). The contents of each issue included such disperse items as a chronicle of current events, a chapter of a serialized novel by a serious author (Victor Hugo) or a popular one (Fernández y González), a calendar of public activities, poetry, a rebus, an article on domestic economy, and reproductions of engravings showing a marked taste for exotic subjects.

My colleague Hugo Achugar has pointed out that a very similar critique of the bazaar structures Rubén Darío's story "El rey burgués," in *Cuentos completos*, ed. Ernesto Mejía Sánchez (Mexico: Fondo de Cultura Económica,

1950), 55–59. For Darío's king, the poet is simply one more specimen in a collection built upon the acquisition of the costly and the exotic.

23 By contrast, Ramón Gómez de la Serna, in "Lo cursi," argues for the existence of two varieties of kitsch, "perishable and exaggeratedly sentimental kitsch and immortalizable and sensitive kitsch," defending the latter as "the spontaneous and naïve adornment that wants to embrace us facing the void. There is warmth in its persistence and desire for company" (26, 35). He stresses the importance of the nineteenth century's acceptance of kitsch as a "vital ingredient, a keeper of the peace, a safe anchor for its time" (32). In *Lo cursi y otros ensayos* (Buenos Aires: Editorial Sudamericana, 1943), 7–54. See also Francisco Ynduráin, "Lo 'cursi' en la obra de Galdós," *Actas del Segundo Congreso Internacional de Estudios Galdosianos* (Las Palmas: Cabildo Insular de Gran Canaria, 1980), 1: 266–82, for an inventory of kitsch artifacts in Galdós's novels.

24 Pérez Galdós, "El coleccionista," 197, 199.

25 Emilia Pardo Bazán, "Coleccionista," in *Obras completas*, ed. Federico Sainz de Robles (Madrid: Aguilar, 1947), 2: 1696–98. Isabelita Bringas is also characterized by "hábitos de urraca" 'the habits of a magpie.'

26 Isabelita can claim a spiritual brother in Maxi Rubín, who is similarly distracted by a collection of worthless odds and ends. As Maxi is about to commit the crime of breaking open his piggy bank, the narrator remembers his only other infraction of note: "The only thing he had done, years ago, was to rob his aunt's buttons to collect them. Instincts of the collector, which are a variation on avarice!" (5: 168). Even Máximo Manso, for all his abstraction from worldly concerns, is not immune to the collector's greed, a fact taken advantage of by that perennial borrower of money, doña Cándida: "Knowing my weakness for collecting trinkets, my enemy [Cándida] always used to bring a piece of porcelain, a print, or a bagatelle" (4: 1196).

27 Jean Baudrillard, *For a Critique of the Political Economy of the Sign*, trans. Charles Levin (St. Louis: Telos Press, 1981), 32.

28 Eugenio Donato, "The Museum's Furnace: Notes Towards a Contextual Reading of *Bouvard et Pécuchet*," in *Textual Strategies: Perspectives in Post-Structuralist Criticism*, ed. Josué V. Harari (Ithaca: Cornell University Press, 1979), 213–38, especially 224–25.

29 The contradictory logic of the structure of supplementarity receives its fullest treatment in Derrida's lengthy discussion of how speech is valued over writing in Rousseau's thought. The *supplément* pretends to be simply an adjunct, an improvement on an already perfect and originary plenitude of presence, yet inevitably comes to substitute for a default or absence that is interior rather than exterior to that origin. See Jacques Derrida, *Of Grammatology*, trans. Gayatri Chakravorty Spivak (Baltimore: Johns Hopkins University Press, 1976), 141 ff. Despite the supplement's cumulative function, its capacity to be added on, Derrida notes the essential and paradoxical poverty at the heart of this concept: "As substitute, it is not simply added to the positivity of a presence, it produces no relief, its place is assigned in the structure by the mark of an emptiness. Somewhere, something can be filled up *of itself*, can

accomplish itself, only by allowing itself to be filled through sign and proxy. The sign is always the supplement of the thing itself" (145). In this light, the serial collection becomes less a compensation than a perennial insatisfaction, a reminder of the imminent defeat that haunts representation, whether visual or linguistic.

30 Pérez Galdós, "El coleccionista," 202.

31 E. H. Gombrich, "The Museum: Past, Present, Future," *Critl* 3 (1977): 457.

32 On the nomenclature of the *passe-partout*, see Jacques Derrida, *The Truth in Painting*, 7–8, 12–13.

33 Ramón María Tenreiro, "Galdós, novelista," *La Lectura*, 20.1 (1920): 335. As forerunners of the realist novel, the *costumbrista* essayists followed a similarly conservatorial policy. Seeing how the nation's traditional modes of life were threatened by the encroachment of progress, they described typical scenes in their articles, thus using the perdurability of literature and the printed word as a hedge against their eventual disappearance.

34 Leopoldo Alas, "Los últimos libros de Galdós," *La España Moderna* 10 (October 1889): 184.

35 Donato, "The Museum's Furnace," 237.

36 Hamon, *Introduction à l'analyse du descriptif*, 73.

37 Pérez Galdós, "La sociedad presente como materia novelable," 26.

38 Donato, "The Museum's Furnace," 224.

39 Germán Gullón, *La novela como acto imaginativo* (Madrid: Taurus, 1983), 72.

40 Tanner's remark is included in a round table discussion reproduced in "Realism, Reality, and the Novel," ed. Park Honan, *Novel* 2 (1969): 206.

41 Ricardo Gullón, *Técnicas de Galdós*, 183–255. Casalduero espouses a related interpretation: for him, Galdós learns to confront reality with spirituality, mimesis with imagination. However, he insists that this response to the crisis of representation is found principally in Galdós's later works, from 1892 on. See *Vida y obra de Galdós*, 186–88. This diachronic classification of Galdós's novels seems unnecessarily rigid, since the author clearly has recourse to the antimimetic throughout his long career. The fantastic, the oneiric, and the metafictive dimensions are in fact staples of Galdós's work, appearing in even his earliest writings.

42 León, *El museo: teoría, praxis, utopía*, 58.

6 Reading and the Frame-up of *El doctor Centeno*

1 In *S/Z*, Barthes postulates five codes (proairetic, semic, cultural, symbolic, and hermeneutic) that govern the legibility of texts (25–28). The idea that literary competence is derived from the readers' ability to understand and manipulate conventions is propounded by Jonathan Culler, *Structuralist Poetics*, 113–30. He defines competence as "what an ideal reader must know implicitly in order to read and interpret works in ways which we consider acceptable, in accordance with the institution of literature" (123). Umberto Eco, in *The Role of the Reader* (Bloomington: Indiana University Press, 1984),

prefers the term "intertextual frames." These refer not to rules governing real-life experiences but to knowledge of literary topoï and narrative schemes, derived from previous experience with texts (21–22).

2 Rimmon-Kenan, *Narrative Fiction*, 123–24.

3 Menakhem Perry, "Literary Dynamics: How the Order of a Text Creates Its Meaning," *PT* 1.1–2 (1979): 45.

4 Marvin Minsky, *The Society of Mind* (New York: Simon and Schuster, 1985), 247.

5 Culler, *On Deconstruction*, 196.

6 Emilia Pardo Bazán, "Carta magna," dated April 26, 1884 (La Coruña) and published May 6, 1884 in *La Epoca*; later reprinted in her *Obras completas* (Madrid: Renacimiento, n.d. [1892]), 6: 142. The enthusiastic embrace of the first volume by the public had augured a more favorable reception for the novel than it ultimately achieved. In a letter to Galdós dated June 24, 1883, Clarín wrote regarding *Centeno*: "In Spain, this is a novelty and a great triumph: that when the second volume comes out, the first one is already in its second edition. Keep it up, keep it up." In *Cartas a Galdós*, ed. Soledad Ortega (Madrid: Revista de Occidente, 1964), 213. Important reviews that appeared at the time of the novel's publication include those by Luis Alfonso in *La Epoca* (July 30, 1883), José Ortega Munilla in *El Imparcial* (May 28, 1883), Eugenio de Olavarría y Huarte in *América* (April 1, 1884), and Leopoldo Alas in *El Día* (August 5, 1883 and March 15, 1884).

7 William H. Shoemaker, *The Novelistic Art of Pérez Galdós* (Valencia: Albatros-Hispanófila, 1980), 2: 188.

8 José Ortega y Munilla, letter to Galdós, in *Cartas del archivo de Pérez Galdós*, ed. Sebastián de la Nuez and José Schraibman (Madrid: Taurus, 1967), 199.

9 Among the *Novelas contemporáneas*, *El doctor Centeno* is not alone in offering a problematic interpretation of its title. Another example of how Galdós deliberately misleads his readers can be found in *La desheredada*, where the plebeian Isidora Rufete cannot in fact be disinherited from the Marquesa de Aransis, since her genealogical claims are completely unfounded. In this instance, the title functions as a kind of "intentional delay in revealing Isidora's representational signification." See Gilman, *Galdós and the Art of the European Novel*, 111.

10 Montesinos, *Galdós*, 2: 70. He confesses, "It must be my own blindness or confusion, but I am unable to see either the reason for the title or even for its continual presence in this work." For Montesinos, the novel is characterized by its "odd structure that we have not yet understood" (72, 73).

11 For a consideration of all these possibilities, focusing on the category that narrates precisely what did *not* happen, see Gerald Prince, "The Disnarrated," *Style* 22.1 (1988): 1–8.

12 See the interesting discussion of names and naming in *El doctor Centeno* as a means of inventing and controlling reality through the arbitrariness of language in Akiko Tsuchiya, *Images of the Sign*, 48–49.

13 Robert Kirsner, *Veinte años de matrimonio en la novela de Galdós* (New York:

Eliseo Torres, 1983), 121. Shoemaker, *The Novelistic Art of Pérez Galdós*, 2: 188–89, similarly labels *Centeno* a prologue.

14   Casalduero, *Vida y obra de Galdós*, 77.

15   Cecil Jenkins, "Reality and the Novel Form," in *The Monster in the Mirror*, ed. D. A. Williams (New York: Oxford University Press, 1978), 5.

16   Geraldine M. Scanlon, "*El doctor Centeno*: A Study in Obsolescent Values," *BHS* 55 (1978): 245. The importance of pedagogical and cultural themes to the successful integration of the novel's two parts is elaborated in Gloria Moreno Castillo, "La unidad de tema en *El doctor Centeno*," in *Actas del Primer Congreso Internacional de Estudios Galdosianos* (Las Palmas: Cabildo Insular de Gran Canaria, 1977), 382–94.

17   Germán Gullón, "Unidad de *El doctor Centeno*," *CHA* 250–52 (1970–1971): 582, 581. Rodolfo Cardona, "Nuevos enfoques críticos con respecto a la obra de Galdós," *CHA* 250–52 (1970–1971): 58–72, views the pairing of Miquis and Centeno as an expression of Galdós's doubled and divided image of himself as a writer: the youthful dramatist whose creations are inspired in an unbridled imagination (Alejandro) and the more mature novelist who, through study and observation, achieves a more balanced vision of life and literature (Felipe). What previous readers have condemned as the text's implied incompatibility with its own discourse would appear to find an analogy in Cardona's discussion of the nonidentity of the author's various selves.

18   Tsuchiya, *Images of the Sign*, 54.

19   Hans Robert Jauss, "Theses on the Transition from the Aesthetics of Literary Works to a Theory of Aesthetic Experience," in *Interpretation of Narrative*, ed. Mario J. Valdés and Owen J. Miller (Toronto: University of Toronto Press, 1978), 139.

20   Culler, *On Deconstruction*, 200.

21   David Simpson, "Literary Criticism and the Return to 'History,'" *CritI* 14 (1988): 731. Following the Derridean line, J. Hillis Miller concurs that imagery of the line and the aesthetic unity it confers are deeply embedded in Western thought and art, adding, "Such a [presupposed] unity always turns out to be spurious, imposed rather than intrinsic." See "Ariadne's Thread: Repetition and the Narrative Line," *CritI* 3 (1976): 74, and similar arguments in his "Ariachne's Broken Woof," *Georgia Review* 31 (1977): 44–60.

22   Leopoldo Alas, "*Tormento*," in *Galdós, Obras completas* (Madrid: Renacimiento, 1912), 1: 122–23.

23   Leopoldo Alas, *El Día*, August 5, 1883.

24   Hillis Miller, "Ariadne's Thread," 68–69.

25   Sherman H. Eoff, *The Novels of Pérez Galdós: The Concept of Life as Dynamic Process* (St. Louis: Washington University Studies, 1954), 13.

26   For a comparison of *El doctor Centeno* and the picaresque, see Eoff, *The Novels of Pérez Galdós*, 14. Cardona establishes the intertextual links between Galdós's novel and Goethe's *Wilhelm Meister* in "Nuevos enfoques críticos," 67–71. On the relationship between *Centeno* and Golden Age literature, including Calderonian theater, see Gustavo Correa, "Pérez Galdós

y la tradición calderoniana," *CHA* 250–52 (1970–71): 221–41, and also his
"Calderón y la novela realista española," *AGald* 18 (1983): 15–24, especially 19–20. A suggested reading of *Centeno* as a parody of *El licenciado
Vidriera* is offered by Alfred Rodríguez and Mary Jo Ramos, "Notas para una
relectura de *El doctor Centeno* en el centenario de su publicación," *AGald*
19 (1984): 143–46. Cervantine influence, particularly that of the *Quijote*, is
especially pervasive in *Centeno*. Shoemaker, *The Novelistic Art of Pérez Galdós*, 2: 205–6, touches on some of the salient points of comparison. For a
summary of bibliography dealing with Galdós's thematic and formal debt to
Cervantes and the *Quijote*, the reader may consult Anthony Percival, *Galdós and His Critics* (Toronto: University of Toronto Press, 1985), 84–86 and
222–23.

27   Miller, "Balzac's Illusions Lost and Found," 167. Peter Brooks, in *The Melodramatic Imagination*, likewise sees in this concluding scene Rastignac's
achieved melodramatic understanding of the struggle in which he is engaged,
a struggle which is in itself hyperbolic and is symbolized by Rastignac's
"standing on the literal heights of the cemetery." Such heightening and excess permit Rastignac "to raise Paris itself to the status of meaning, to see
society and the city as a landscape endowed with clear, represented signifi-
cations" whose hidden drama cannot be pierced by the hero's visionary gaze
(140). Peter Bly recognizes the symbolic value of similar scenes in *El doctor
Centeno*: "Felipe's elongated perspective of events [during Calvo Asensio's
funeral] due to his position atop a lamppost is an example of Galdós's skill-
ful use of distance in this novel to underline the deformed vision of Spanish
reality that he is presenting. This distortion is also present in the protagonist's
initial view of Madrid from a hilltop." See his *Galdós's Novel of the Historical
Imagination* (Liverpool: Francis Cairns, 1983), 37n.

28   Honoré de Balzac, *Le Père Goriot*, in *La Comédie humaine*, ed. Marcel Bou-
teron (Paris: Gallimard, 1951), 2: 1085.

29   Concerning the opening of the novel one critic was moved to exclaim: "What
a way to begin a novel! . . . *El doctor Centeno* begins by breaking with established practices that the first chapter of every novel be some singular event
whose inexplicable mystery becomes the hook to string up the reader's spirit,
until he finishes the book, and after the money that it costs is obtained, he
is let down so that he may go on his way." See J[osé] Ortega Munilla, *El
Imparcial*, May 28, 1883.

30   Montesinos, *Galdós*, wonders: "He [Centeno] is the character who joins the
world of the Polo family with that of Miquis, but what is the purpose of that
union? Miquis and Polo never come into contact" (2: 72).

31   Hillis Miller, "Ariadne's Thread," 68. Early on, Hafter perspicuously identified a particular type of internal repetition in Galdós's works, based on
pairings of characters or doublings of the story. He labeled these examples
of "ironic reprise" because although the repetitions superficially appeared
to highlight antithetical relationships, a closer inspection revealed that such
oppositions actually tended to dissolve in a fundamental identity of themes,

motifs, and motives. See Monroe Z. Hafter, "Ironic Reprise in Galdós' Novels," *PMLA* 76 (1961): 233–39.

32 The *mise en abyme* is a special case of frame embedding, in which the contents or structure of both inner and outer frame are identical. The definitive study of this figure can be found in Lucien Dällenbach, *Le récit speculaire* (Paris: Seuil, 1977).

33 For instance, Montesinos, *Galdós*, 2: 78; Diane F. Urey, "Isabel II and Historical Truth in the Fourth Series of Galdós' *Episodios Nacionales*," *MLN* 98 (1983): 189–207, especially 189–90; Antonio Regalado García, *Benito Pérez Galdós y la novela histórica española, 1868–1912* (Madrid: Insula, 1966), 366.

34 Peter Brooks, *Reading for the Plot* (New York: Random House, 1985), xiii, 35.

7 Criticism, the Framing of the Canon, and the Nineteenth-Century Spanish Novel

1 Hans Ulrich Gumbrecht, " 'Phoenix from the Ashes' or: From Canon to Classic," *NLH* 20 (1988–1989): 150–51.

2 Urbano González Serrano, "*Doña Perfecta*: Novela original de Pérez Galdós," *El Imparcial*, July 31, 1876.

3 Leopoldo Alas, "*Lo prohibido*," rpt. in *Leopoldo Alas: teoría y crítica de la novela española*, ed. Sergio Beser (Barcelona: Laia, 1972), 243.

4 Alas, "Del naturalismo," ibid., 137.

5 For further discussions of Krausism and its promotion of the novel and literary criticism as tools of instruction and social and moral improvement, see Juan López-Morillas, *El krausismo español* (Mexico: Fondo de Cultura Económica, 1956), and his introduction to *Krausismo: estética y literatura* (Barcelona: Labor, 1973), 9–30.

6 José Ortega y Gasset, "La deshumanización del arte," in *La deshumanización del arte y otros ensayos de estética*, ed. Paulino Garragori, 3d ed. rev. (Madrid: Alianza, 1984), 30.

7 Aleixandre's comments are featured in a survey of opinions of twentieth-century writers on Galdós, including Baroja, Cela, Azorín, Zunzunegui, and Laforet. "Revisión de Galdós," *Insula* 82 (October 15, 1952): 3. The questions posed by the survey were: "What impression do you retain of your first encounter with Galdós's work? Do you believe Galdós had some influence on your work or that of the writers of your generation? How do you view Galdós today and what role do you think he occupies in the history of our novel?"

8 Juan Goytisolo, *Disidencias* (Barcelona: Seix Barral, 1977), 155.

9 Cited in Fernando Valls, *La enseñanza de la literatura en el franquismo, 1936–1951* (Barcelona: Antoni Bosch, 1983), 161.

10 On this topic see Manuel L. Abellán, *Censura y creación literaria en España, 1939–1976* (Barcelona: Península, 1980), 41, 49–50; Valls, *La enseñanza de*

la literatura en el franquismo, 160–63; and Percival, *Galdós and His Critics*, 34–36.

11 A detailed history of the treatment of *La Regenta* and its author, including the stony silence maintained by many critics at the time of its publication, can be found in María José Tintoré, *"La Regenta" de Clarín y la crítica de su tiempo* (Barcelona: Lumen, 1987).

12 Gonzalo Sobejano, *Clarín en su obra ejemplar* (Madrid: Castalia, 1985), 177.

13 Francisco Blanco García, *La literatura española en el siglo XIX* (Madrid: Sáenz de Jubera Hermanos, 1891–1894), 3 vols.

14 Emilia Pardo Bazán, "Un jesuita novelista (El P. Luis Coloma)," *Nuevo Teatro Crítico* 1, no. 4 (April 1891) (Madrid: La España Editorial, 1891), 55.

15 Emilia Pardo Bazán, *La cuestión palpitante*, ed. Carmen Bravo-Villasante, 2d ed. (Salamanca: Anaya, 1970), 31.

16 In this study I generally oppose literary to nonliterary or extraliterary criteria in the process of canon formation and consolidation. I am well aware that one may plausibly argue that no act of literary evaluation is totally free of self-interested perceptual biases, and that for some the distinction between an ideal critic whose cognitive appreciation of aesthetic form would result in objective and universal value judgments and a practical critic whose dicta are influenced by the political and social relationship he or she bears to the reading audience is in fact a straw man opposition, particularly since the ideal critic is a construct that exists solely on paper.

Paralleling the tendency in contemporary criticism, especially marked in Derrida and Foucault, that sees embedded in literary structures an articulation of modes and relations of power, Barbara Herrnstein Smith argues that "the recurrent impulse or effort to define aesthetic value by contradistinction to all forms of utility or as the negation of all other nameable sources of interest or forms of value—hedonic, practical, sentimental, ornamental, historical, ideological, and so forth—is, in effect, to define it out of existence; for when all such particular utilities, interests, and sources of value have been subtracted, nothing remains." In "Contingencies of Value," *CritI* 10 (1983): 14. Approached from this angle, the distinctive feature of Hispanic value judgments regarding the nineteenth-century novel appears to be the baldness with which the aims of canon formation (and canon busting) have been presented, with little attempt to disguise their local, parochial motivations.

17 Abellán, *Censura y creación literaria en España*, 87–96.

18 Marcelino Menéndez y Pelayo, "Contestación del Excmo. Sr. D. M. Menéndez y Pelayo [a Benito Pérez Galdós]," *Discursos leídos ante la Real Academia Española en las recepciones públicas del 7 y 21 de febrero de 1897* (Madrid: Est. Tip. de la Viuda e Hijos de Tello, 1897), 68.

19 Jonathan Culler, "Issues in Contemporary American Critical Debate," in *American Criticism in the Poststructuralist Age*, ed. Ira Konigsberg (Ann Arbor: University of Michigan, 1981), 12.

20 Claudio Guillén, *Literature as System* (Princeton: Princeton University Press, 1971), 12–13.

21 John Rutherford, *Leopoldo Alas: "La Regenta"* (London: Grant and Cutler, 1974), 9.

22 Gullón, *La novela como acto imaginativo*, 36. One marked exception is the interest that has been generated in the field of semiotics, as evidenced by such studies as Tarrío's *Lectura semiológica de "Fortunata y Jacinta"* and María del Carmen Bobes Naves's *Teoría general de la novela: semiología de "La Regenta"* (Madrid: Gredos, 1985).

23 Francisco Caudet, "Introducción" to *Fortunata y Jacinta* by Benito Pérez Galdós (Madrid: Cátedra, 1983), 1: 12.

24 Cited by Noël M. Valis, "Benito Pérez Galdós' *Miau* and the Display of Dialectic," *RR* 77 (1986): 415.

25 See Farris Anderson, "Ellipsis and Space in *Tristana*," *AGald* 20.2 (1985): 61–76, for a recuperation of this novel: "*Tristana* is a coherent novel and, paradoxically, a complete novel, if by 'completeness' we understand compliance with aesthetic principles established within the work rather than with expectations that are externally imposed" (62).

26 John W. Kronik, "The State of the Art: American Contributions to the Appreciation of Eighteenth and Nineteenth Century Peninsular Literature," *The American Hispanist* 2.18 (May 1977): 3.

27 Roland Barthes, *Writing Degree Zero*, trans. Annette Lavers and Colin Smith (New York: Hill and Wang, 1968), 67. Barthes's discussion of realism as a local construct that seeks to project itself as a universal essence finds its analogue in the work of other theorists intent upon revealing the subjective, invented structures of fields considered to be objective and immune to the devices or processes of the fictional. As examples, one might cite the rhetoricizing of science through a series of interpretive paradigms, treated in Thomas Kuhn's *The Structure of Scientific Revolutions* (Chicago: University of Chicago Press, 1962) or the narrativization of history explored by Hayden White in his *Metahistory* (Baltimore: Johns Hopkins University Press, 1973).

28 Frank Kermode, "Novels: Recognition and Deception," *CritI* 1 (1974): 112.

29 On realism as transcription and the nineteenth-century opposition of multiple reproduction to originality, see Noël M. Valis, "The Perfect Copy: Clarín's *Su único hijo* and the Flaubertian Connection," *PMLA* 104 (1989): 856–67.

30 Robert Scholes, *The Fabulators* (New York: Oxford University Press, 1967), 11.

31 Germán Gullón, "Problemas del pluralismo crítico: *Pérez Galdós: 'Fortunata y Jacinta'*," *HR* 49 (1981): 186.

32 Richard Rorty, *Philosophy and the Mirror of Nature* (Princeton: Princeton University Press, 1979), 273–95, 333–42.

33 Terry Eagleton, *Marxism and Literary Criticism* (Berkeley and Los Angeles: University of California Press, 1976), 71.

34 Jameson, *The Political Unconscious*, 193.

35 Eagleton, *Marxism and Literary Criticism*, 5.

36 Frank Kermode, "Institutional Control of Interpretation," *Salmagundi* 43 (1979): 74.

37 Walter Benjamin, *Charles Baudelaire: A Lyric Poet in the Era of High Capitalism*, trans. Harry Zohn (London: NLB, [1973]); Jonathan Culler, *Flaubert: The Uses of Uncertainty*, rev. ed. (Ithaca: Cornell University Press, 1985).

38 Emilio Alarcos Llorach, "Notas a *La Regenta*," in *Clarín y "La Regenta"*, ed. Sergio Beser (Barcelona: Ariel, 1982), 243.

39 Harriet S. Turner, "Vigencias de Clarín: vistas retrospectivas en torno a *La Regenta*," *Arbor* 116 (1983): 380.

40 Gullón, *La novela como acto imaginativo*, 133.

41 In *The Novel Histories of Galdós*, Urey writes that "novel and history are interchangeable and indistinguishable modes of discourse because they both necessarily rely on the same narrative strategies. However diligently the reader may pursue some absolute point of reference, some sure knowledge of the past in the novel or in history, in Galdós's novel histories this effort is constantly undermined. While the *Episodios nacionales* may give us a better understanding of many aspects of Spain's past, they also always tell us that the past they create is an illusion" (13).

42 Laura Rivkin, "Seeing, Painting, and Picturing in *La Regenta*," *HR* 55 (1987): 321.

43 Gerald Graff, "The Politics of Anti-Realism," *Salmagundi* 42 (1978): 4–30.

44 Eduardo Mendoza, *El misterio de la cripta embrujada*, 7th ed. (Barcelona: Seix Barral, 1982), 20.

45 James H. Kavanaugh, "Ideology," in *Critical Terms for Literary Study*, ed. Frank Lentricchia and Thomas McLaughlin (Chicago: University of Chicago Press, 1990), 314.

46 Terry Eagleton, *Literary Theory: An Introduction* (Minneapolis: University of Minnesota Press, 1983), 201.

47 Stanley E. Fish, "How Ordinary Is Ordinary Language?", *NLH* 5.1 (1973): 52.

48 Charles Altieri, "An Idea and Ideal of a Literary Canon," *CritI* 10 (1983): 43.

49 Among the obligatory readings on the subject of the popular novel in Spain are Juan Ignacio Ferreras, *La novela por entregas, 1840–1900* (Madrid: Taurus, 1972) and *Introducción a una sociología de la novela española del siglo XIX* (Madrid: Editorial Cuadernos para el Diálogo, 1973); Jean-François Botrel, "La novela por entregas: unidad de creación y consumo," in *Creación y público en la literatura española*, ed. Jean-François Botrel and Serge Salaün (Madrid: Castalia, 1974), 111–55; Joaquín Marco, *Literatura popular en España en los siglos XVIII y XIX* (Madrid: Taurus, 1977), 2 vols.; Leonardo Romero Tobar, *La novela popular española del siglo XIX* (Madrid: Fundación Juan March, 1976); Peter B. Goldman, "Towards a Sociology of the Modern Spanish Novel: The Early Years," *MLN* 89 (1974): 173–90, and 90 (1975): 183–211; Alicia G. Andreu, *Galdós y la literatura popular* (Madrid: Sociedad General Española de Librería, 1982); Francisco Ynduráin, *Galdós entre la novela y el folletín* (Madrid: Taurus, 1970); Iris M. Zavala, "El triunfo del canónigo: teoría y novela en la España del siglo XIX (1800–1875)," in *El texto en la historia* (Madrid: Editorial Nuestra Cultura, 1981), 11–68. An

overview of scholarship in the field to date can be found in Victor Ouimette, "'Monstrous Fecundity': The Popular Novel in Nineteenth-Century Spain," *Canadian Review of Comparative Literature* 9.3 (1982): 383–405.

50   Constance A. Sullivan, "Re-Reading the Hispanic Literary Canon: The Question of Gender," *IL* 4.16 (Second Cycle: May–June 1983): 93–101. See also her "On Spanish Literary History and the Politics of Gender," *JMMLA* 23.2 (1990): 26–41.

51   Smith, "Contingencies of Value," 26.

52   See, for instance, the use of this term in John O. Stark, *The Literature of Exhaustion: Borges, Nabokov, and Barth* (Durham: Duke University Press, 1974).

53   Ricardo Gullón, *García Márquez o el olvidado arte de contar* (Madrid: Taurus, 1970), 44.

54   "Revisión de Galdós," 3.

55   Gullón, *La novela como acto imaginativo*, 35. The phrase I use to describe García Márquez's mode of narration is borrowed from the title of Harold Brodkey's *Stories in an Almost Classical Mode* (New York: Knopf, 1988).

56   Scholes, *The Fabulators*, 21.

57   Andreas Huyssen, *After the Great Divide: Modernism, Mass Culture, Postmodernism* (Bloomington: Indiana University Press, 1986).

Index

Hazel Gold is Associate Professor of Spanish at Emory University.

Library of Congress Cataloging-in-Publication Data
Gold, Hazel, 1953–
The reframing of realism : Galdós and the discourses of the
nineteenth-century Spanish novel / Hazel Gold.
Includes index.
ISBN 0-8223-1334-0 (hard : alk. paper). — ISBN 0-8223-1367-7
(pbk. : alk. paper)
1. Pérez Galdós, Benito, 1843–1920—Technique. 2. Realism in
literature. 3. Spanish fiction—19th century—History and
criticism. I. Title.
PQ6555.Z5G65   1993
863′.5—dc20   92-39376